WHITE MEN ON RACE

WHITE MEN ON RACE

Power, Privilege, and the
Shaping of Cultural Consciousness

JOE FEAGIN AND EILEEN O'BRIEN

Beacon Press
Boston

Beacon Press
25 Beacon Street
Beacon, Massachusetts 02108-2892
www.beacon.org

Beacon Press books
are published under the auspices of
the Unitarian Universalist Association of Congregations.

Printed in the United States of America

05 04 03 8 7 6 5 4 3 2 1

This book is printed on acid-free paper
that meets the uncoated paper ANSI/NISO
specifications for permanence as revised in 1992.

Composition by Wilsted & Taylor Publishing Services

Library of Congress Cataloging-in-Publication Data

Feagin, Joe R.
    White men on race : power, privilege, and the shaping
of cultural consciousness / Joe Feagin and Eileen O'Brien.
        p. cm.
Includes bibliographical references and index.
    ISBN 0-8070-0980-6 (alk. paper)
    1. White men—United States—Attitudes. 2. White men—United
States—Interviews. 3. Whites—Race identity—United States. 4. African
Americans—Public opinion. 5. United States—Race relations. 6. United
States—Social conditions—1980– 7. Elite (Social sciences)—United
States. 8. Social classes—United States. 9. Public opinion—United States.
I. O'Brien, Eileen, 1972– II. Title.

    E184.A1F39 2003
    305.896'073—dc21   2003011632

CONTENTS

INTRODUCTION

One of the greatest Americans of the last century, W.E.B. DuBois, once said that *the* problem of the twentieth century was the color line. We can extend this insightful comment, for this color line is still in many ways *the* problem of the twenty-first century. Indeed, virtually every week, the national news media report on some type of debate or conflict over issues of race, ethnicity, racism, or immigration in the United States.

At the center of these issues are white Americans, and especially elite white men. This book is about this rather neglected group of white Americans. Surprisingly enough, the views, perspectives, and proclivities of this group have received relatively little detailed attention in the research literature or in popular magazines and periodicals. Indeed, we know considerably more about the views of ordinary white men and women than we do about the white men in the local, regional, and national elites.

As we were writing this introduction, news programs were reporting on highly controversial remarks made by Trent Lott, the former leader of the Republican Party in the U.S. Senate, and once one of the most powerful white men at the very top of the U.S. elite. Remarking nostalgically on Senator Strom Thurmond's run for president in 1948 as an outspoken segregationist, Lott said that the people of Mississippi voted for Thurmond and that "we're proud of him. And if the rest of the country had followed our lead, we wouldn't have had all these problems over all these years either." Lott soon apologized for this and earlier remarks supportive of Thurmond, who had run under the banner of "Segregation Forever." Soon Lott was also apologizing for other actions such as his cozying up to neo-confederate groups, and for his votes against extending the Voting Rights Act.[1] Somewhat belatedly, the white-dominated mass media linked their discussions to the fact that many in the Republican Party had long catered to the racial views of white voters to garner support. In the debates over Lott's remarks, however, it became clear that many white men, among many others, did not agree with his remarks or with the Republican Party's often racialized strategy to secure white votes. Though some leading white officials said they thought Lott did not mean what he said, eventually many white leaders tardily censured his remarks as unacceptable, including President George W. Bush. Clearly worried about the impact on moderate voters' opinion, many Republicans moved to prevent Lott from becoming Senate majority leader, and Lott withdrew.

While only a few white leaders have so far used this incident as an occasion to call for aggressive enforcement of civil rights laws and new efforts to end systemic racial discrimination in the United States, a number of the nation's white leaders did go beyond condemning Lott's nostalgic remarks to censure the racialized strategies that many conservative white Republicans and other conservatives have used to try to win over white voters. Thus, former president Bill Clinton spoke out strongly against Lott's remarks, and further noted that many Republicans have "tried to suppress black voting, they've ran on the Confederate flag in Georgia and South Carolina." He added, "Look at their whole record. He embarrassed them by saying in Washington what they do on the backroads every day."[2]

Over time, white commentators in the mass media gave Lott mixed reviews. Three days after Lott's comments, for example, columnist Robert Novak made a comment that was typical of some early assessments: "I don't think he was at all serious, and I don't even think we should dwell on it." It took a few more days for the Lott remarks to get critical reviews in most major national newspapers and on major television news programs. Several white commentators deserve credit for their critical analyses of Lott's actions early on. One of the first columnists to examine the story critically was Salon.com columnist Joe Conason, who suggested that "the attitude that ignores or downplays Lott's remarks is what used to be called 'institutional racism.'"[3] Clearly, such critical assessments of Senator Lott's racialized remarks and actions indicate that there is still significant debate within the white male elite over how to discuss and handle the continuing reality of racial prejudice and discrimination in the United States. In this incident we see that numerous white men disagree with the subtly or overtly racist actions and strategies of yet other whites, and will indeed speak out about them. Clearly, there is *diversity* of opinion within the white male elite on racial matters.

As we will see in the chapters that follow, the nearly one hundred respondents in our sample provide much insight into how white men in the upper reaches of U.S. society think about a significant range of racial issues. While only a few are from the top echelons of the national elite, most are powerful or influential men, at least in their local communities. Moreover, while they share the views and opinions of ordinary white Americans on many racial issues, they often seem more complex and nuanced in their views. Most also differ in that they have a greater ability to shape community and national views on racial matters than do most Americans. We will also see that, as was the case among the prominent whites debating the Trent Lott episode, there is significant diversity in their views and understanding of racial matters. One significant finding is that almost none of our respondents share Trent Lott's nostalgia for a time of legal segregation and blatantly racist discrimination. They therefore demonstrate that there has been a major shift in this regard among whites in the upper reaches of U.S. society. Many of them seem critical of the openly racist past and view the move away from the era of legal segregation in positive terms. Indeed, numerous respondents are willing to take, at least some of the time, interpretive positions contrary to the white majority's views on racial matters. Still, as we will also see, many of these men are now hesitant about, or opposed to, aggressive efforts to continue in the direction of eradicating racial inequality. And only a handful, albeit a significant handful, report that they have spoken out routinely and aggressively against the forms of racial prejudice and discrimination that they encounter in their daily lives. In our view, this latter group of white men suggests the direction in which the country's white population and leadership now need to move.

It has been a half-century since the famous 1954 *Brown v. Board of Education* decision, a decision that played a significant role in accelerating and influencing the racial desegregation of U.S. society over the subsequent decades. This powerful decision was made by nine white men who stood against the tide of white public opinion at the time. Indeed, a white man, Chief Justice Earl Warren, organized the unanimous opinion against initially strong opposition within the high court. Whatever the social and political factors lying behind it, and they were indeed complex, this court decision was a sign of commitment by a certain sector of the white male elite to the stated U.S. ideals of fairness, justice, and equality. It was a watershed event for U.S. society, one whose impact and implications are yet to be fully assessed. Of course, we should be clear that it was courageous African-American parents, their community supporters, and their lawyers who brought this pivotal lawsuit in the first place, and it was they and millions of other African-American parents and children who actually had to deal with the hostility of the many whites who resisted the desegregation decision at the local level. Moreover, it is these and other African Americans who have also had to suffer in recent years, as many in the white elite have moved away from a serious commitment to the full desegregation of all institutions in U.S. society.

Our interviews with white executives, managers, administrators, and professionals make clear much of the thinking in the white elite, and in white America generally, that has led to backtracking on earlier commitments to sustained and full desegregation of society—commitments that once looked like they would move our society forever away from the fundamental reality of racial inequality. As we will see, too, there are numerous dissenters over this backtracking to be found in the white male elite, yet they remain in the minority. Whether U.S. society can ever get on the track to full and meaningful racial desegregation and the ending of racial inequality remains to be seen.

1

"RACE" IN AMERICA

In his 1944 book *An American Dilemma,* Gunnar Myrdal, the Nobel Prize–winning social scientist, examined anti-black prejudice and discrimination in the United States of the 1930s and 1940s. In his introduction, he notes that his initial focus was on what he saw as "the Negro problem." Once in the field, however, he discovered there was no Negro problem but rather a "white man's problem." Myrdal belatedly realized that white Americans had not only created the system of racial oppression directed at black Americans, but maintained it over time for their own benefit. [1]

Today we need to recover this insight, because most whites still do not see the problem of "race" in America as a "white problem." Recently, another Nobel Prize winner, Toni Morrison, has called for research on the "impact of racism on those who perpetuate it." Continues Morrison, "It seems both poignant and striking how avoided and unanalyzed is the effect of racist inflection on the subject."[2] Following this advice, we examine here the racial experiences, perspectives, and inclinations of about one hundred white men who generally occupy important positions in major U.S. institutions. Among the most important things one can know about such individuals or groups are their assumptions and understandings about the social worlds around them. Coming from a powerful social stratum, the views examined in this book are part of a complex macrocosm with a framework of taken-for-granted assumptions and understandings. Using a sociological approach, we seek to describe something of the collective mentality of the social stratum to which our respondents belong.[3] Covering a range of topics from how they first encountered African Americans to views on interracial dating, affirmative action, immigration, crime, and other important policy issues, these men enlighten us on how they view the condition of the United States as we move well into the twenty-first century.

Significantly, whites of European descent are now a decreasing proportion of the world and U.S. populations. They are a statistical minority in half the country's one hundred largest cities and in three states: California, New Mexico, and Hawaii. If current migration trends and birth rates continue, by no later than the 2050s white Americans will be a statistical minority of the U.S. population. This demographic trend presents an ongoing challenge to the historical, social, and political dominance of white Americans, and especially to those in the white elite. To make the picture more complex and conflict-ridden, these demographic changes come at a time when numerous studies still show substantial racial prejudice and discrimination directed by whites against African Americans and other Americans of color in areas such as housing, employment, education, and public accommodations.

In the midst of these dramatic social changes, where do influential white men stand on important racial and ethnic matters? Will their perspectives on these critical matters enable them to provide able leadership, as these demographic trends become ever more substantial and result in increasing pressures for social, economic, and political changes?

THE SYSTEM OF RACIAL OPPRESSION

In the United States, racial prejudice and discrimination remain pervasive and imbedded in a system of racism that provides significant advantages for white Americans at the expense of African Americans and other Americans of color. This system includes not only racial stereotypes and prejudices, but also a racial ideology, powerful racialized emotions, a range of discriminatory practices, and the institutions in which the foregoing are imbedded. The result of this is significant inequality in resources, privileges, and power. This racial system is the material and ideological construction of the dominant white group. It is not a natural reality, but rather a construction that provides privileges to whites over black Americans and other Americans of color.

In this book, thus, we are centrally concerned with the social realities, contexts, and frameworks associated with this racialized system. We are not interested in characterizing any particular person as a "bigot" or a "racist." Such characterizations make the problem of contemporary racial discrimination and inequality too individualistic. Instead, we examine here the expression, transmission, and rejection of racialized ideas and understandings within a key group of white Americans.

Here we look for the prevailing social patterns, as well as important deviations from and rejections of common patterns. We examine the impact of the historically racialized social system on the often complex and nuanced ways in which influential, upper-income white men view their lives and experiences, the lives and experiences of racial "others," and the socioracial reality of U.S. society as a whole. We prefer not to describe an individual as a "racist" because we view the racial views and proclivities of individuals as *socially* generated, transmitted, and situated, and as imbedding the frequently multifaceted and conflicting racial ideas, images, and inclinations that have pervaded the white population since at least the seventeenth century. As we will explain further below, we emphasize the surrounding social frameworks of racial ideology, privilege, and power that have an impact on the perspectives, attitudes, and, everyday lives of all white Americans.

Because they are systemic, racial stereotyping and discrimination are part of the experience of everyone who lives in the United States. Short of becoming a hermit, there is no way for anyone to avoid this racist system. In both its early and modern forms, this system is concrete and materialistic, advantageous for whites, and destructive for those who are not white. For nearly four centuries, white-generated racism has been structured deeply into the rhythms of everyday life across the nation. Not surprisingly, recent research shows that racialized ways of thinking, imaging, and acting intrude at an early age.[4] Consider these realities: A person's parents are usually determined by the racial practices of this society, such as the pressures to choose a mate from one's own racial group. Typically, one's place of residence is determined by access to places and material resources that are shaped by the racially discriminatory system, past and present, including lack of access to better-paying jobs and good-quality housing for many Americans of color. In addition, the food one eats, the clothes one wears, and the schools and churches one attends are affected to some degree by access to resources that are determined by one's position in the racial hierarchy. Even dying and being buried are often influenced by the discriminatory system. Most aspects of one's life, through every part of the life cycle, are shaped by the racial discrimination and inequalities systemic in the United States.

Historical Contours of Racial Oppression

Even a brief review of the historical evidence reveals the deep reality of racial oppression in the United States. This system of oppression meant long centuries of slavery and legal segregation for African Americans. In the modern era, slavery and segregation have been replaced by large-scale, informal discrimination. In addition, other Americans of color have faced racial oppression in various forms at the hands of white Americans. In this book, we often emphasize the relationship of white Americans and black Americans because this relationship has been central to the development of systemic racism in North America. But racial animus and discrimination also target other Americans of color. The racially inegalitarian system has long included a general privileging and unjust enrichment of white Americans, and an unjust disadvantaging and impoverishment of those Americans who are viewed by whites as darker-skinned and inferior. Thus, there is only one racialized system, and it was created by white Americans and applied to all people of color.

Fundamental to this system is that it reproduces itself across many generations of societal structures and processes. As a result, it maintains the racial hierarchy and its unequal access to resources and privileges. Without these societal structures and their constitutive organizations, racial oppression would not persist and thrive. Among these are the generally white-run firms and other organizations that provide the majority of the country's jobs, the white-controlled financial institutions that control most capital for economic development and housing, the white-dominated political and legal institutions that make and enforce the laws, and the white-controlled public and private schools that provide much of the education. As each new generation matures, it inherits racially inegalitarian organizations and institutions, as well as a racial ideology that rationalizes them. At all social class levels, most whites underestimate the extent of the racial resources and privileges passed down from distant and proximate predecessors. This intergenerational process of social inheritance appears fair to the majority of whites, and mainly the result of hard work by generations of whites. However, the reality is that most whites in each later generation have inherited an array of economic, social, educational, and political resources and privileges that were, at least in part, unjustly and unfairly gained in earlier generations because of the oppressive systems of slavery, segregation, and informal discrimination targeting Americans of color. In a recent book, a white slaveholder's descendant underscored this point: "If we did not inherit money, or land, we received a great fund of cultural capital, including prestige, a chance at an education, self-esteem, a sense of place, mobility, even (in some cases) a flair for giving orders."[5]

Today, most whites benefit, directly or indirectly, not only from these social inheritances but also from continuing discrimination in workplaces, housing, schools, and politics. Whites do not have to be overtly prejudiced, nor do they have to discriminate knowingly, for this structure of racism to persist. Racial inequality is perpetuated by social inheritance processes that pass on privileges and resources from one generation to the next. Numerous social, political, and economic resources and privileges—such as access to good housing and good-paying jobs—are disproportionately allocated to whites. Today, on average, white families garner much more income and have much greater economic wealth than black families—and the average white American lives more than six years longer than the average black American. Most whites, knowingly or unconsciously, help to perpetuate the racist system by making choices of friends, mates, neighborhoods, schools, and churches along the same racial lines as those before them. Most whites inherit significant social networks that are heavily or exclusively white and that provide access to important social contacts or capital. Once networking is in place, it tends to persist over the generations. Thus, whites' lives are shaped as much by the racialized system as the lives of those who are oppressed by it.

THE UMBRELLA IDEOLOGY

From the seventeenth century onward, the system of labor exploitation and oppression, initially developed by whites for Native and African Americans, was rationalized in shared understandings and ideas, in a collective racial ideology. People often engage in extensive "symbolic labor" to construct a range of fictional representations used to defend or hide important societal realities.

Engaging in such symbolic labor over several centuries, whites have constructed an array of "sincere fictions" about white America and white Americans, as well as about the racial "others." Here the adjective *sincere* indicates that these racial fictions are generally thought to be faithful representations of societal realities by those who adopt them. Such socially constructed fictions often conceal the underlying realities of racial discrimination and oppression by portraying these realities as normal and natural. Sincere fictions operate to prevent people from seeing, or seeing clearly, that their society is pervaded by discrimination and oppression.[6] For example, anti-black discrimination has involved physical, psychological, or symbolic violence directed against its victims, and these realities are often hidden from collective recognition by whites in a society with a strong set of "liberty and justice for all" ideals.

This symbolic labor is a continuing process in which, as conditions change, the dominant group refurbishes or revises, often in subtle ways, the old stereotyped views of subordinate racial groups. Today, as in the past, a broad racial ideology and consciousness provide the umbrella framework that encompasses the racial stereotypes and understandings common across the society. These are not just individually held, but are part of a societal framework of knowledge about racial matters. Stereotypes and prejudices do not exist alone but group themselves in sets, which are in turn part of the collective ideology and consciousness. For example, stereotypes about African Americans having a poor work ethic are frequently linked in many white minds to images of African Americans as preferring welfare, views that are in turn commonly linked to ideas and feelings about the superiority of white values, families, or culture. Such a broad racial consciousness in turn plays a role in white choices of friends, mates, neighborhoods, schools, and workplaces. This consciousness—which can be conscious, half-conscious, or unconscious —involves a complex mental structure that enables whites to process information not only about the white ingroup but also about racial outgroups. One need not know or accept the entire ideology for it to have some impact on thought, emotions, or action. Indeed, even the most liberal or antiracist whites often reflect some aspects of the racialized consciousness in their thought or actions. This awareness exists substantially because of the constant reinforcement of racial thinking and feeling in most societal sectors and institutions, and especially in the omnipresent mass media. For white people, this racial awareness represents an individualized manifestation of the collective racial ideology long dominant in this society. This reality means there is a dominant societal framework of racialized "knowledge" in the United States that extends well beyond individual people and local groups.

Over many generations, elite groups of white men much like our respondents have played an important role in the creation or maintenance of this societal framework. Periodically, some in the upper classes have worked to undermine aspects of the dominant racial ideology, but the majority in any given historical era have accepted at least certain important aspects of it. Generally, the racial imagery or discourse generated by ordinary whites becomes societally important only when it is incorporated into the umbrella ideology by influential white men.

Among those at the top of the white elites are U.S. presidents. Analyzing the ideas and actions of major presidents, Kenneth O'Reilly has described numerous incidents that show how U.S. presidents mostly do not follow, but rather lead, the white population on major racial issues. He shows that the comments and actions of many presidents have operated "to nurture and support the nation's racism."[7] In the past and present, many men in elite groups have actively fostered, maintained, or enhanced racialized thinking and consciousness. In contrast to ordinary white Americans, upper-income whites often have much sway beyond their interactions with family and friends, for they tend to dominate higher-level communications throughout the society, such as those in the media, advertising, corporate and professional settings, education, church pulpits, and politics. "Through talk, tales, stories, gossip, anecdotes, messages, pronouncements, news accounts, orations, sermons, preachments and the like, definitions are presented and feelings are expressed."[8] Elite white men are powerful substantially because they dominate a broad range of organizations that have major resources and power.

Cultural Superiority and Cultural Deficiency

Over several centuries, this racial consciousness among white Americans has added and deleted many ideas and images. Certainly, one of the oldest and most fundamental ideas of racial thinking, especially in the United States, is that those called "whites" are racially superior to those who are not, such as those originally named (by whites) as "black" Americans. This racialized thinking was central to justifying the enslavement and legal segregation of African Americans and their exploitation for the gain of whites. This thinking early took the form of viewing African Americans—and, soon, other Americans of color—as biologically, genetically, and intellectually inferior to white Americans. Today, however, this notion of white superiority in biological and intellectual terms is expressed by what seems to be a decreasing minority of influential whites, such as in the book *The Bell Curve*.[9]

While the majority of whites no longer declare their support for the full range of flagrantly racist stereotypes of the past, many still hold to a perspective that some researchers have variously termed "modern racism" or "color-blind racism."[10] This contemporary perspective places some accent on white superiority, but now in cultural terms. Unlike those holding to traditional racist thinking, many whites who hold to the cultural-superiority view can accept black individuals who do not fit their stereotypes as more or less exceptions to the group, and they do not assume that a black person is unfit to participate fully in society by virtue of skin color. Those whites holding to this contemporary perspective often hold both negative and positive views of black Americans. Nonetheless, this cultural-superiority perspective generally envisions white Americans as having different and better values, customs, families, or communities than African Americans and many other Americans of color. Thinking from within this viewpoint, whites blame the victims and emphasize inferior values—such as an alleged lack of commitment to hard work and education or a supposed lack of religious values—that whites believe account for why black Americans have not done as well socially or economically as whites. Surveys of whites show that many still view blacks as less hardworking and ambitious, or as more aggressive or violence-prone than whites.[11]

These prevailing images indicate that a majority of whites frequently think of black America in terms of the low-income neighborhoods often seen and stereotyped on news programs. Missing in the typical white view of black America is the knowledge that many black neighborhoods are substantially working class or middle class, and that the majority of black Americans live in such neighborhoods or in racially integrated neighborhoods. Moreover, in most of these maligned low-income neighborhoods, usually only a *minority* of the residents exhibit the antisocial behavior often condemned by whites as typical of black America. In most low-income neighborhoods, the majority of people hold to traditional work and family values, and still hope to succeed despite discrimination and their very difficult living environments.[12]

This modern cultural-superiority perspective can be at least as harmful to its targets as traditional racial attitudes focusing on biology. For one thing, African Americans are constantly reminded that they themselves are thought to be blameworthy for their continuing problems. They and some other Americans of color must endure—and develop strategies to counter—the steady drumbeat of white complaints in the media, in schools, and from politicians about the alleged differences between whites and people of color in culture and personal, family, and community values. Many whites frequently misperceive African Americans in negative terms that help support visions of white cultural and value superiority. In Ralph Ellison's *Invisible Man,* his black protagonist makes this sage comment about how whites view him: "I am an invisible man. . . . I am a man of substance, of flesh and bone, fiber and liquids—and I might even be said to possess a mind. I am invisible, understand, simply because people refuse to see me."[13] African Americans often report that whites do not see past their physical characteristics to view them as full human beings with many of the same concerns as whites.

The view of black Americans as having, compared to whites, substantially different and inferior values, customs, propensities, and behaviors—as well as widely problematical marriages, families, and communities—seems common among white Americans. Yet there is no evidence for such great divisions between black and white Americans with regard to values and the customs and issues of ordinary life. There is consensus among blacks and whites on the values necessary for a good life and family, and for achieving the American dream. Survey research shows substantial similarities between blacks and whites in beliefs in the value of hard work and self-sufficiency, in their determination that they and their children will succeed, and in other values that facilitate achievement and social mobility. Overwhelming majorities of both groups view good relationships with family and friends and commitment to religious beliefs as very important to success.[14] One prominent researcher, Jennifer Hochschild, has summarized the survey data thus: "In short, black and white Americans occupy the same moral domain when they think about the American dream as an ethical imperative, and they occupy almost the same perceptual realm when they think about the validity of the American dream in their own lives. Up to now we have only one hint of serious disagreement—beliefs about how much discrimination blacks face in their daily lives."[15]

Psychoanalyst Jessica Benjamin has emphasized the significance for society of the interpersonal processes of human recognition and human misrecognition. She argues that "domination and submission result from a breakdown of the necessary tension between self-assertion and mutual recognition that allows self and other to meet as sovereign equals."[16] Throughout the interviews, many elite white male respondents indicate that they do not recognize African Americans, especially as a group, as such sovereign equals. In this regard, they seem much like the majority of white Americans, who generally have difficulty in recognizing black men and women as being much like themselves. The repeated messages of misrecognition create mental blueprints for white and black Americans and thus become central to the reproduction of the institutional structures of racial privilege and inequality. More or less stereotyped understandings often creep into white attitudes, assessments, and commentaries about African Americans, and stereotyped understandings can undergird even apparently nonracial analyses of group differences and related social matters.

The contemporary white cultural-deficiency ideology often tends to ignore or play down the pervasiveness of current discrimination. From this perspective, many whites believe that the 1960s civil rights laws took care of most serious racial discrimination. Surveys indicate that the majority of whites see the U.S. social system as fair and egalitarian, and some get angry that black Americans do not see the country in the same way.[17] Moreover, old-fashioned racist thinking has been replaced in the minds of many whites by thinking that accepts modest desegregation in many areas, but is opposed to a full-scale racial integration of the society by means of antidiscrimination programs.[18] African Americans and other Americans of color are frequently seen as making illegitimate demands for societal change. White support for racial change often ends when such programs are large-scale and seem to seriously endanger white resources, privileges, and social comfort. As we will see in later chapters, many respondents have strong negative views or serious misgivings about the continuing use of government affirmative action and other antidiscrimination programs. While many understand the reasons such programs were originally set in place, and often support their use in the past, they take the position that discrimination is declining, and now many or all such programs are no longer needed.

A majority of whites indicate in surveys that they sincerely believe that racial discrimination is no longer a serious problem for black Americans. Thus, one recent *Washington Post*/Kaiser/Harvard survey found that a substantial majority of whites felt that African Americans had societal opportunities that were equal to, or better than, those of whites. Half or more of the respondents felt that black Americans had a level of education equal to or better than that of whites, were as well off as whites in jobs held, and had health-care access equal to or better than that of whites. Some 70 percent agreed with one or more erroneous beliefs about current white-black differentials, yet the data clearly show that white Americans are significantly better off than black Americans in such areas. Striking, too, is the fact that only a fifth of these whites thought that African Americans today face "a lot of discrimination."[19] Many whites, including many of our respondents, recognize that some discrimination exists, yet downplay its character, significance, or extent in the contemporary United States. Even more striking, perhaps, is the fact that a majority of whites do not see the centuries of slavery and segregation as bringing whites substantial socioeconomic benefits. Another national survey found that most whites did *not* think that whites as a group had benefited from past or present discrimination against black Americans.[20]

One contradictory aspect of the contemporary racial ideology is the way in which those who adhere to it often express verbal commitment to racial tolerance and color-blindness, while still being opposed to serious and aggressive attempts to eradicate ongoing discrimination and inequality. Historically, the country's prominent leaders and founding documents have emphasized the values of liberty, justice, and equality. At the same time, racial oppression and inequality have long been basic features of U.S. society. In *An American Dilemma,* Myrdal attempted to explain this ongoing contradiction. He argued that most whites were indeed adherents of the American creed, which includes the "ideals of the essential dignity of the individual human being, of the fundamental equality of all men, and of certain inalienable rights to freedom, justice, and a fair opportunity."[21] In his view, this equality ethic was in great tension with widespread discriminatory practices, a tension he termed "an American dilemma." The problem of anti-black racism was solvable in principle, for all whites needed to do was to live up to this egalitarian creed. Yet this conclusion was then, and still is, naive. Over nearly four centuries, the majority of whites, including the majority of those in elite positions, have not revealed a serious commitment to *fully* implementing these ideals of equality and justice for African Americans and other Americans of color.

If one examines how far the United States is from equality in both opportunities and outcomes as we move into the twenty-first century, it is clear that this egalitarian ethic does not often enough, at least in practice, guide the country's white leadership or indeed the majority of white Americans. It is a hypothetical ethic that often operates to deflect a real understanding of the realities of continuing racial discrimination and inequality. The past and present history of the United States indicates that the vested interest of most whites lies in keeping a structure of racial inequality that works to their advantage, regardless of verbal commitments to egalitarian ideals. Thus, in an early 1990s study, the European media scholar Teun van Dijk examined what top members of political, media, and corporate elites in Europe and the United States thought about racial issues. He found that "much elite text and talk about minorities may occasionally seem to express tolerance, understanding, acceptance, or humanitarian worldviews, although such discourse is contradicted by a situation of structured inequality largely caused or condoned by these elites." Many of these elite whites spoke publicly about their color-blindness, and against racial discrimination, yet did not support government policies that would actually end that discrimination and its accompanying inequality. Many whites in the mass media, educational, and corporate elites expressed humanitarian ideals of tolerance, yet also regularly problematized the values, cultures, or immigration of racial outgroups.[22]

Today, most white Americans seem to be in agreement with this elite perspective. In surveys, the overwhelming majority of whites indicate a commitment to the ideals of equal opportunity and equal respect for all people. A majority of whites assert egalitarian values, insist that they are color-blind, and believe that they are fair in dealings with others.[23] Indeed, a common statement made by whites would go something like, "I do not see color. I treat [or view] people the same whether they are white, black, pink, or green." Those who adhere to this color-blind view typically assume that racial discrimination is much less frequent today and what remains is basically a problem of a few bigoted individuals and not of social institutions. As legal scholars Lani Guinier and Gerald Torres have recently put it, this "rule of colorblindness disguises (sometimes deliberately) or normalizes (sometimes unwittingly) relationships of privilege and subordination." They add that racial differences are often relegated by color-blind advocates "to celebratory holidays that capture the nostalgia of a time when we once thought we were different, but whose celebration reaffirms how essentially 'the same' we truly are."[24] It appears that most members of the country's elite have worked for several decades to foster this color-blind perspective, which in effect helps to camouflage the continuing stereotyping and widespread discrimination directed against Americans of color.

Central to the thinking of the majority of whites, in regard to these various racial matters, is a constant and enduring approach to the social world that is centered in and framed from a white-American perspective. It is not just that the racial outgroup is viewed as culturally deficient; it is that the viewpoint on this matter is consistently white-framed. As we will see in numerous interviews in this book, as well as in interviews in other research studies that we will cite, white Americans frequently have a difficult time looking at the world from the perspective of those who are not white. There may be occasional sympathy from some, but strong and sustained empathy across the color line is relatively uncommon. For most white Americans, including those who are relatively liberal, the framing of important racial issues, from the extent of racism in the society to the multiracial future of the society, is generally done from the white-interested point of view.

ATTITUDES UNDER THE UMBRELLA: CONCRETE STEREOTYPING

In the late 1990s, at a town meeting on racial issues in Ohio, a white college student admitted to the audience that he was fearful of poorly dressed black men. Then-president Bill Clinton, who was the moderator of the meeting, commented, "That's a pretty gutsy thing for you to admit. Do you think that's because of television crime shows, or because of your personal experience?" Significantly, the student spoke sincerely and indicated that the views did not come from his own experience, but rather from things he had heard in the media.[25]

Stereotyped ideas and images are more than ordinary bits of human knowledge, for they generally influence the ways in which we sort out the world around us. Integral to the system of racial discrimination are specific stereotypes and prejudices that whites hold about African Americans and other Americans of color. Stereotypes generalize negative characteristics viewed as representative of people in subordinate racial groups, while prejudices involve negative feelings about the latter groups and tend to accompany stereotypes. Stereotyped images of racial groups are abstract images that transcend the experiences of one individual; they are part of a stock of racialized "knowledge" that groups make available to those within them. Such collectively transmitted knowledge is generally inaccurate or fictional, but is believed to be true by adherents. The stereotyped and prejudiced views that many white Americans hold about Americans of color offer a make-believe foundation for white dominance in the society. Such racialized knowledge often takes the form of sincere fictions about racial others and about whites themselves.[26] Indeed, since the seventeenth century, no group has been more central to white thinking about whiteness and the racial "others" than African Americans.

Since national opinion surveys were first conducted in the 1930s, white respondents have indicated that they believe in an array of racially stereotyped images of African Americans and other Americans of color. Now, as in the past, views that the racial others are lazy, violent, or welfare-prone are still strongly expressed. While surveys indicate a significant decline since the 1930s in the percentages of whites publicly articulating a large range of racial stereotypes, today a majority of whites still admit to survey researchers that they accept at least a few racial stereotypes about African Americans and other Americans of color. A large minority admit that they harbor numerous racial stereotypes. In the early 1990s, for example, an Anti-Defamation League national survey asked whites to evaluate eight stereotypes of African Americans, such as that African Americans "prefer to accept welfare" and have "less native intelligence." Three-quarters agreed with one or more of these stereotypes, and a bit more than half agreed with two or more. A majority of college-educated whites in the survey also publicly agreed with at least one of the anti-black stereotypes. Several other surveys have shown a similar pattern, with significant proportions of whites accepting anti-black stereotypes.[27] A 2001 national survey found that more than half of white respondents agreed with one or more of four negative racial stereotypes of African Americans, and one-third agreed with two or more.[28] In addition, numerous studies of white students have found that almost all are well aware of the standard black stereotypes, and that the majority accept some of these as true.[29] While most no longer see African Americans as biologically inferior, a majority of whites admit to accepting at least one of the stereotypes about African Americans being lazy, desirous of welfare, violent, or paranoid about discrimination. A majority of whites still attribute the difficult conditions that African Americans face to alleged failings of black individuals, families, and communities. Moreover, in surveys the majority of whites indicate that they do not see U.S. society as fundamentally racist or still pervaded by widespread discrimination.[30]

Because many whites often give socially desirable responses to these relatively brief survey questions, such surveys tend to underestimate the degree to which whites today hold negative stereotypes and prejudices directed at Americans of color. When whites, including white college students, are given more time to discuss their views, they often articulate more stereotypes and racial animosity than they do on short-answer survey questions.[31] Two studies have shown that whites are less candid about their views in public settings than in private settings. One recent study increased the privacy of the settings in which white respondents expressed their views, and found that, as the privacy of the settings increased, so did the expression of negative attitudes toward black Americans. Another ethnographic study noting comments made by ordinary whites in private places found that many still used blatant racial slurs and overtly racist categorizations of African Americans and other Americans of color. When numerous whites discussed racial matters out of the public eye, especially with white acquaintances or relatives, African Americans and other Americans of color were often the targets of hostile and stereotyped commentary.[32]

Some social-psychological research using white subjects shows that those who openly reject some racial stereotyping, especially in settings where the expression of that stereotyping is easy to control, may still reveal some racial stereotyping in situations where they are less able, or less concerned, to control the deeply held stereotypes. If these whites think that those around them will not censure them for acting in racially biased ways, they may act in such a fashion. Another key psychological finding is that racial stereotypes prime most people to impute certain characteristics to the individuals thus stereotyped, whether they agree with those stereotypes or not.[33] Negative stereotypes of African Americans as lazy, unambitious, or happy-go-lucky are well-known among almost all white Americans. A random encounter with a black person may activate in the mind a stereotype that is unconsciously held, even for those who are relatively unprejudiced.[34] Yet there is a major difference among whites in the responses to the activated stereotype. The more prejudiced whites are likely to have other racial beliefs that coincide with the activated racial stereotype, and thus they are more likely to allow the recalled stereotype to shape their thinking and actual behavior, while less prejudiced whites are more likely to counter the triggering of a stereotype in their minds by conscious processing that refuses to think or act on the activated stereotype.[35]

As we have noted, in some research on racial stereotyping, a majority of educated whites indicate that they agree with at least a few of the prevailing stereotypes of African Americans. Much anecdotal evidence also supports this finding. For example, the distinguished philosopher and artist Adrian Piper, an African American, has described how influential and well-educated whites at major universities and other prestigious institutions frequently make rather negative comments about African Americans in her presence, because her light skin gives them the impression that she is white. Piper adds this trenchant point: "For part of the tragedy is that the racism I witness when their guard is down is often behavior they genuinely do not understand to be racist. So the revelation is not only of racism but of ignorance and insensitivity."[36]

Similarly, in the mass media we occasionally get reports of white executives, police chiefs, or sports officials forgetting the public etiquette and using stereotyped imagery or common racial slurs. Thus, in the mid-1990s *The New York Times* revealed that several top executives at Texaco, one of the country's largest companies, were secretly taped by one of their number while discussing a lawsuit by African-American employees who contended that they faced serious discrimination. The recording revealed that some white executives had discussed destroying documents involved in the lawsuit and called African-American employees "black jelly beans" who "seem to be stuck to the bottom of the bag." Materials filed with the lawsuit indicated that another white executive in one Texaco office had commented on a discrimination complaint by a black employee, saying he would "fire her black ass." When a subordinate pointed out that company policy protected her, the executive reportedly replied, "I guess we treat niggers differently down here."[37]

Still, it is probably not such overt animosity and blatant stereotyping among elite or ordinary whites that is the most serious problem today for African Americans and other Americans of color. It is the somewhat more subtle stereotypes, such as some accenting cultural inferiority, that seem to influence the views and actions of whites more than the old blatant stereotypes and prejudices.

SOCIAL CONTEXTS OF RACIAL THOUGHT AND ACTION

Some traditional psychological views of human behavior heavily emphasize the individual over the group, as in this influential statement by psychologist Floyd Allport: "There is no psychology of groups which is not essentially and entirely a psychology of individuals. . . . Within his organism are provided all the mechanisms by which social behavior is explained."[38] However, social groups obviously precede in time and importance the arrival of new individuals. For most whites, their personal views on many topics, including their perspectives on racial outgroups, not only are socially derived but also serve a significant social adjustment function. As they grow and mature, most whites learn and more or less conform to many of the prejudices and stereotypes of relatives, friends, teachers, and coworkers. Racial prejudices and stereotypes, as well as more subtle understandings of their racial position, help whites fit into the groups in which they spend much of their lives. In this sense, all such racial knowledge is rooted and localized. While individuals may have their own distinctive framing for bits of knowledge, these bits are imbedded in, and are elaborations of, group knowledge. Karl Mannheim, a leading sociologist of knowledge, once noted that "Strictly speaking it is incorrect to say that the single individual thinks. Rather it is more correct to insist that he participates in thinking [to] further what other men have thought before him."[39] Thus, all whites find themselves in social settings where they participate in inherited patterns of thought. Ready-made ways of thinking about racial issues and interactions are inherited or adapted from previous generations by means of early and ongoing socialization.

In the case of white Americans, as we suggested previously, the racial stereotypes and prejudices are not just about negative thoughts, images, or feelings directed at outgroups, but rather they are usually rooted deeply in a positive sense of the ingroup's *position* in the racial hierarchy. From the seventeenth century onward, white Americans as a group have had the superior hierarchical position in terms of power, resources, status, and opportunities. Today as in the past, the sense of having the superior social position is a basis for whites having negative images of people of color and positive images of whiteness.[40] Coupled with this is the view that the dominant group deserves its privileged and disproportionate access to social resources, prestige, and status.

It is likely that most white Americans learn this sense of group position, and of white cultural superiority and others' cultural inferiority, at an early age, typically from observing how parents, teachers, and friends speak and act. Certain common racial ideas and images become part of a collective white consciousness and unconsciousness—the "collection of widely shared individual memories, beliefs, and understandings that exist in the mind at the nonreporting level."[41] These ideas and images are roughly similar for most whites because they are socialized as children and adults in more or less comparable sociocultural contexts. Within important social networks, the frequent use and repetition of bits of knowledge, such as particular racial images and stereotypes, keep them in circulation.

French sociologist Maurice Halbwachs explained that there is no point in seeking where these bits and pieces of knowledge are "preserved in the brain or in some nook of my mind to which I alone have access: for they are recalled to me externally, and the groups of which I am a part at any time give me the means to reconstruct them, upon condition, to be sure, that I turn toward them and adopt, at least for the moment, their way of thinking." Indeed, individual knowledge hangs together because it is "part of a totality of thoughts common to a group."[42] The sincere fictions about the ingroup or racial outgroups that are held by white individuals connect directly to the ongoing collective efforts that reinforce these images and understandings. Thus, even though they come from many different areas of the country, have many different occupations, and have been through many different educational systems, the majority of whites—including a majority of our respondents—often report broadly similar understandings of African Americans and other Americans of color. Certainly, our respondents differ to varying degrees in their views on racial matters, yet the majority seem to carry in their heads some relatively similar bits of knowledge in regard to the historical and contemporary dimensions and contours of racial categorization and action in U.S. society. Indeed, it is the ongoing pressures of relevant social groups that impel people to use, reuse, or elaborate these bits and pieces of human knowledge.

Nonetheless, within this sample of elite white men, there are some who have developed a much more liberal, even radical, perspective on racial matters and relationships in this society. One question we will ask later is why this is the case. One reason for the more liberal views of some of these men seems to be that they have had experiences with unconventional racial relationships or alternative social groups, today or at key points in their lives. While much learning about racial stereotyping and prejudices takes place in traditional white family and peer groups, these are not the only settings that can have an impact on racial views. A few of the men have at some point developed very close relationships with Americans of color, and these relationships have made a great difference in their lives and their thinking. For some others among these respondents, experiences within other types of alternative social groups have been important in generating some liberal or radical understandings about these issues. For example, the 1960s was an unusual time in U.S. history in that the major protest movements provided numerous social settings where an alternative, more progressive view of racial issues could be learned, reinforced, and recalled in supportive environments. For some of the men, early experiences with these groups and movements have been critical to their more progressive thinking about racial matters to the present day. For yet others, more recent experiences in multiracial groups and settings have helped to reshape, sometimes significantly, their views toward contemporary racial and ethnic issues.

The men who are willing to take an avowedly antiracist position add an important element to the overall picture of white men's views and actions on racial matters. Historically, the United States has had a long tradition of antiracist thought and action, not only among African Americans and other Americans of color, but also among some white Americans. Among all groups of Americans, antiracist thought and action has arisen dialectically in response to racist thought and action. Since the seventeenth century, there has been a long history of a brave minority of white men and women speaking and working against racial oppression and against the ideology that legitimizes that oppression. For example, in the mid-1700s bold white men like Anthony Benezet asserted that the "notion entertained by some, that blacks are inferior in the capacities, is a vulgar prejudice, founded on pride and ignorance."[43] For centuries, numerous white men and women have not only spoken out like this against oppression but have actively participated in antiracist movements. Many whites were active in antislavery movements in the nineteenth century, and many more participated in the civil rights movement of the 1960s. To the present day, antiracist whites have worked alongside Americans of color in attempts to bring down the walls of systemic racism in ways small and large.

THE CONSEQUENCES OF SEPARATION AND SEGREGATION

A key to understanding the social context of much stereotyped thinking about racial matters is the fact that most whites live in what might be termed the "white bubble"—that is, they live out lives generally isolated from sustained and intensive equal-status contacts with African Americans and other Americans of color. How has this segregated social reality been constructed and reinforced over many generations?

This social segregation is rooted deeply in centuries of large-scale residential segregation. Current research indicates that all U.S. metropolitan areas are still very segregated along residential lines. For example, using 2000 census data, researchers have calculated statistical indices of residential segregation for the thirty largest metropolitan areas. These statistics show high levels of residential segregation. On the average, fully *two-thirds* of the white (or black) residents of southern and northern metropolitan areas would have to move from present residential areas in order to create proportional desegregation in residential housing arrangements in those areas. Smaller cities often have lower, though still substantial, levels of segregation. Between 1980 and 1990, and again between 1990 and 2000, there were modest decreases in the (still high) level of white-black segregation in most of the largest metropolitan areas. Yet the decrease for 1990–2000 was *less* than that for 1980–1990, so the modest rate of change may be slowing.[44]

Not surprisingly, a substantial majority of whites have no sustained equal-status contacts with African Americans, especially in informal settings such as social clubs or residential communities. Interestingly, in one recent survey, 42 percent of whites said that there was a black person that they personally felt close to. However, when asked for first names of their good friends, just 6 percent actually listed a black person. Most whites who said they had a close black friend apparently did not.[45] Research indicates that some whites have had no significant contacts with African Americans, while many others have only had contacts with black domestic or yard workers, brief contacts with black store clerks, or contacts limited to (often lower-ranking) black employees in their workplace. Clearly, only a modest number have had ongoing equal-status relationships. Some social science researchers have studied what is termed the "contact hypothesis," which suggests that interactions between white and black Americans must generally be between those of roughly equal social status for the contact even to have the possibility of lessening white prejudices and stereotypes.[46] Contact between people of unequal status, such as between servants and employers, is not likely to have major positive effects in regard to changing racial attitudes.

As we will see in later chapters, most of our respondents do not indicate that they have had close contacts on an ongoing, equal-status basis with African Americans. This lack of contact is the case for most white Americans. Since most whites at all class levels live, as a rule, in relatively segregated settings, they typically garner many ideas about racial outgroups from close contacts with white neighbors, friends, and relatives, as well as from the mass media. This general isolation of whites from black Americans, as well as from other Americans of color, helps to explain many white misrepresentations, misunderstandings, and stereotypes about racial outgroups.

White views of Americans of color often seem to be made from a distance either in time or space. For all whites, this distant or distancing view can result in insensitivity or ignorance about the conditions of people across the color line. Our respondents generally root their racial understandings and views locally, often tying them to particular times and places in their lives. As influential as they are, even powerful white men are born into a highly racialized society that is *not* of their own making. Their parents and other key adults, as well as older children among whom they grew up, have likely communicated to them certain negative racial attitudes, interpretations, and ideologies. For most, their family settings involved, at best, limited or unequal contacts with African Americans. If the contacts occurred early on, they were likely to have been with black domestic workers or other servants, while later contacts have often involved black acquaintances in elementary and high schools, college settings, or military service. Only a modest number of these men discuss close and sustained equal-status contacts with African Americans or other people of color in their neighborhoods or at work. As with other whites, most seem to have had few discussions of significant racial matters with African Americans or other Americans of color on a recurring basis.

Since the white majority has no, or very few, recurring and sustained equal-status contacts with African Americans, their views seem to be significantly influenced by omnipresent mass media images and interpretations. As two communications researchers have recently put it, "Lacking much opportunity for repeated close contact with a wide variety of blacks, whites depend heavily on cultural material, especially media images, for cataloguing blacks."[47] These media-screened communications help explain how negative stereotypes and related racial understandings persist, even when there are some societal norms against stereotyping. Various research studies show significant racial bias in television and other media presentations of white and black Americans. Thus, the mainstream media offer a limited range of accounts of the lives of African Americans—mainly stories about entertainers, sports figures, and criminals. Local television news tends to present, disproportionately, whites as victims of crimes and blacks as the perpetrators. Significantly, mass media stories about African Americans are much less likely to accent achievements and societal contributions than do stories about whites. Whites are also disproportionately called on as media commentators and experts on a range of important public issues. Whites tend to generalize from negative media images of African Americans to traditional views of the latter as a particularly problematical group. Heavy reliance on the media leads many whites to very mistaken notions, such as the common view that African Americans are one-third or more of the total U.S. population or that they make up most of the violent criminals.[48] Reliance on biased media presentations can facilitate and support racial stereotyping and insensitivity.

Social and residential segregation tends to breed lack of knowledge about and insensitivity toward groups and communities beyond the boundaries of the segregated life. Thus, another serious aspect of social separation is the emotional segregation. We see recurring insensitivity and distancing in many white commentaries on the situations of African Americans and on other racial matters. There is often a missing emotional component in whites' commentaries about the difficult life conditions often faced by African Americans and other Americans of color. Only a minority of whites seem to empathize much with the pain and misery faced by those who are the continuing targets of stereotyping and discrimination. Thus, the unjust suffering of African Americans appears to be more or less invisible to the overwhelming majority of white Americans.

THE RESPONDENTS

This book is an exploratory analysis of how a significant sample of up-per-middle-class and upper-class white men think about a variety of questions on racial and ethnic relations in the United States. These men were interviewed by college students, who were each asked to interview white men in "elite positions." In this book, we use the term "elite" in the standard dictionary definition: "A group of persons who by virtue of po-sition or education exercise much power and influence."[49] As a group, these white male respondents fit this description of people with substan-tial education, influence, resources, and status.

Typically, elite men like these respondents have resources that are multiple and cumulative and include substantial economic resources, bureaucratic and other organizational resources, educational capital, and political influence. In general, these men also have a social rank that places them in the upper reaches of U.S. society.[50] As we have suggested previously, U.S. society is not made up of a loose group of isolated indi-viduals, but rather of a set of distinctive social strata with subgroups and social networks. The upper strata in this social structure are character-ized by important local, regional, and national networks.

Our respondents are not all members of the same networks, for they live in different cities, states, and regions. In a process of snowball sampling, we began with numerous different starting points and have respondents from different social networks.[51] Approximately two hun-dred interviews were initially gathered, but for this book we have drawn only on the interviews of the approximately one hundred respondents with the highest incomes. Our respondents mostly range in age from their 30s to their 60s, and all hold important occupational positions. We should note, too, that these men do vary in social, economic, and polit-ical influence and power. Some are at the top of powerful organizations, and thus have significant national power and influence. Many others are one or more tiers below that top level, yet are still successful entrepre-neurs; key executives in various types of businesses, corporations, and government organizations; senior academics and administrators; prom-inent local physicians and attorneys; and other important professionals. These latter individuals usually seem to be part of local elites, although they may not have national or regional influence.

CONCLUSION

In many ways, elite white men are like other white Americans. They often share the common negative views, images, and attitudes that are held in regard to African Americans and other Americans of color. The evidence at hand strongly suggests that today the majority of whites in elite positions, as well as the majority of ordinary whites, desire to maintain many, if not most, white privileges as well as their control over major organizations and institutions.

As we will see in chapters that follow, some of these upper-class and upper-middle-class men frame their negative views on racial matters gently and subtly, while others are more open about their negative views. Many have ambivalent or contradictory attitudes, often mixing relatively liberal interpretations of some racial issues with conservative interpretations of other racial matters. And several articulate a firm antiracist perspective.

Clearly, these elite men are different from lower-middle-class and working-class whites—the majority of whites in this country—in one important respect: They have greater power to sustain or eradicate the negative racial attitudes, images, interpretations, and actions directed at African Americans and other Americans of color. Most have substantial power to reshape the practices, laws, and institutions of this society in the direction of a more egalitarian democracy. For that reason, we will give special attention those respondents whose views and inclinations are distinctive in their explicit willingness to consider significantly dismantling the structures of ongoing institutional racism. They often express views that diverge from majority positions on racial matters in key respects, and offer the greatest insights into how the country can move toward a more egalitarian and nonracist democracy. We will return to these important issues in the concluding chapter.

2

THE WHITE BUBBLE: LEARNING ABOUT
WHITENESS AND THE RACIAL OTHERS

Just where and how do whites learn their views of those they see as racial "others"? The way that whites think and feel about racial matters as adults is commonly shaped by family and school contexts in which they grow up. Childhood and adolescence are important times for learning much about the surrounding social world, including conventional racial attitudes and personal understandings about racial matters. In this socialization process, a person typically adopts inherited ways of thinking about racial issues and interactions, yet may rework some of these views to fit within his or her own personal orientation.

Family and school settings are localized places where individual knowledge about racial and other societal matters is regularly learned and called forth. Recall Maurice Halbwachs' idea that our knowledge and understandings about life and society do not languish in some isolated nook of our minds, but instead are constantly recalled, used, and reinforced in the processes of social interaction. In this chapter's comments from respondents, we see the impact of certain traditional white interpretations of the racial world, as well as the often distinctive framing of these inherited views by those who have labored hard to come to terms personally with these social inheritances. Racial understandings and images are here localized, learned, and called forth in particular life experiences. These men utilize inherited racial views to interpret concrete personal experiences with members of racial outgroups, however limited these contacts may be. Their views are often rooted, subtly and deeply, in a sense of the privileged white position in the racial hierarchy. This sense of position may be signaled in overt or subtle ways, and it can be a basis for both positive images of whiteness and negative images of the racial others.

This chapter mostly examines accounts of the respondents in regard to their early contacts with African Americans and, less often, other Americans of color. For the most part, these experiences were limited to certain spheres of their lives, particularly to home, school, and military settings. Few respondents indicate that they have lived in residential communities with a significant number of African Americans. They mostly discuss relationships with African Americans who were not equal in social status to them, or more equal status relationships that were relatively brief in duration. Very few attest to lifetime friendships with African Americans. Numerous respondents are eloquent in discussing the reality and character of their racially isolated lives, past and present, and often have some sense of the significance of that reality. In this regard, these men seem much like other white Americans, for research studies have found that most whites have grown up with no, or few, sustained equal-status contacts with black Americans.[1]

LIVING IN ISOLATION AND SEGREGATION

In the interviews, a question about first contacts with African Americans generated an interesting array of answers. Some cite experiences with particular black people, while others focus on events or incidents from early periods in their lives that seem memorable to them. Yet others talk about their first awareness of discrimination, such as contact with patterns of legal segregation. They often extend their evaluations of their contact, or lack of contact, with African Americans into the present day. The accounts tell us much, not only about their early contacts with African Americans, but also about their thinking and emotions in regard to an array of racial matters today and in the past.

Residential segregation has been central to everyday life in the

United States in recent decades, just as it has been historically. It is hard to overstate just how segregated whites and blacks have been across the United States, especially in regard to residential settings. Note this sensitive and nuanced statement from one influential manager. He answers a question about his first contact with a black person this way:

> That is really interesting, because where I grew up as a kid—I got to be almost in college and . . . working in local retail organizations and other things where I really started to come across black people for the first time. It was almost as if, you know, we were totally segregated from them, and you really have no particular opinion one way or another. It is part of your everyday life. I think the first black person I remember was when I worked in [names store] and he was a salesman inside, just a everyday type of person, but I was never, even to this day, confronted with face-to-face living conditions, working conditions, with people from cultures other than white. I have basically been immune from that, so it's, so it's almost like ignorance. [I] never had to worry about, you know, a situation where it really infringed on how I felt about what I was doing. There was always another neighborhood, another side of town, there was little or no effect on how I felt. And my relationships with black people other than work are negligible. . . . To this day, I can honestly say that I have never had a person, black or Hispanic, or whatever, [as a] friend.

Residential segregation has created, and continues to create to the present day, a situation of lack of contact—which, as this respondent notes perceptively, means a certain ignorance of people of other cultural backgrounds, both black and Hispanic Americans. Like most other white Americans, this insightful respondent has grown up and still lives in isolation from black Americans. Most whites have no substantial equal-status contacts with African Americans, at least until they go off to college or into full-time work.

A corporate executive uses similar "we" and "they" language in reflecting on his generally segregated experience while growing up, a limited social contact with African Americans that continues today.

> We just didn't hang out together. I mean, they sort of kept to themselves and we kept to ourselves. I mean, that's just the way it was. It's still that way today, I think. I mean, if I had occasion, I suppose, to so-

cialize or knew somebody that was black that, you know, I could have over to my house—[I do] not entertain a lot—but I wouldn't have any compunction about asking them over. But you just don't, it just isn't, it just hasn't been in my life that that's been the case.[2]

Note, too, that this lack of experience with African Americans leads to a social framework of thinking about those outside one's experience. In these commentaries, we see a subtle framing in terms of a language of "I" and "we," in comparison with "them." These linguistic distinctions come with inherited patterns of living in a racialized society. In these accounts, the respondents do not indicate any racial hostility, but rather a resigned sense of the inevitability of segregation from Americans of color. We see an acceptance of social segregation as if it were the natural order of things, such as in the comment that "you just don't" socialize.

EARLY CONTACTS WITH DOMESTIC WORKERS AND OTHER SERVICE WORKERS

While some respondents had no significant contacts with African Americans until they were older, others offer accounts of a few African Americans whom they encountered or knew about in their early years. Given their upper-class or upper-middle-class status, it is perhaps not surprising that these men often indicate that their early experiences were with black persons significantly lower in social status than they were. Like many other white Americans, their first contacts were often with a black domestic worker, sanitation worker, or other service worker.

One perceptive respondent distinguishes different categories of black people with whom his family has had contact, encounters that likely influenced his own views of racial matters. In an account that indicates much reflection, he makes a number of points about the black people with whom he has had contact over the years.

> Growing up in white-bread New England, there were no blacks. The only black families there were actually the families of the guy who was president of [names corporation] and a guy who was a successful business man. So the blacks we met there were really "white blacks." When I moved to another state, though, the experiences were totally

different, because these were more, should we say, "urban blacks." And although I don't remember my first experience of meeting a black person, I would assume it was my—believe or not—my grandfather's chauffeur when I was five years old. So, to me, blacks at that point were people that waited on you and—or on the train, as conductors and chauffeurs and so forth. When I moved to a big city, though, I have to admit I've had some pretty . . . bad experiences, with some black people who were really "urban blacks." Challenging, and being pretty bad, pretty rude. So it does change your perception. But I guess my first memory of dealing with black people were, they were really, frankly . . . servants.

Here, too, we see a high level of early segregation of young white people from African Americans. This respondent's first youthful contact of consequence involved a servant in the critical family setting. This family reality had its impact in lessons taught to him as a child, which he articulates well. One lesson was that whites have a superior position in the racial hierarchy of society. As a young white person, he came to see blacks as people destined to wait on whites. For numerous respondents, such early contacts lead to a similar early sense of a superior white position.

Reflecting at some length on racial matters, he also distinguishes—in a somewhat distancing fashion—two other categories of black people that he has encountered, what he terms "white blacks" and "urban blacks." The "white blacks" are, specifically, the two black families that he knew about in his area, a very small group that had social status relatively close to that of his family. The choice of the term "white blacks" is telling, because it suggests that, in his view, economically successful black Americans have given up substantial aspects of black identity and culture, and are now significantly assimilated to white culture. While he does not give details about his encounters with the other named group, the "urban blacks," in one city some blacks—perhaps lower-income African Americans on the streets—have been "pretty rude" in interactions with him. Of the three groups mentioned, this latter group may be the one in which African Americans have the greatest freedom from pressures to conform to white norms and ways of interaction—and thus have the greatest freedom to be assertive with a white man. At least, it is only in the case of this group that he reports negative impressions.

Numerous respondents note that their first encounters with African

Americans were with a black service worker. These contacts were often sustained over some time, involved significant affection, and remain significant in their memories. For example, a manager for a large company describes his first contact with a black person.

> I can go back to when I was probably six or seven years old, we had a lady, a black lady who worked for my mother. Her name was Sally. . . . And I loved the woman and she took care of me for a while, and that did not last, only because my parents did not have the money to afford to continue to do that. So that was my first meaningful experience with a nonwhite individual.

Particularly for whites from affluent backgrounds, first contacts with black Americans have often taken place within the household setting and at an early age. In this comment we see a major theme that recurs in numerous interviews: that of a black person as a sort of substitute parent for whom the child developed fondness or love. Thus, one physician used the term "second mother" for the black person encountered in his early years.

> My very first contact with a black person was with a black maid who essentially raised my sister and I—and who was in a very real sense for us a second mother. And . . . most of the people I knew growing up in the South had a very similar situation.

In many cases, in the past and in the present, black domestic workers have functioned as substitute parents in regard to supervising and raising white children. It is not just among Southern whites that close and affectionate relationships with a black person, usually a black woman, have developed in the formative years. Using similar language, another respondent notes that his first contact with a black person was intimate and at home.

> Honestly, the first black person I ever met was probably a household employee at my parent's house a long time ago. I went to parochial Jewish schools, so I didn't encounter many growing up and going to school, and I went to a ninety percent white private preparatory high school. . . . There was only one housekeeper from the time I was about five . . . so my very formative years were spent with her—and I spent a lot of time with her—so she was a second mother for me.

He, too, uses the same language of "second mother" to describe this long-term relationship. For many white Americans, close contact with a black domestic worker in their youth may be the longest extended contact with a black person that they have over the course of their lives.

In another account, a black man is described by a respondent as having functioned as a substitute father. One business leader remembers his early years thus:

> My first experience with a black person was when I was a young boy and, ah, my mother and father had a black chauffeur. And I thought he was the most wonderful person in the world, because he taught me how to drive a car, and paid a lot of attention to me as a young boy that my father didn't seem to have the time to spend [on], because he was away working and so forth.

Here the first experience is with a type of servant usually found only in the wealthiest of American families, the chauffeur. In his case, the black servant served as a substitute father and teacher. This poignant comment not only indicates a problem for many children in upper-class families but also illustrates the fact that many of the men now in the country's top social class have themselves come from wealthy families of origin.

We see further evidence on the point about wealthy families of origin in the comments of this executive. Here he remembers his first experience with a black person at a close relative's house.

> I still remember her name, she was very nice.... She was actually the cleaning lady who came and cleaned the house. My grandmother had two maids, they happened to be white, they were live-in maids. So, the black was the cleaning lady.... Her husband I remember, because he was very nice, too. He was a porter on the trains in those days, and she gave me—she used to have tips that were Indian head pennies.... It was neat at the time. So my first encounters with black Americans was through, I suppose, through the service—that was with service people, if you will.... They weren't part of my social group, growing up.

The huge socioeconomic gap between this respondent and most of the U.S. population can be seen in the fact that his grandmother not only had live-in maids but also a cleaning woman. Again, as a child, the respondent gained a clear sense of a higher position in the socio-racial hierarchy.

The language used in numerous accounts in this chapter indicates the favorable impressions that respondents, recalling early life experiences much later in life, have held of those black domestic workers and other servants who took care of them as youngsters. It is common in the interviews for the men to use terms like "nice" or "wonderful" for these black household workers. Numerous men clearly indicate the youthful affection they had for these workers, who were most often black women.

Significantly, research on black female domestic workers indicates that adult white employers often treat these workers as socially or racially inferior and insist on social deference, such as by using only the first name of a black domestic worker from the initial encounter, yet not allowing the worker to respond in kind.[3] This research indicates that these domestic workers usually do not speak their minds to employers and have to put on a mask of deference and pleasantness, however they may in fact feel. Interestingly, one only occasionally senses a realization of this aspect of the imposed deferential reality—the other side of the early color line—in most respondents' interviews.

When queried about his earliest experience with a black person, one respondent speaks about the role of the black "cleaning lady," who is an important figure in many white families to the present day.

> There was [a] black section of the community where I lived when I was growing up.... We had a cleaning lady who came on Fridays.... My mother or father would pick her [up] at the train. She came up from the city on the commuter train and she came to the house and we paid her and she cleaned. She was there when I was very little, she was there when I was older. And I would guess that my father, who was very thrifty—and that there wasn't much money to be made in the situation. I don't know anything about her except she was there probably in my life for more than fifteen years.... I remember her cleaning me when I was a little kid on the toilet.

The beneficial impact of the toil of black domestic workers on the respondents is clear, as they often indicate in their fond recollections of their youth. Yet few of them do more than hint at its impact on the black women and families. Note here the physical distance traveled. Many black female domestic workers have had to leave their children and commute significant distances to serve white families in heavily white residential areas such as affluent suburbs.

After mentioning a few black schoolmates in elementary school, the previous respondent comments further on the black domestic worker, in response to a follow-up question asking if she was "a nanny in any sense."

> Very limited sense, but ... she wasn't a housekeeper. She wasn't the babysitter, but I am sure there're times when she served for a few minutes in that role and she helped my mother. Maybe if my mother was having a party or something she'd come and be around. She wasn't a maid, but I can recall, with a little embarrassment looking back, the ways that she lived and was a part of our life. Not that we were cruel or mean, but she was very clearly from a different group, and my parents were older, very traditional, and they probably didn't look at her as a friend. I probably looked at her more that way than they did.

Once again we see how the sense of social position in a racial hierarchy is transmitted from parents to children, in this case in the apparently distancing treatment given by parents to the black employee—treatment that the respondent is now embarrassed about. Indeed, he remembers being much more sensitive to her as a person than his parents were.

The difficult and demeaning position of black domestic service workers is not new to this generation of white men. In fact, the comments of one professional in a high position suggest how the current situation of black servants is rooted in a long history of black subordination in servant roles. Replying to a query about his first contact with black people, he describes some household workers.

> They were our servants. I stayed fairly kindly towards them, but they stayed in their place. And we made sure that they did. They worked for us. ... Oh, these were just experiences; I would not call them positive or negative. I didn't pay a bit of attention to it. When I was small—they no longer do this—but they came to the back door. They lived in their own quarters on our place; we had four Negro houses. In fact, two of them bore my last name; they were descendents of slaves that never left. We treated them very much like family. If they needed anything, they always had it. A lot of them left after the Sec-

ond World War and went [north] to go to work, and they were treated terribly by the Yankees, who didn't understand them, [who] didn't want them there. And they all came back. They left for an integrated society and returned to a segregated society by choice.

Like other respondents, this Southerner uses the distancing language of "us" and "them," and indicates that he learned early about the superior social position of whites. His family made sure they kept "their place" as part of the social structure of the local community. Yet his emotional reaction to the black servants was not like other respondents quoted above, in that he says he did not have positive or negative experiences. One also sees in his remarks the ways in which the sense of white privilege and position are passed down over numerous generations.

Several respondents indicated in their interviews that their early experiences with African Americans were not with domestic household workers, but rather with African Americans in other blue-collar and service jobs. Thus, remembering early contacts, one respondent discusses some of these other service workers.

> My father was a building superintendent in New York City and had people working for him, handymen, doormen, elevator operators, et cetera, and, probably because I was the boss's son, everyone was very, very nice to me.

He notes the deferential reality of the social hierarchy. Note, too, the recurring theme of "niceness" in regard to black service workers, this time those encountered outside the home.

In contrast, one professional remembers some blacks in apparently lower-level building service positions as more threatening.

> I think when I was a little boy there were some black men who used to live in the basement of an apartment house down the street where they worked to tend to the building. And they were the superintendents of the building, and they ... would walk the streets occasionally, and they were often drunk. And it was a neighborhood of 95 percent white Jewish people. And they were looked down upon as low-life people with whom you didn't have anything to do on a social basis. ... Well, I can't change what my experience was, that was my experience. It was not that there was something in their nature that

made them worse or better than white people. But my only experience with black people as a child was people who worked in very menial positions like stoking furnaces and cleaning hallways, and I didn't know then that there were black or Hispanic or other nonwhite populations who were other than menial workers.

In recounting their early contacts with African Americans, numerous respondents do not speak about black people with whom they had close personal contacts, but rather about black people whom they saw at more of a distance, as in this respondent's account. In his mostly white community, the black men who kept up buildings were viewed in negative terms by white parents, who apparently taught children that the black men were "low-life" types and should be kept at a physical and social distance. Once again, the respondent reportedly learned a key lesson in his youth about the significant difference in the socio-racial positions of whites and blacks.

In most of these accounts, we see the central role of the *family* and close relatives in socializing children into knowing their social position in the social and racial hierarchies. The contacts with household and other service workers often took place in or near a home setting, as did lessons about how to treat black workers and how to view them in their proper social place. Other lessons about racial attitudes and actions were also taught in these family settings, some blatant and some very subtle. For example, the lesson about avoiding certain black people noted in the previous account was echoed by other respondents. In response to a question about first contacts, a medical professional recounts an early lesson in racialized thinking.

> I think it is interesting, because my first real recollection of thinking of someone as being black was with my grandmother. There were, there were black people fishing down behind where she lived, and I was visiting. There was definitely some clear paranoia. We weren't allowed to talk, we didn't go there. And that is my first recollection in my mind as a child identifying some one as "black" or not.

Frequently, the lessons children learn about racial thought and practice come from observing what influential adults do in their daily lives. In yet other cases, relatives impart, openly and directly, their own racial images and fears. Here, a lesson about distancing black people is characterized by this sensitive respondent as "paranoia." For most whites, it seems clear that the earliest socialization into racial attitudes begins among close relatives, particularly parents, aunts and uncles, and grandparents. While some children rebel against parental views on various matters, including racial matters, many others accept some version of their relatives' views.

In these accounts of experiences with black domestic and other service workers, we see a recurring image of African Americans as being consigned to, or appropriate for, work that services whites. The experiences of these respondents with black workers are often specific and localized in family settings. It is in such settings that numerous elite white men learned, consciously or unconsciously, about the advantaged social position of white Americans and the subordinate social position of African Americans in the immediate community and, sooner or later, the larger society. Throughout these accounts we also sense the reality in which white and black Americans have long lived in U.S. society: one consisting of two distinct social worlds, often segregated yet periodically or regularly overlapping.

OTHER CONTACTS WITH BLACK AMERICANS: EARLY SCHOOL YEARS

Family contexts were not the only settings for respondents' early contacts with African Americans and other Americans of color. School settings were also important. In this section we focus on the interaction of our respondents with black Americans in elementary school and other preteen settings.

Interaction in Elementary School and Youth Organizations

In reflecting on some early experiences with young black people, one perceptive respondent, quoted above, also reports that a black service worker in his city had a little girl.

> His daughter was in my class later on in school and she was very nice. But they lived in a different part of the community, we didn't see them very much, and outside of the school. . . . I don't remember much other interaction, but she was probably one of two or three

African-American children in the class. We called them "Negroes" in those days.... I'm sure that we thought that many of these children didn't have our academic ability or skills; they may not have. I would say that most of the African-American children that I went to school with did not succeed to the degree that the other kids in the school did.... So they were programmed in different ways into the business or the shop or general education programs. But some of that was clearly a self-fulfilling prophecy, that they were not given opportunities, or that they may have not had whatever ... would be comparable to a computer in the fifties—an encyclopedia—or somebody that takes them to the library, or the support of academic orientation in the family.... My parents both went to college and talked about things that were not intellectual but certainly were at a higher level than the parents of people who didn't go to college.... Yeah, we had kids in the schools [who] couldn't compete. They were athletic, they dropped down [in] the schools.... Their only interest in schools was school sports. They got no support, encouragement, I guess, to do much else.

Across the United States, school desegregation has rarely been linked to residential desegregation. The black man's daughter went to school with this respondent, yet did not live in his residential area. In most towns and cities, the implementation of school desegregation without parallel residential desegregation has created situations where children in all racial groups usually have few interracial contacts with other children outside school. Note here the way in which cultural capital, in this case educational resources, is routinely passed down from one white generation to the next. In contrast, most black parents, like those of the little girl, did not have similar resources to transmit. In this perceptive account we see an acute awareness that lack of resources for black children had an inevitable impact on school performance and internal tracking, which in turn doubtless helped to shape many white youngsters' negative views of the abilities of black children. The personal framing of racial understandings can thus be aided, at an early age, by observations made about racialized conditions and consequences inside and outside the desegregated school setting.

For a number of these men, early contacts with black youth came outside home and school settings in various youth organizations. Thus, another professional recalls his first contact with African Americans.

> I remember it very well. It was a young [boy] in my Boy Scout troop that I was a member of. He was really the only black person that I knew personally. He was a very affable boy, and he tried to please people which, looking back at it now, he was trying to fit in with the rest of the kids. He was a nice boy.... I remember he could walk on his hands, which was absolutely, incredibly impressive. He had strength that was clearly upper-body strength, and coordination and balance. That he could walk on his hands, and it was a pretty cool thing.

Now, many years later, this man recalls well certain distinctive characteristics of the only black youngster that he knew personally. His comments on the black boy's affability are further examples of the niceness theme that we have previously noted in other respondents' recollections of early contacts with black domestic workers and their families. Another theme in this account, which can also be seen in several other comments in this chapter, is an accent on the athletic ability or physical prowess of black youngsters whom whites have encountered.

After describing his early years in a rural school that had some religious diversity but no black students, another respondent continues with an account of the black children encountered in the urban setting to which his family later moved.

> So my first contact was with black children in Little League. I can remember very specifically a black boy who played on my team in little league.... He was smiley, friendly, always laughing and was never without a smile, so it was probably a pretty good exposure for the first time.... I came to know them through this association. I can remember a kid by the name of [gives name] which was a, which was a superb athlete and this was on a Little League all-star team that had a number of kids who would make a distinctive mark on athletics in their lifetime.... But ... there was another kid by the name of [gives name], and I bring them up just because they represent such a disparity in life's accomplishments that I think that they are worth looking at and examining.... He ... hangs around in this area. He doesn't really have a job, doesn't have a career. I don't know that he has ever really been productive for the community or for society at large, other than just existing.

Two of the aforementioned themes appear here. One black youngster is described as having been affable and thus having shaped a certain image of black people in the respondent's mind, an image seen as positive. Yet another child was an excellent athlete and apparently grew up to be a productive citizen. However, a third black youngster has not had a very productive life, as the respondent sees it. From the latter example, he draws this conclusion:

> Therein lies what I feel is the real basis of a lot of racial issues, and that is education, productivity within the community and society base, for the good of society as well as economically for one's own welfare. And I think if you begin to break down and look at what we consider a lot of current racial issues, therein lies the basis of those racial issues.

For him, as for many Americans of all backgrounds, education is seen as critical for human productivity and development. Particular experiences with a few black youngsters, and observations about their development, are linked to his explanation of larger racial issues in the society.

Drawing on his own experiences, this professional develops some ideas on when and how children learn negative racial understandings.

> I think children for the most part did not have inherent prejudices. . . . I think that at age nine or ten or eleven it's unusual that children would have an already developed social prejudicial system in place. Nothing happened specific along racial lines which would have led me to [be] prejudiced at that time. I think that children are exposed by the comments that their parents make. . . . There may have been prejudicial comments made within my home along racial lines, but probably equally or more so along ethnic lines. I think in specific response, in how I felt in my first contact with a black or my first meaningful contact with a black where there was actually a conversation, I didn't come away thinking that there was anything extraordinary about these people. I felt that this was a happy, friendly kid.

This man offers a brief but interesting analysis of children and prejudice. He views himself as not being prejudiced even as an older child—a common view among many Americans—and this assessment has some plausibility. Yet recent research on white children as young as three to five years old does indicate that many already know at least some racial and ethnic stereotypes, and many hold some prejudices, which they do sometimes act on and which they often hide from parents and other adults.[4] The respondent suggests some experiential data that may help to explain this apparent contradiction, for it is likely that most white children are exposed to significant racial and ethnic stereotypes and comments made by influential adults such as their parents. Here again we see that the learning of racialized images or understandings is localized in home settings, where white (and other) youngsters participate in thinking what others have thought before them. Yet, as in this case, many people are not robots, and they retain or apply learned racial and ethnic understandings in their own particular ways.

Negative Recollections

While most respondents' memories from their preteen years seem positive or mixed, at least as they view them, a few recall more negative encounters with black youngsters. Unlike the reports of many respondents who grew up in all-white or virtually all-white areas, the following two men report growing up in racially diverse areas of large cities.

One man remembers the racial tensions in the large city where he grew up some decades back.

> I think the first experience I remember was in [large city] in the summer, when I was seven or eight years old. And I grew up in a mostly Italian neighborhood, and they built, you know, government housing across a big boulevard.... That first summer after that housing was occupied, the whites from my neighborhood and the blacks, also now from my neighborhood, started hanging around in the same recreational park. And I remember, not myself being personally involved, but I do remember there being tension between the teenagers of the different races.... That was my first contact. In other words, being in that park, and seeing that unfold, that was my first contact.... I know it was a bad time in the neighborhood as far as how the older people were reacting to what was going on.

This man grew up in a predominantly white big-city area, yet lived just across a boulevard from African Americans in new government facilities, presumably a public housing complex. His account suggests the balkanized character of the cities in which many Americans have grown up, cities with racially segregated communities that are sometimes immediately adjacent to one another. For decades, U.S. metropolitan areas have had a high degree of residential segregation. Indeed, only about five percent of city neighborhoods are both racially diverse and stable; the other 95 percent are segregated or are currently integrated but becoming more segregated.[5] In this respondent's interesting account, his first observations of African Americans were made in regard to racial tensions between teenagers at a nearby park—and with knowledge of white adults' likely negative reactions to that cross-racial tension.

In his detailed interview, an executive also reflects upon being raised in a diverse urban area and going to a naturally desegregated school.

> I grew up in a somewhat diverse neighborhood in a big city, so I was used to going to school with black kids and such.... My first contact was on my first day of kindergarten, getting beaten up by two black kids. And they took my milk money, and I made a mistake then that I haven't made since, and that's that I ratted them out. I went and told, and I got waled after school as a result, because I went around with the principal and identified the kids who had done it, and that was an important lesson. So I guess that was my first encounter that I remember with black kids.... I felt beaten up and stupid, and ... very scared.... But that—and the discrimination against black kids even in my school was, many examples of that—I saw that a whole lot. Vivid examples that have stayed with me.... I was confused. Confused and scared. I'm not sure it was because the kids were black. But confusion is the word that applies to—because then when I saw how the black kids were treated by some of the teachers in some circumstances, I was confused because, I mean, I just didn't understand why they would do that.

In this recollection of a negative first contact with two black children, this respondent recalls feeling both scared and dumb, which apparently reinforced a fearful view of black boys in his mind at the time. Yet, as a perceptive youngster, he also took note of the substantial discrimination that the black children faced at the hands of teachers. This description of a complex set of cross-racial experiences demonstrates that some of these white respondents have shaped their understandings, and emotional reactions, in concrete encounters with black Americans, though these were probably not sustained equal-status encounters.

Queried about an initial contact with a black person, another articulate respondent provides this account from a private elementary school setting.

I grew up in a place with plenty of black people. Most of them came in with the Navy, there was a large Navy base there.... There was a kid by the name of [gives name], and he was in the first and second and third grade with me, in grammar school. And we used to walk back and forth to school together and we were very good friends. It was, he was, it was a private school.... [Looking] back on [my] first experience, I just remember we used to walk back and forth to school together, we used to, we used to walk part of the walk to school together, probably a mile worth of it and we used to have a lot of fun together. And that's my first experience. And later on as he grew up and sort of became a punk and seemed to fall victim to a lot of the things black males fall victim to in this society, for, for whatever reason, I always remember being a little bit disappointed....

In this account of education in a private school, the contact over several years with a black child was positive, even a good friendship. Then, without bridging comments, the respondent moves from a comment about having a "lot of fun together" to the judgment about his former friend becoming a "punk." He assesses this black youngster's later development negatively and links his disappointment to a generalization about what he sees as common traps for black men.

In the next example from an interview with a corporate official, a white youngster's initial contact with a black child was negative because of the respondent's prior fearfulness.

The first time I ever came in contact with a black person I can remember very well, it scared me to death. I was in day camp, at the shore club that we belonged to, my parents. And it was a rainy day at the shore club and the guy who ran the shore club was a gym teacher at a high school. And in order to—maybe we had had two or three days of rain—but he took the entire day camp to that high school because they had a couple of indoor gyms. And ... we were playing basketball, and one of the kids from the high school day-camp thing was a black kid. And I must have been nine, eight or nine, and we were going after this ball, and this black kid jumped on top of me; and was I afraid, that something was going to happen just because he was a black kid, and I was a white kid. I hate to say that I thought something was going to come off or something, but I had never been touched by black person before.... I thought about it for quite some time.

While this incident happened many years earlier, the respondent still has vivid memories of a first physical encounter with a black youngster during play. Racial images and stereotypes are usually learned early, in this case prior to camp experience and likely from parents or friends. In this case the learned images came into play and shaped a white youth's fearful reactions to contact with a black youth. The white child's fear of being touched suggests just how blackness can loom large and threatening in white imaginations.

CONTACTS IN THE HIGH SCHOOL YEARS

Some of the strongest recollections of first or early contacts with African Americans are from the high school period. While many respondents did not report high school experiences, those who did usually indicate that they had some impact on their thinking. Contacts in the high school setting sometimes have more impact than those in elementary school because they can involve more socializing or communication between white and black youth. In these accounts of contacts, which vary in extent, we see the ways in which social interaction can call forth or shape racial views and understandings. Interestingly, once again, these encounters and experiences are often in athletic settings, a dimension of white-black relationships we have seen in earlier years. Numerous respondents report initial contacts with black students while playing sports like football, basketball, or baseball.

After noting that he only had contacts with black servants in his earliest years, the director of a company discusses his experiences in high school.

> And then as I got older, in the high school that I went to, it was vastly, predominantly white. I think there was only two or three blacks in the whole school. Again it was a private day school. I played football with them, they were good football [players], they were very nice.

Like other elite male respondents, this man spent some years in private school settings with very few black students. He is aware of how segregated he was from black youngsters and notes that his few contacts were with "very nice" black students in the athletic sphere. For numerous respondents, contacts with blacks in the sphere of athletics seem to be the main contacts of their teenage and college years.

Another respondent in corporate America notes that he grew up in an East Coast city during a period when a lot of Latin American immigrants were coming into that particular area.

> But my first involvement with somebody of a different color was probably in high school, although I did have some situations with Puerto Rican—Hispanic people, I should say—Hispanic people in junior high school. But the thing that I remember about my first encounter with a black person was sports. And since I was always, you know, fairly athletic, and I played basketball, my first involvement with someone who was—you know, black—was in sports. . . . There was an absolutely lovely young man by the name of [gives name] . . . and he played on our high school team. . . . And I remember inviting him . . . to play basketball at this park, and we had a great afternoon. And then I brought him up to my house where he had soda or something, and so it was a very positive experience, it was a very enjoyable experience. . . . But I do remember my mother saying to me that, you know, did I want to bring black people into my house? My mother had . . . a different point of view, that there was a separation between white and black. And . . . I tried to treat everyone as human beings, no matter what their color.

This man's analysis is sensitive and revealing. After early contacts with some Latino students in junior high, this respondent first encountered a black person at the high school level. Once again, sports teams provide the arena for the interracial connection, in this case a rather positive one. While his mother questioned him about bringing a black person to his house, he managed not to adopt her view that whites and blacks should be separated. While racial attitudes are often transmitted and learned in family settings, we see in this case that outside experiences can also be important, to the point of countering some views expressed by adults in the home.

One professional comments in some detail about a good friendship in high school.

> I was very fortunate in high school. My best friend at that time was black, and I had two or three other real close friends who were white, and there was no racism in my little town. I mean, there were two or three families that were black, and everybody loved them. . . . They were hardworking, their parents were working and nice people.

There wasn't prejudiced thoughts against them. In fact, my best friend became president of our class for four years, because he was a good student. He was a good person, he was an athlete.... It was an advantage for him, probably, in a small town, being a little bit different.... I met this person in sixth grade, and because we were both very, very good athletes early, we were well known in our little town, and it just progressed all through high school. And the same thing happened in terms of our popularity, in terms of our involvement in clubs. It was kind of intertwined just because of our beginnings in sixth grade, so they were all good feelings, of that particular black person.

Unlike the accounts given by other respondents, in this case it was not just contact on the sports fields that brought these youngsters together, but also academic achievements and clubs. Interestingly, his glowing account accents hardworking black families. While this respondent is liberal in his racial views, here he seems to be unaware of the racism very probably faced by black families there, as well as of the discrimination that was likely faced by his friend. This perspective is not surprising, for previous research shows that relatively few whites have the ability to understand clearly and deeply the discriminatory aspects of life faced by black Americans.[6]

Having come of age in a diverse environment, a respondent quoted previously adds comments about the role of sports in his high school setting.

I came from a very racially mixed area, so that my earliest memories are always of black and white together.... Participating in sports in my large, racially mixed high school meant that I was—I dealt with a lot of blacks competitively and socially because a lot of our social activities were based on sports-related things. Teams would get together for parties and stuff. So I felt very comfortable with blacks. I certainly didn't have any perceived or unrealistic perceptions of black people. As a matter of fact, that was always something that was easily talked about. If there was an issue that came up that had something to do with suntanning, or whatever, that we always made jokes about how we didn't want to get any blacker than we are, et cetera. But to actually have a feeling on my part that I treated anyone differently because of the color of their skin, I didn't notice that.

In the following section of the interview, he continues by noting that this early experience was of a "mild racial climate" when compared to more difficult racial climates later on. Once again, we see the ways in which social interaction can elicit or influence racial understandings and emotions. Still, as he relates it, this man's experience with black Americans in the high school setting was mostly limited to sports-related activities. They were comfortable for him and did not link to "unrealistic perceptions" about African Americans, by which he apparently means racial stereotyping.

In the last few school accounts, we see the way in which black students are perceived, usually some years later, in generally positive terms, though the descriptions of them are somewhat superficial and limited to just a few personal characteristics. In the interviews we rarely get a sense of black acquaintances as fully developed and complex human beings. This is also the case in the next two accounts. Responding to the question about his first experience, another respondent comes up with these interesting reflections:

> [My first contact was] probably growing up when I was very young, in urban [names state], where there were lots of black students in the grade school that I went to. But we moved away when I was [in] second grade, so those are not memories that I have fairly well captured. In high school ... there were really only a handful of black students. [Gives name], a year ahead of us, was a very popular, very congenial, very well-liked guy in the class. He happened to be black, but he was extremely well accepted and a lot of that I suppose was that he was a great guy, but also he did not threaten the population of white students at all. There just weren't enough black students.... There's no question that that's positive.... The few that were in our class were good guys, well thought of.

Those respondents who did have contacts in high school usually note that there was only a handful of students. Here, the black male student who is recalled was "very congenial" and "well-liked," adjectives once more suggesting the black amiability theme. There is a glimmer of deeper insight in his comment that this student was not threatening to whites because there were so few black students there—a situation that might well have been different had there been more black students. We sense here, as well, the relative racial isolation of the school experience.

Clearly, school integration at the high school level set up the possibility for some young whites to have more meaningful contacts with black students than they had earlier. The next respondent makes a similar comment about a student at his school. After citing his relatives' admonition to stay away from black people when younger, this professional continues with an account of his first real interaction.

> I think probably my next interaction, which would probably be social or more involved, would have probably been in high school—which was the first time when there was a black student in the school that I attended. And that was actually very positive, very nice. We weren't close friends, but knew each other. We saw each other in class, but there was no differences or animosity. . . . I don't think there was any difference—because he was black—in the way he was treated, or [in] the way he treated anyone else in that experience. . . . I mean, he was living in a definitely white community where he was the minority, and I don't know if that was his way of dealing with it. But it made the interaction easier for me, and I am sure for him also.

Commenting in a fashion almost identical to the last respondent, this respondent reports positive interaction both because of the black student's style of interaction and because of the few black students. Here the theme of niceness is mentioned together with a view that there were "no differences or animosity."

After recounting his close relationship with a black servant when he was young, a broker notes how interaction with black students at high school shaped his views: "But my views were shaped in the course of political debate in high school and whatnot, when we were discussing racial relationships in high school and junior high school, and that's where we formed our ideas or discussed our ideas." Those men who had high school contacts likely had some such discussions, though most do not add the details that this man did. Manifestly, the views of white teenagers can be reinforced or shaped, to some degree, as a result of observations of and discussions with black youth in school situations. Interestingly, the memories of numerous respondents have a certain similarity, forming what seems to be a sort of collective memory, in regard to friendly relationships with "nice" black students.

Yet we should also note what these men usually do not report. Generally speaking, these often perceptive men do not seem to have gained from these interactions much of a sense of what life is like on the other side of the color line. What they learned from this usually limited, school related interaction seems circumscribed. In their comments on school contacts, from first grade to graduate school, only a few explicitly note the racial prejudice or discrimination that their black acquaintances were likely encountering. For most, it appears that in school, as now, their racial attitudes have involved some variation on a "color-blind" position that sees relatively few difficulties with racism for black people, young and old. It seems probable that they, like other whites, would have developed deeper relationships, and deeper understandings about racial matters, if they had had substantial interaction beyond the school context, such as in home neighborhoods and churches.

We should note, too, that a few of these men recalled first contacts with black people during their high school years as not being so positive. Thus, one respondent remembers this encounter:

> I had parked my car with a friend to get a hot dog outside, and I had my father's car. A black fellow drove up, parked next [to] me—and saw a young white kid in a fancy car, and he took his door and slammed it into the side of my father's car. It created a bit of a situation at the restaurant. At the time it was an outdoor drive-in, so there where a lot of people outside. It was summertime. And that's the real first time somebody black did something that I thought was just [an unprovoked] incident.... I guess I would say I, I felt threatened, unduly. In a, in a non-provoked situation.

This man draws from this car-door incident (a common occurrence in parking areas) the conclusion that this black man was jealous about his affluence. Central to his account of an early contact with a black man is a strong recollection of feeling threatened.

THE COLLEGE YEARS

A number of the respondents noted that significant contacts with African Americans came later on in life, during their college years or time in military service. These settings can provide some opportunities for contacts of somewhat more equal social status. Interracial contacts that involve more equal social status can reduce certain blatant stereotypes and prejudices. However, this does not mean that such contacts result in full-fledged, close friendships.

When asked to describe his first contact with a black person, one executive in a major company makes this interesting statement about his college years:

> The first black person that I ever had any significant contact with was [names a prominent black American], when we were at college. Because he was from the same socioeconomic background that I was, I really didn't focus that much [on] the fact that he was black. In fact, I remember one situation when we were sitting at dinner and someone made a racial remark that they regretted considerably, later on, and wouldn't have made it if he had been focusing on the fact that we had a black person sitting at our table. Because he was so much like us in terms of his background—the way he talked, the same values—we didn't focus on the fact that he was black and we were white.... I think it was healthier that we developed a friendship that didn't focus on the fact that there were racial differences.

As this man recalls it, the fact that this black student apparently spoke in a white, middle-class dialect of English and had similar values resulted in white students being less conscious of his being black. This is reminiscent of an earlier respondent's comments about "white blacks" who seem well assimilated to white-normed social settings. Here, for the white students, the interaction may have countered to some degree their tendency to racial stereotyping and perhaps made them cognizant of class differences among African Americans. The research literature noted in chapter 1 suggests that stereotyping and prejudices are most likely to be reduced if interracial interactions are with persons of roughly equal status, recurring, informal, and friendly. Still, the liberal consciousness of certain white students was limited, for at least one of them made racist comments in front of the black student. Moreover, this cross-racial relationship apparently did not involve much open discussion of difficult racial experiences and issues. This suggests that the black student probably did not discuss racism very often and that the whites were likely unaware of his problems with campus racism, problems that the overwhelming majority of black students report in recent studies of college and university campuses across the United States.

A number of these men seem to have been affected by the social movements and conflicts of the 1960s, including, for some, long-term effects on their racial images and views. In response to an interviewer's question about how friendships with African Americans came about during his college days, a corporate manager offers one of the more striking examples.

> Oh, it was most likely through social activities or class. Where you drank. Where I started out college, there weren't a lot of bars, and it was a social environment—and it was, again, this was 1963.... [There was] a lot of social turmoil on the campuses and the freedom marches and the riots. It was a racially sensitive time, and the colleges were probably the center of that sensitivity. And I was never on a campus that wasn't wholly engaged in fighting against discrimination.... So the relationships were formed in class, they were formed socially ... they were formed through some of the political action that went on, and no one particular form took any precedence over the other.

Later in the interview, this perceptive respondent discusses how his college and other experiences in the 1960s have kept him from accepting arguments in popular books that suggest that black Americans are more inclined to deviance than whites. Asked why he is skeptical of this stereotyping, he replies: "A couple of things.... Certainly, one is generational, having gone to college in the sixties. Having been a long-haired hippie traveling in the South in the sixties was an eye-opening experience. And so that kind of experience stays with you." His observations of what happened to black Americans and his own experience as a "deviant" person during this period have made a major difference in how he views racial stereotyping and other racial issues to the present day.

While much learning about racial issues takes place in family and early school groups, these are not the only settings that can have an impact on the racial views of white Americans. For some of the men, alternative, nontraditional groups and relationships have periodically been important in generating understandings about racial images and issues. As can be seen in this commentary, the 1960s were an unusual time in U.S. history, in that they provided many new group settings where a more liberal and progressive view of racial issues could be learned, reinforced, and recalled in new and supportive social environments.

Indicating first that in his elementary and high school years he had

no significant contacts with African Americans, one executive continues
with a description of a more integrated college experience.

> And I came East, the East Coast—that was the first experience with
> ... black students, and a sizable number in the university. And I had
> a good friend in architecture school who was ... black.... So it's al-
> ways been a very neutral, in my view, a neutral and balanced [experi-
> ence], and I don't think that I have, that I've grown up with racial
> stereotypes, because they weren't in the environment. So I've only
> grown ... to know and think about them in a more heightened time,
> [during] the late sixties, of black consciousness and things like that.
> So [I was] a college student, so there was more thinking, more sen-
> sitivity, more awareness, so again it's sort of like having a neutral
> background.

He then adds that in those college years he was close to a black student
who was talented in a number of ways, including being one of the best
students in his class. As he sees it, his early years were not a period of developing stereotypes; he reports becoming more sensitive to racial issues
in college. Like several other respondents who went to college in the
1960s, he had at least one black person he considered a good friend and
was very aware of the black consciousness movements of that period.

The political turbulence of the 1960s had some negative effects on
other whites. For example, one professional provides insights on the impact of black organizations when he lived in the West.

> If I ever had a negative exposure to blacks, it would have come during
> the late sixties in California during the era and the rise to power of the
> Black Panther organization.... There was a large black population in
> [names city], which I would have had little or no contact [with]. But
> there was some, I think there was some general sense of fear and in-
> timidation by the militaristic stance of the Black Panthers, which
> were very active in that area at that time. It was a time of unrest and
> upheaval. It was a time of race riots and so there was a sense of uneasi-
> ness in dealing with blacks in general or maybe a sense of concern,
> maybe, for one's welfare when you were in predominantly black
> areas.

This fear of going into black communities is still common among
whites today, fueled by the extensive housing segregation of U.S. society.
Moreover, for decades many whites have expressed fears about assertive

black organizations such as the Black Panthers. Beginning in the 1960s, white fears of these new and assertive black organizations were significantly accelerated by white police officials and media commentators, who often circulated one-sided, exaggerated, or mythologized images of such organizations. In reality, these groups did much good in their communities, such as by providing meals for children and surveilling white police officers' interactions with black people in communities where police brutality was a serious problem. In spite of their community self-help orientation, they received consistently negative portrayals in the white-dominated mass media. Lingering images in the minds of some whites who remember the negative media images of the 1960s may still shape some of their views of black Americans.

OTHER CONTACTS WITH AFRICAN AMERICANS

A few of these men speak about significant contacts occurring during their time in military service. For instance, there is the following comment from one respondent: "It was very positive, sort of. It didn't make any difference what race you were, it was just that you had something to do together, whether you were in basic training or what, you did it, that's all!" Basic training in the military can create a situation of roughly equal status, at least in regard to how one is treated by the training officers, a situation of common goals and experiences. In his interview, the respondent then generalizes, "I don't think I've ever had a negative experience with a black person, or Hispanic, or an Oriental." Clearly, he is upbeat about his contacts with Americans of color, though he is apparently not aware that "Oriental" is now seen as a derogatory term by many Asian Americans.

Similarly, an older physician describes his first memory of significant contact with a black person.

> It was when I was in the Army, and I was doing my internship and in my internship group there was one black colleague, and we were stationed in the South in the military hospital—and at the time there was, segregation still existed in the South. . . . We would do things socially together, and one evening we were all going out for dinner, including our, our black colleague—we didn't call him black in those days, we called him "colored"—and we went to a restaurant and they

refused to serve him. So there were about six or seven of us all total, and we all decided at that time in a rather embarrassed way that we would just leave the restaurant and not patronize them anymore.

In this case the discriminatory treatment of the one black colleague taught a group of well-educated whites a lesson about the negative character of legal segregation, a basic lesson that is still etched on this respondent's mind some decades later. The fact that a group of whites somehow agreed in this case doubtless reinforced the lesson about the proper responses to such racial injustice.

This sensitivity to blatant discriminatory practices during the period of legal segregation—which did not end until relatively recently in U.S. history (the late 1960s)—can be seen in several other interviews. Replying to a question about early contacts with African Americans, yet another professional does not discuss black individuals, but speaks about his first encounter with racial segregation.

I can't tell you the first experience with, with an individual, but my first experience in race relations came . . . before my teenage years. My family and I went to Florida on a vacation, and this was in the late forties or early fifties. And we were in the store and my brother and I went for a, to get a drink of water out of a fountain. And there were two fountains there, one said "black" and one said "white." . . . I turned on the black fountain because I wanted to see what black water would look like. . . . I never even thought of the fact that this was for, that one fountain was for black people, and one for, was for white people. And it just, it boggled my mind, and I'll never forget that. . . . So, if you ask me for a specific person I don't remember it, you know, I guess mainly because I grew up in a relatively white community. But I [didn't] ever feel threatened, you know, as a child by black people or people of different color.

Having grown up in a white community, this respondent does not now remember his first particular contacts with African Americans. However, he does recall vividly his rude introduction to the South's system of comprehensive racial segregation. Several decades later, he still recalls his youthful shock at learning the meaning of the sinister signs "black" and "white" on water fountains. This account encourages reflection on the ways in which young whites have been taught about how to operate in a racially segregated system, for such knowledge is not instinctive. They must be socialized into the etiquette required in such a system.

In response to a question about first contacts, a few respondents discuss events after going to high school and college and make some comments on how later experiences with black Americans had an impact on their past or current views. To take one example, after recounting an early experience with a black woman who worked in his home, one manager discusses what he considers to be the next most memorable event involving black Americans.

> I had been out of college for three years when I was a sales representative, and I used to make calls on several black physicians and it was a very positive experience because these were obviously very bright, highly educated individuals. In addition to that, they were very nice people. And quite frequently they were looking after my welfare, by suggesting that I only call on them during certain hours ... because they were located within black areas. . . . So they were nice people who were looking out for my welfare.

We have shortened his account of this experience considerably, but one can see here that his work-world experience with black physicians was positive, and he emphasizes their niceness. He also remains impressed that they were concerned with a white person's safety in "black areas."

CONCLUSION

The interviews are revealing about early contacts and encounters with African Americans. While numerous respondents reported no significant early contacts, some did have contacts that they saw as consequential, although the timing of these contacts varied considerably. It is clear from a review of the interviews that most such contacts took place in a limited range of situations. The most common initial contacts were with black domestic workers or other servants in home settings, with black students in public and private schools, in certain college and graduate school settings, and in the military.

It is also important to note what they do not report. Few discuss ongoing contacts with black people who have lived in their residential neighborhoods or who have regularly visited their homes as their guests or as guests of their parents. Given the extensive residential segregation of U.S. society, which was even greater in the past than now, this is perhaps to be expected.

However, we were somewhat surprised at the modest number of men who note initial or important experiences with specific black Americans in their workplaces. In later chapters, we will see that some do mention certain interpersonal contacts with black employees, yet even then, few comment on having close and ongoing equal-status contacts. Perhaps one reason for this is their own high positions in the economy and society, positions where there are usually relatively few black Americans.

Given this circumscribed range of contacts, what do these white male respondents seem to have learned from experiences with black Americans? Numerous respondents had their first significant experience with black workers in their family home or with other black workers doing service work near or outside the home setting. In these cases, they usually report what they recall as a positive experience, with recurring comments on how "wonderful" or "nice" these black domestic workers and other servants were to them. In several cases, a black worker sometimes functioned as a substitute parent. This theme of niceness is common in the interviews and continues in numerous discussions of contacts with black students, though often with just one or two, in elementary and secondary schools. These students are often described in remarkably similar language as nice or friendly. Often, contacts in elementary and secondary schools were with black youngsters in various sports settings. Similarly, college contacts often involved those made in sports settings, though there is more diversity in the reports of college life.

Interestingly, these college experiences, including those in sports settings and some associated with 1960s social movements, seem to have had a mostly positive impact on the respondents' views of black Americans. Thus, sports contacts seem to break down barriers in the immediate school settings, though it seems that these friendly sports-linked relationships mostly did not carry over to more extensive social relationships off the playing field. While we do not have the detailed accounts necessary to make a conclusive judgment, it appears that the black students mentioned in these accounts rarely became *close* friends of these respondents. At least, the respondents generally do not indicate this happening.

Indeed, the reported interactions themselves usually seem to have been limited in character, for the interviewees rarely mention serious discussions of issues of racial stereotyping or racial discrimination with their black acquaintances. Generally speaking, it seems that the interpersonal contacts at school and college remained at a more or less surface level. Such contacts seem to have allowed numerous respondents to regard black acquaintances in a distant way, rather than in a way that encouraged deeper understandings of the difficult experiences with prejudice and discrimination likely faced by these black students.

One reason for this is the character of the social settings themselves. Few whites understand that most historically white public spaces in the United States—including schools, colleges, and workplaces—are white-normed as well as demographically white. These spaces are pervaded by white-determined norms, and they are generally white in their major cultural components. For that reason, such settings generally seem normal and unexceptional to the whites who spend their lives in them. However, black Americans often experience these settings as unwelcoming or unsupportive. For example, some research indicates that many black students have found historically white school and college settings to be so racially negative or hostile that they do not consider returning for reunions or homecomings.[7]

Recall that some social scientists have proposed an equal-status-contact hypothesis in assessing white contacts with black Americans. This view suggests that, as a general rule, interaction between white and black Americans must be between those of roughly equal status for that interaction to have even the possibility of reducing traditional racial prejudices and stereotypes. Prejudices are most likely to be affected by equal-status interaction if that interaction is cooperative, interpersonal, and friendly, and if it involves people with similar social backgrounds and common goals. It also helps if the contacts are in social settings with imbedded egalitarian values.[8] Most interracial interactions in U.S. society do not meet all these requirements. Recurring contacts between people of unequal socioeconomic status and in hierarchical social positions, such as those between upper-class or upper-middle-class whites and black domestic workers, between high-salaried white professionals and low-wage black service workers, or between white upper-middle-class students and black working-class students in an integrated school setting, will not be likely to consistently reduce much stereotyping by the whites involved, nor will such contacts likely generate an understanding of the blacks' struggles with stereotyping and discrimination.

In the case of the contacts reported in this chapter, those with domestic workers and other servants clearly were not equal-status contacts. Such contacts often seem to have reinforced, albeit sometimes subtly, the respondents' sense of their hierarchical and advantaged position in society, as would be predicted by those social scientists who have articulated the equal-status-contact hypothesis. Still, some of these early contacts with domestic workers and other servants have had positive effects, in that they left the respondents with images of the kindness and friendliness of these black Americans.

Later contacts at various levels of schooling, though at least somewhat more equal in social status than the home contacts with domestic servants, often seem to have had much the same effect. On the one hand, there is the common feeling of the niceness and friendliness of the black students that they had contact with. On the other, there is still a certain social distance from typical black acquaintances and at least a hint that such contacts reinforced the whites' sense of higher social position. Very few of the school contacts appear to have generated intimate or ongoing discussions of racism in society or, apparently, long-term and close friendships. One reason for this may be that even the contacts in the school settings, though often friendly and cooperative, may not have been truly equal-status in terms of socioeconomic backgrounds, since the majority of our respondents come from the upper-income classes and the black students there were likely to be from working-class or lower-middle-income backgrounds.

Indeed, this reality of more or less unequal social contacts may help to explain some of the findings in later chapters on respondents' racial views and attitudes. There we often find a mixture of positive and negative views of black Americans, as well as of various racial issues in U.S. society. This mixture may well have its roots in the character and range of early experiences that the respondents have had—or not had—with black Americans.

In our interviews only a few respondents report truly intimate contacts with black Americans in their homes or neighborhoods. Those who do note such contacts usually offer much insight into the character of interracial relationships and their significance, not only for the individuals involved, but also for the larger society. This closeness and intimacy, such as in an interracial marriage or truly close friendship, can have profound effects on the racial attitudes and views of those whites involved. For example, one professional in our sample makes clear how these close contacts can have a major and lasting impact.

> Well, I grew up in a suburban community, which was a lily-white community.... The only black person in the whole area was a fellow named [gives name] ... and he always hung out at our house, and then he and I became good friends, and during my first marriage I used to actually visit and see him a lot.... I know that he was the first black person that I really became friendly with, you know, that I had, really had any kind of a relationship with.... I mean, we all have our heroes, you know, the Dr. Kings and the Malcolm X's, and stuff like that, but as far as, you know, face to face, person to person, he would be the first person.

Here the friendship seems to have been close because it lasted beyond his youthful years. Rare, too, is the fact that, apparently as a young white person, he admired Martin Luther King, Jr. and Malcolm X, an inclination that may have facilitated his forming a close friendship with a black person.

Elsewhere in the interview, he explains that a bit later in life he married a black woman. This relationship has had a major impact on his thoughts and feelings about a range of racial matters, both in his life and in the larger society. Thus, in response to an interviewer's question asking what it is like being "white in a society of growing racial and ethnic diversity," he replies with much insight.

> Well, you know, I don't consider myself totally white.... Physically, I'm white, I know.... But my wife and my love is a black woman and my son is this little golden boy. He's over there [points to photo].... I don't really permit myself to think of myself as just white, you know. Now, maybe that, part of that's out of an abhorrence to what the whites have done ... to the Native Americans and the African Americans, and how intolerant as a group we've been. But I remember years ago being at a party with my wife, in a local city.... And on the ride home, and it was a party that was all white people, sort of yuppies, and it was a polite, nice party. But there was no music, no real

liveliness to the party at all and if you're, if you're around people of color they usually have music on, you know, a lot of, a lot of warmth.... And when we were riding home, I said, "Geez, we were the only black people there," and that was just, you know, sort of a spontaneous comment. And she started laughing, you know.

This articulate respondent's closeness to a black person has made him much more sensitive and empathetic than most whites in regard to the racial intolerance that black Americans face. One likely reason for this is his conversations with his wife about the everyday discrimination that she faces, as well as his own experiences with her in situations where she faces that discrimination. His experiences in the interracial relationship have even inclined him sometimes to view himself in the category of "black," which is, after all, a socially constructed and *not* a biological category. Abandoning traditional stereotypes and making a strong identification across the color line is very difficult for most white Americans, for it involves, among other things, a deep understanding of the problems African Americans face in this racist society and a willingness to take on the position of the racialized other.

In previous work, Joe Feagin has suggested that those whites who come to deeper understandings of the attitudinal and action-linked racism faced by black Americans tend to go through

> three different stages: sympathy, empathy, and what might be called autopathy. The initial stage, sympathy, is important but limited. It typically involves a willingness to set aside some racist stereotyping and hostility and the development of a friendly if variable interest in what is happening to the racialized other.... Empathy is a much more advanced stage of development in that it requires a developed ability to routinely reject distancing stereotypes and a heightened and sustained capacity to see and feel some of the pain of those in the outgroup.[9]

The third stage involves understandings and feelings that go beyond empathy to what has been termed "autopathy" or "transformative love," a stage where one actually experiences some of the pain of racial intolerance and discrimination. In a pathbreaking book, white law professor Sharon Rush has described the profound impact on her life that has come from raising a black child over nearly a decade in a southern city.

Her experiences in defending her child against racism, she notes in a book aptly titled *Loving Across the Color Line,* have dramatically transformed her views in an antiracist direction.[10] The new understandings across the color line, what Rush calls "transformative love," involve whites intentionally placing themselves in the discriminatory settings of loved ones and thus enduring some of hostility and pain of those settings. The comments of Rush and the white professional above suggest that feeling the pain of racial hostility or discrimination directly from joint experiences with black Americans who are close friends, partners, or other loved ones may be an excellent way to break down traditional white biases and misunderstandings about black Americans and about racism in U.S. society.

3

PERSPECTIVES ON WHITENESS

Previous research indicates that many, if not most, white Americans have never given much thought to the meaning of being white in America. Whites at all class levels typically do not see being white as a central part of their social identity. Indeed, most whites identify more with their ethnic or religious heritages (such as Jewish, Italian, or Irish ancestry) than with their racial status as whites. Whiteness as a racial identity maintains its privileged position in part by remaining mostly unexamined, yet at the same time being the standard by which racial "others" get measured. Like other whites, many elite white men say that their whiteness is something they rarely think about, and they often have difficulty answering questions about what their whiteness means to them. It would appear, at first glance, to be unimportant in their lives.

Yet, on deeper probing, we find that some sense of whiteness is often important in their lives and in much of their thinking about the social world. Although whites like many of these respondents may sometimes profess not to notice racial categories, whether theirs or someone else's, they are often aware of how being white has helped them get into the privileged positions they occupy. Indeed, on contemplating a society that is becoming increasingly multiethnic and multiracial, some express concern that whiteness is no longer the surefire boost for success that it once was. Some also display a complex type of awareness of being white, a view that includes both the knowledge that whiteness works in their favor and, sometimes, the perception that they are now "victims" in a multiracial society that is in the process of taking away certain traditional privileges. This racialized awareness is not something that an individual develops independently. It is a manifestation of *collective* understandings and consciousness. As we suggested in chapter 1, there is a dominant societal framework of racial knowledge and understandings that extends well beyond particular individuals. Most whites—elite men as well as other whites—may profess to be color-blind at points, to not see people in terms of their color but in terms of their abilities. Yet the majority of whites do seem to be cognizant, at some level of their thinking and feeling, of what being white means in their lives.

As we have suggested previously, "race" as a categorical social grouping is a material and ideological *construction* by human beings, a social construction that has long been used to distinguish those who are racially superior and deserving of certain substantial rights and privileges from those who are somehow inferior and therefore undeserving. "Race" is a relational concept that cannot be fully understood without comparing the meaning of one racial category, such as "white," with that of other such categories, such as "black." Analyzing the meaning of whiteness in people's lives almost inevitably means taking into consideration the relationship of whiteness to not-whiteness.

On being asked to reflect on whiteness, many whites initially articulate a more or less color-blind response, often devoid of much reflection, such as some variation on the statement that they "don't see race." Yet, on further questioning, many whites couple the sincere notion of being color-blind with explicit knowledge that their once-exclusive and privileged status is being threatened by certain contemporary racial conditions or changes, such as the movement in the United States to an increasingly multiracial reality. Once they begin to compare their situations to those of black Americans or other people of color, many whites, including many elite white men, are articulate about what being white today actually means. Although being color-blind, feeling privileged, and also feeling victimized may seem contradictory ways to feel about one's socioracial status, as we will see, this cluster of views is a more or less logical product of how racial categorization and related matters are seen by many whites today.

TRYING NOT TO SEE WHITENESS

An interesting pattern often emerges when whites are asked to reflect upon their own whiteness. They frequently begin with a socially acceptable statement, such as "I don't see myself as white." However, eventually they follow this opening with statements that indicate an awareness of what being white means, especially vis-à-vis people of color. Reporting on interviews with several dozen white women in the West, Ruth Frankenberg has noted that their color-blindness is a "now you see it, now you don't" type of discourse because of this cycling dialectic.[1] It is particularly difficult for elite white men to maintain a consistently color-blind discussion of whiteness, because their education and orientation generally involve significant awareness of the social and political realities of the society, and because most spend substantial time in a variety of workplace and other societal arenas where color plays an important role. As we noted in chapter 2, they typically live lives that are relatively segregated in terms of home neighborhoods and close friendships, and that may be the reason why it is possible for them to ignore their whiteness to some degree. However, once they are asked to contemplate such racial conditions as the difficult situations of African Americans and other people of color, they often do have an ability to discuss and explain, articulately, how much their whiteness distinguishes them and their lives from those of the racialized others.

In one comment, for example, one well-off respondent initially asserts the unimportance of his whiteness this way: "I don't have a strong identification of myself as being white—more of being an individual.... I am white, but it is not that important to me. I tend to identify myself more along my political and social criteria rather than by racial criteria." However, when the interviewer asks about the racial makeup of his neighborhood, he replies with a clear awareness of the meaning of whiteness.

> It is very white, very suburban, not as Waspy as many areas around here, but it is mostly white.... I chose the area because of its safety, the quality of its education for my children, and the fact that I got a very good value on my home. [Q: Do you think that the education and the safety has anything to do with the fact that it is an all-white community?] The fact of the matter is, in communities that are largely black populations, that there are more problems in the schools and with

safety. That's not due to the race of the people, [that's] due to soci-ety—the way society is constructed. More disadvantaged people will lead to poor educational opportunities and high crime. That's so-cioeconomic, not racial.

This man, doubtless like a majority of white Americans, does not prima-rily identify himself as being "white," but rather as just an individual with certain political or social interests. Yet he has a strong sense of the advantaged social position of white Americans, as we see in his compar-ison of his neighborhood with those that are largely composed of black Americans—those communities he characterizes as problematic. Re-searchers examining the array of privileges for whites have identified one of those privileges as the greater ability the average white family has to purchase an affordable home in a neighborhood with little street crime and well-funded schools.[2] Being white means that this man and his fam-ily have to struggle less, and his response indicates that he recognizes this advantage.

In this commentary, we also see two themes that often appear in one way or another in comments made by many white Americans. Signifi-cant here is the safety theme, which is often part of whites' framing of their lives in contemporary U.S. society. Also important is his interpre-tation of the difficult community conditions faced by black Americans in socioeconomic rather than racial terms. Like other white Americans who make similar comments, he does not mention the persisting dis-crimination faced by most black Americans in seeking good housing to rent or own. Even when families of color have the financial means to pur-chase a suburban home, they are often shut out of opportunities by the discriminatory practices of real estate firms and lenders, or by the hos-tility of white neighbors.[3] Thus, the often less favorable socioeconomic conditions faced by black American families in their neighborhoods are ultimately a racial matter.

Also missing throughout the commentaries made by many of these elite respondents is a sense of the diversity in black neighborhoods and communities. There are many black communities that are substantially middle-class or substantially working-class, as well as communities that have concentrations of low-income people, some of whom do exhibit the antisocial behavior often emphasized by whites. Yet it is only these latter communities, with a modest proportion of the total black population, that many whites have in mind when they talk and generalize about black America.[4]

While they may not readily attach the word "white" to their experiences, many of these men understand that they enjoy relative safety and comfort, especially when they compare themselves to other racial groups. One respondent, who is in management, provides this example:

> I don't think being white is really anything that a white person gives conscious thought to. It's something I think a white person probably for a large part takes for granted. And until you exist where as a white person you're [in] a minority situation or in a non-dominant vital situation, I don't think it has a conscious thought given to it.... When I was in Vietnam, I spent ... months as an advisor and I spent most of my time with the Vietnamese. And I oftentimes was the only American and Caucasian there. And even in that environment, with the always obvious language barrier, I didn't really feel that left out or isolated. Also that, and perhaps more of the reason, I was dealing more with the upper socioeconomic groups of Vietnamese.
>
> Perhaps some of the difference is not so much ethnic or skin color as it is economic, socioeconomic factor[s].... I don't deal with those [ethnic problems] except through the newspaper and on the TV.... Most of them tend to be gang-related, and most of gang-related problems seem to be based on drugs.... Since it doesn't directly impact [me], there tend to be things that you ignore and just are glad that you don't have to deal with them.

Like the previous respondent, this man accents the socioeconomic differences as perhaps more important than racial-ethnic differences in his thinking about ethnic relations and urban problems. Although he describes whites like himself as not consciously thinking about whiteness, he also shows a keen awareness that his whiteness has meant feeling comfortable, even when he was abroad in a war zone among people of color. Implicitly recognizing the privileges of his whiteness in the continuing conversation, he notes that he can thus ignore and distance urban problems such as gang and drug problems.

Although many whites profess not to notice or think about racial categories, they frequently make distinctions between their experiences and those of the racial others. Frequently, it is the more liberal whites who have the most insight into this process. Consider the responses of this white male entrepreneur who, unlike the men above, has not been racially isolated.

> I come from a much different background than most people. I wasn't born in wealth.... I grew up where I intermingled with other races, various races, whether it be black, yellow, white. When I was in college I roomed with an African American. So I purposely didn't look at myself as being white.... When people came to me and would say to me that blacks were inferior, I would argue the case. "How could you possibly say that?" So in that regard I saw it, but [not] me personally looking at it.

He continues by describing what happened when his black college roommate asked to visit him at his home.

> Because my foster parents never ... [met him,] they said, "Who is [gives name]? Show us a picture of him." So I showed them a picture, and I knew what was coming. They said, "He's not coming here." ... It was tough when I had to call him, and I said, "... we can't come here, but you know what we'll do, we'll all stay together in the city." He knew what the real story was.

Very aware of the privileges of whiteness, this liberal respondent notes that he was not "born into wealth," so that whiteness seems to be associated in his mind with affluence and wealth. Further, he describes elsewhere in his interview how he has interacted with people from many different groups through multiracial and multicultural business contacts made in other countries. It is these latter contacts, plus those with a black roommate, that have helped to shape his critical attitude to whiteness. Describing an incident with his parents, he indicates a solid understanding of how whiteness involves the power to denigrate the racial others. Yet, in spite of his critical awareness and trying not to see himself as white, he is still part of a group of advantaged white people who are gatekeepers of the racial divide. The norms of whiteness become clear when he tries to step outside of them, for then he, too, gets viewed as deviant.

The fact that many whites do not wish to embrace "white" as a central or salient identity for themselves does not mean they are unaware of the key components that distinguish the white experience of the societal world from that of people of color. As many white men see it, their neighborhoods are safer, quality homes are affordable and accessible, schools are of higher quality, and certain gang- and drug-related problems seem remote from their everyday experience. They seem to feel comfortable or included in most routine societal situations, and the white group to which they belong has both a superior position and the power to exclude others considered inferior, whether they personally approve of such exclusion or not. Constantly, throughout the interviews, we observe how these men reflect in their own thinking the collective consciousness of whiteness and its associated ideas, which have long been pervasive in society.

WHITENESS AND PRIVILEGE

Most white Americans are resistant to the idea that they have major privileges over other racial groups. To acknowledge such privileges means recognizing significant racial disparities in the societal fabric—which recognition, as we have noted, is frequently considered socially unacceptable in this era of assertive color-blindness. White privileges, by definition, are unearned advantages one receives solely by virtue of group membership. One researcher has described an invisible knapsack of these significant advantages in negotiating everyday life, which most whites are taught not to notice.[5] Certainly, most white men, including elite white men, have worked hard to earn the positions they hold today. However, in focusing on white privilege, we are discussing advantages that are gained not so much from work as from holding the conventional white position in society's racial hierarchy. Even when they strive not to think of themselves as white, but as just "American" or "human," in their accounts these men often do recognize some of the important benefits of being white that they have been able to enjoy.

Now You See It, Now You Don't

Several respondents mixed a color-blind discourse about not noticing whiteness with some observations about the character and reality of white privilege as such. This makes them unlike other respondents who prefer to see their privileges in socioeconomic rather than racial terms or who do not see themselves as part of a white group with particular benefits, even when other whites are discriminating. One executive, for example, would prefer not to see the world in racial terms, but in response to the interviewer's probing acknowledges his *racial* advantage over similarly situated people of color.

> I would be more inclined to ... view myself with others who have done or are going to do or would like to do the sorts of things that I have done with my life, whether they were black, pink, or purple. I don't think there's much difference.... I think that people ought to be judged on the merits of what they do or have done or plan to do. [Q: And do you think that's the way it works?] Well, I think that it's more difficult for people who are not white to be successful in society.

The phrase "whether they were black, pink, or purple" is a common indicator of color-blind discourse, which interestingly mixes a category of real racial significance in society (black) in the same list with meaningless categories that do not signal real racial realities (pink and purple). The naming of nonracial categories (green and purple seem to be favorites in such lists) is common among many whites who comment on how they see racial matters in the United States. Such artificial categories are a clear indicator of the sincere fiction of color-blindness. Yet the respondent himself then points out the contrast between his color-blind and meritocratic ideals and the harsher societal reality, when the interviewer asks him about how society really works. Even some who employ color-blind imagery realize that it often does not reflect everyday reality.

Another respondent strives to uphold this color-blind ideal, yet also questions the veracity of whites who say they would trade places with those in subordinate racial positions. In doing so, he reveals the fictional basis of the color-blind outlook.

> I never gave it much thought through the years, but ... the more you think about it, and deep down you start to think that everyone is basically the same, and it's just their outer looks might be different.... I think that growing up in a white society, most people that grew up white, I really don't think they would say, "Well, if I grew up black or in another ethnic background [things would be the same]," or trade places. Like, if they say that, I really don't believe it. I think that in this country here, it started off as a white society, it developed that way, and anything that wasn't white, was thought of as a second- or third-rate citizen, so anybody that would want to trade places with them

> [would experience that]. Well, maybe you would want to bring those people [blacks] up to a higher standard. But I don't know if those people [whites] would want to change from a white to a black.

Like many other whites, he admits that he has not thought much about being white over the years. While he suggests that "everyone is basically the same," he also points out that this is not the way the world works. Recognizing clearly that whites have had a privileged position in the racial hierarchy, he suggests that most would really not trade places with those who are racially oppressed.

This hypothetical scenario of changing places with someone who is not white is brought up by several respondents in order to reflect on the topic of what whiteness means. Since most indicate that they have not thought much about being white, this "trading places" line of thinking gives them a chance to reflect on the relational character of racial categories. One professional uses this technique in trying to define what it means to be white.

> It really doesn't mean very [much].... I never thought of it as an issue. I guess there's some safety in numbers, that you feel a little more secure as a white person and probably [have] greater opportunities in most fields of endeavor. But aside from that ... I never really thought of myself ... in terms of black and white. There are times when you feel, I probably did better economically and socially as a white person than if I were black.

Even though this speaker has not given much thought to whiteness, he acknowledges he has more privileges, such as more security and opportunities, than a similarly situated black American. Taken together, these last few quotes, as well as others in this and other chapters, demonstrate that numerous whites, with some conscious reflection, are themselves able to poke holes in the color-blind notions and myths that are common across white America.

"If I Were Black ..."

Amazingly enough, some white men, including a few members of the elite, have on occasion expressed the desire to be black, or so they say for public consumption. For example, the New York real estate developer Donald Trump once insisted to an interviewer, "A well-educated black has a tremendous advantage over a well-educated white in terms of the job market." To this odd notion he added, "I've said on one occasion, even about myself, if I were starting off today, I would love to be a well-educated black, because I believe they have an actual advantage."[6]

In contrast, many of our perceptive respondents indicate that they are well aware that being black is not desirable in the United States. Abandoning the pretense of color-blindness, some are expressive and thoughtful about the ways in which their lives would have been different if they had not been white. They clearly have thought, at least occasionally, about the meaning of whiteness, and they identify certain privileges, specific to their own circumstances, that they believe have come about by virtue of being white in a color-conscious society. A retired professional comments thus:

> What is it like to be white? I guess it's a question of what is it like to be in the mainstream, as opposed to what is it like to be a minority. What is it like to always be in a room where you feel you're in control, as opposed to what is it like to always be in a room where you feel you don't know when things are stacked against you. . . . I can't give you anything other than that except that, it's just kind of led you to believe that you were in control.

One specific benefit of being white is the omnipresent sense of having the dominant position, of being in control and not having to worry that things may be "stacked against you." Again, the comparison of being in the minority versus being in the majority is sensitively relied on to arrive at some understanding of the relational category of "white."

One reflective manager similarly contemplates what it would be like to be black in order to arrive at a definition of whiteness. He suspects his opportunities in business would have been much more restricted as a black man.

> I have thought from time to time what it would [have] been like to be, to have been born black . . . how it would have changed my life. And I suspect that being white provides some advantages that make things . . . easier. I'm sure that it makes things easier in my relationships with [those with] whom I do business. . . . I feel that if I were . . . black I'd probably be looked upon differently.

In the world of business, many deals are made through developing personal relationships with those one feels comfortable with. Words like "easier" do not adequately describe the positive consequences in the business world of having contacts and networking relationships. Many clients and contracts are secured or lost based on the quality of relationships and networking in the business arena. Something as subtle as easy associations and networking with many other businesspeople provides whites yet another item for their invisible knapsack of white privileges.

Looking at other business issues, one entrepreneur is clear about how white privilege was an asset that helped him develop his successful business. Like other men quoted in this book, he discusses his privilege by way of imagining how his climb would have been different if he had not been white.

> As a white person, the biggest thing that I can see is that I had a chance to grow and develop—primarily, we are talking economically. Opportunities were presented, and I am positive because I was a white person I was able to take advantage of those opportunities.... I'm my own boss [of a] retail business. And I assure [you] that if I was a black, even if I had the opportunity, because I was black I probably wouldn't have gotten the opportunity to begin it. But even if I was, I wouldn't have been successful. That's taking into context who I am, I have been successful. As a white person wanting to open my own [store] in a ... predominantly white neighborhood ... there is no question that I had the opportunity and also I could be successful at it.... Historically, even in the black neighborhood, ... [business is] all dominated by whites. So, as a white person, I think the greatest difference is that the opportunities that I have had were much more numerous ... that I have had to work on.

This respondent brings out an important aspect of systemic racism, today as in the past, when he underscores the fact that business opportunities are not equal across U.S. communities. As a white man, he has the privilege of entering most neighborhoods (whether predominantly black or predominantly white), obtaining the required loans, securing the necessary insurance, and gaining a large enough clientele to ensure success. He has worked hard, but doors were open to him that were not open to others. Numerous research studies on the discrimination that black Americans face in setting up businesses back up these perceptive contentions.[7]

It is perhaps easier to see the reality of discrimination when one is an executive who handles personnel issues for a company or other large organization. Having held such a position for some time, one respondent speaks in an informed manner about how his life might have been different if he were not white.

> I almost feel blessed, to answer your question. I am glad I'm white, because then I don't have all the uphill battles that Afro-Americans have or, not so much Asians, but some Hispanics and Native Americans. They really have a difficult time assimilating in this country.... The more you look different from the norm, the more you stand out, and [the] more potential for discrimination. I'm glad I don't have that problem of having to grow up as a black in this country and go through the torment that they have to go through.... Prejudice [and] being called names simply because you have a very dark skin. It's crazy how some white people treat other people just simply because of their color of their skin. The way they are treated when they go into a store, just [that] they may not be served as well, they may not be treated as courteous as a person who may be white.... Statistically it's also proven, there is no question in my mind. I've seen employment for many years and blacks do not have an equal opportunity for employment. They don't have it.

Having greater than average sensitivity to the struggles with discrimination routinely faced by African Americans and other people of color, this man feels blessed to be white and not to have to face such torment. From getting good service in stores to having greater employment opportunities, he recognizes the range of white privileges that he has. This man speaks from an interesting personal history because, as he adds in his interview, his first job after graduating from college was as the only white employee in a workplace. There he experienced being in the minority in an employment setting, and now he recognizes the overall advantages that whites today reap in U.S. society.

Putting the shoe on the other foot, and generally drawing upon their own business or employment experiences, leads some elite white men in the sample to recognize at least some of the privileges whites have today. While significant career advancement certainly requires hard work, numerous respondents acknowledge that the climb would have been a lot more arduous had they not been white. Interestingly, these benefits of whiteness that they enumerate from their vantage points are seldom fully discussed in the public discourse of the country. School and media discussions tend to accent Horatio Alger–type stories of economic achievement, which try to convince the listeners that anyone, no matter what their racial or ethnic background is, can make it to the top of the economy and society through hard work. As we will see below, numerous well-educated whites are even convinced that whites face at least as many barriers today as black Americans and other people of color in areas such as employment, an erroneous notion often encouraged by mass media discussions and representations. Thus, speaking decisively about the character of white privilege separates the men in this section from many other whites, of similar or lesser socioeconomic status.

THE SENSE OF LOSING POSITION AND CONTROL

A substantial number of the men interviewed for this study are not so convinced of the reality of white privilege, either theirs in particular or that of whites as a group. While we see some diversity in their views, they share a general perspective that is increasingly held by many white men in various social classes. Within their social networks, similar bits of racial knowledge are kept in circulation. While many of these respondents recognize to some degree that whiteness has had benefits for them, they also feel there has been a recent societal shift in the direction of shortchanging white men, who are too often becoming the targets of "reverse discrimination." Most do not deny that white privilege has been part of their experience, a safety cushion that has guaranteed them perks and has helped them get to where they are now, but they sense this advantage slipping away as the society becomes more multicultural and multiracial. They often express concern, fear, or resentment that they are having to, or might soon have to, give up some of the substantial privileges that white men have historically enjoyed.

One businessperson provides an example of this concern over losing social position or control in the society. Here he reflects perceptively on an interviewer's question about what being white will mean to him in an increasingly nonwhite society.

> Well, I think that it's kind of scary.... It's going to be tougher for white males like myself, or those just trying to start out, to get a job.... I believe we have a certain advantage being white in today's so-

ciety. There is definitely an advantage, being a white male. . . . Twenty years ago it wasn't as competitive . . . the workforce wasn't as diverse as it is now, so I took for granted being a white male—saying to myself, "Oh, this great white male, I should have no problem getting a job. I have an advantage, I have a step up on people." So now, in a sense, I don't take it for granted.

Like the men quoted in the previous section, he clearly recognizes that whiteness (or white maleness) has historically meant that one had greater ease in finding employment. Judging from his comments and those of other respondents in the rest of this chapter, the prospect of a more racially mixed society seems to threaten the sense of economic security that has historically typified the white male experience, especially for those in the middle and upper classes. They sense that the more or less guaranteed position in society that white men could traditionally count on is becoming less certain.

Such a guaranteed place seems to be considered a right by some white men, because they have enjoyed it for so long. This manager provides one variation on this perspective.

Being white means that I was very lucky. I never had any of the problems—of being . . . offered jobs, education, housing. It was definitely, too, an advantage and I don't think anyone can deny that. . . . Being white definitely meant I was able to acquire the better things in life, [live] in the better neighborhoods and not really have to worry about any prejudices. . . . This is my own opinion. I just think that quotas and affirmative actions really have just gotten a little bit, not really out of hand—but how long do you let certain ethnic backgrounds or racial backgrounds use something like that as a crutch at the beginning or a helping hand at the beginning? To where now it just seems to me, being white, a male, that we're being boxed into a corner where everybody has certain privileges or rights and full force of the United States government behind them. That really starts to infringe on what I consider my rights.

In addition to the employment opportunities already discussed, this man mentions unproblematic access to education and housing as some other white privileges. He recognizes and describes his whiteness as an advantage he has had over others in acquiring these things. Yet now, to him it seems that everybody has these rights and privileges, and this new situation seems to "infringe" on what he views as his own rights and privileges. If everyone has equal access to these assets, then they are no longer the privileges that they once were.

Many white men like this respondent not only perceive some loss of certain privileges, but also seem to have a sense of losing the traditional white position in the social hierarchy. Some even articulate the view that white men are now, to a serious degree, the victims of new types of discrimination, as we will see in some detail in the next section. One manager describes this feeling of being a new minority, but then adds this comment in response to a question asking if he benefits from being white:

> I'm still part of a traditional white ethnic ruling class that has been in power, and that has certain mores and standards and lifestyles and speech patterns, and givens and understanding and recognition in the ways that you do business. So I'm accepted by many people for that reason. [Q: Do you like that?] Sure, I like being accepted, sure. I like fitting in easier than having to work harder, yeah.

Again we see the importance of the white privilege of fitting well into and maneuvering through a white-dominated business world. Unmistakably, the respondent recognizes the major advantages that he has, as a member of what he terms the "white ethnic ruling class," one of the few respondents to explicitly use such a concrete term for those who dominate the society.

Interestingly, the movement of people of color into certain select fields has led many whites, like Donald Trump, to exaggerate black progress and advancement in general. One respondent suggests a variation on this view as he reflects on black advances over recent years.

> What is it like to be white? Well, for some reason I think that whites do have privileges that they shouldn't have over blacks. But I think that blacks in my lifetime have moved tremendously into positions of [status]. But you couldn't conceive when I was a boy that there would be a chief of staff in the U.S. Army [who was] a black man. That was just inconceivable. You couldn't conceive of [it], actually, even in sports; in my younger years, there were no black players in major sports. And today, all the major sports are dominated by the blacks and not the whites. Whites are now in the great minority.

While this man explicitly recognizes that whites have unjustly gained privileges, he couples this with the theme of great black progress, which one sees in commentaries on the state of the country by many other white Americans. Many whites are impressed by the fact that black Americans have attained greater status than ever before in some military branches and in certain professional sports. These changes are real, yet they seem much greater advances in the minds of many white Americans than in the minds of most black Americans, who are aware that few black Americans have made it into top positions in many key areas of society outside of sports and the military.

WHITE MEN AS VICTIMS

As we have seen, most of these white men have a strong sense of their groups' position in the social hierarchy. Some also link their sense of social position to the view that whites (or white men) generally deserve their privileged access to resources, prestige, and status. Today, a sizeable group of white men also believe that they are losing these privileges because a takeover of the country by Americans of color is under way. Unlike the previous respondents, some of these men do not explicitly acknowledge white privilege in their own lives and careers. Instead, they argue that it is Americans of color, particularly African Americans, who now seem to have significant, even unfair, societal privileges. We periodically sense the resentment expressed by those elite men who cannot clearly see their own advantages—or the racialized others' disadvantages—and thus believe that they are now victims or scapegoats in regard to racial or related social problems for which they do not feel personally responsible.

Color-Blind Victims

In the contemporary United States, many whites feel burdened or slighted because, as they frequently note, they adhere to the idea of color-blindness. Such whites often profess not to be prejudiced or discriminatory, claiming not to see themselves or others in racial terms. In addition, race-conscious programs and policies aimed at more fully including the racial others into society are viewed as betrayals of color-blind values. In this regard, we often encounter the sincere fiction that most whites are naturally benevolent and non-discriminatory without the prodding of government or the insistence of people of color, who are often viewed as the only ones bringing up the outdated matter of "race."

Those taking this perspective tend to minimize the widespread and systemic character of contemporary discrimination, often accompanied by a myopic or misinformed view of historical discrimination against African Americans and other Americans of color. Some whites do not realize, for example, that slavery's end was followed by nearly a century of government-sanctioned legal segregation, much anti-black violence, thousands of lynchings, and few rights for blacks in U.S. society. From the beginning to the present, the country's history is hardly one of color-blindness. In fact, until very recently in U.S. history, most white Americans have routinely worked to include or expand racial prohibitions and distinctions in law, education, government, the economy, and virtually every other aspect of public and private life. To claim that white Americans have a long history of deeply ingrained color-blindness—in contrast to African Americans and other people of color, who allegedly focus much too heavily on race—is a sincere fiction of great consequence. Moreover, the fact that many whites express these views in roughly similar ways suggest that they are not individually generated, but rather have been constructed and reinforced within important family, friendship, workplace, and associational groups. Human beings are what they are because of the important reference groups in which they live every day. An individual's views and knowledge about such racial matters generally hangs together because it is "part of a totality of thoughts common to a group."[8]

One professional asserts strongly that he is color-blind, yet feels that white men are now the victims of discrimination, at least in his particular city.

> I wish we could look beyond race and not see each other as blacks or whites or Asians or whatever, but just see ourselves as other people who have things to contribute to this society.... I try not to think about race too much.... Although I think I'm living in a city, working in a city that's predominately African American, and I feel negative things about being white.... That if I don't have black people, African Americans, working on my projects, then I can't get projects.

That most of the people that are hired in city government are African Americans. . . . So I feel that it's tough. . . . If I want to advance, [and] if I were to try to advance in city government, that I would have a very hard time doing it, not being African American.

Articulating a common "I try not to think about race" stance, this professional reveals that he does indeed think about racial matters in some depth. Clearly, he feels that being white is sometimes negative, such as when it comes to getting jobs with the local government in a city that now has a large black population. Elsewhere in his interview, he explains that he also did not like the former situation, when the local government excluded blacks from jobs. As a white person who did not support past discrimination, he now seems to feel burdened by apparently having to compensate for that past discrimination today in his hiring practices.

Noting that he is color-blind in his dealings with others, another professional reports feeling like a scapegoat.

Sometimes I feel that the racial problems in the United States are blamed on the middle-aged white male. However, I feel, as a middle-aged male, that I've never created this problem, and I've always worked to resolve that problem. So I don't see . . . myself as being a guilty individual in whatever is being perceived as the racial problem in the United States. . . . I have honest feelings that I don't think that race is an issue in any of my decisions during the day.

From this well-articulated perspective, terms like "blame" and "guilt" are often used to characterize significant aspects of the white experience as we move into the twenty-first century. Especially when whites view themselves strongly as color-blind in their own actions, they feel that matters of race enter into their frames of reference mainly when they are being made to feel guilty for the society's racial problems.

Although he asserts that he does not really see himself as white, this perceptive professional also argues that white men are a singled-out and overburdened group in U.S. society.

I don't think I really think of myself as a white person. Certainly there have been times, because as you go through certain processes, whether it's losing a job or seeing your child go to college and be affected by the fact that they are white when they come from a mid-

dle-class society. It almost seems more difficult for them in the last
ten or fifteen years. And almost more difficult as being a white middle-class American male.... There are things being done for the
women, there are things being done for the blacks, there are things
being done for the Hispanics. And I think a lot of white middle-class
American males feel that they are really carrying a load. [Q: Do you
feel that way?] Sometimes, sure, yeah. Sometimes, [like] April 15th
when you pay your tax bills, you really feel like you're carrying the
load.

From this perspective, other major groups in society now often reap
more advantages than white men, and as a white man who pays substantial taxes he feels shortchanged. In a society where women and people of
color have made gains, whites (or white men) are said to have a more
difficult time in the occupational and educational arenas.

In these and other accounts in this chapter, some white men indicate
that they do not notice, or think much about, being white until they feel
others are singling them out or stigmatizing them for being white or
white male. It seems that it is at that point that they begin to see whiteness as a besieged and beleaguered identity worth noticing as such.

Certainly, a white man can take the reasonable position, which may
well be correct, that he does not knowingly discriminate in his daily
rounds, yet still miss the critical reality of institutionalized racism in his
social worlds—the continuing patterns of subtle, covert, and blatant discrimination that are still maintained by whites as a group. Ignoring this
larger discriminatory reality and its many privileges, even for whites
who themselves may not discriminate, contributes greatly to its malign
persistence in the society.

"Extinct Like the Dinosaur"

In their interviews, some of these elite men did not make much of an attempt to portray themselves as color-blind. They, too, emphasize that
whites, or white men, as the beleaguered or targeted group in U.S. society. We have pointed out the extent to which whites can exaggerate the
presence and power of people of color in society, sometimes perceiving
themselves as "the minority." However, this influential executive goes a
bit farther, by suggesting that white men are becoming almost extinct.

> Well, you're almost becoming extinct, like the dinosaur. I feel you're at a disadvantage today if you're white and a male. There [are] a couple different factors working against you. It's like basically if you're white and you're born here, I believe it's a disadvantage—as opposed to coming into the country, not even being white, especially, and not being born here, you have a greater advantage. It seems like you get more help financially, socially, and a lot more social programs now are out [for nonwhites and immigrants].

This man sees disadvantages for whites, or white men, as coming from increases in power not only of resident Americans of color but also from new immigrants. Significantly, his perspective is not just his own, for it seems to be shared within important networks of white men across major institutional sectors in the society. One interesting idea articulated by many whites, including this respondent, is the largely fictional notion that government programs have provided more help for nonwhites and immigrants than for native-born whites. And the "almost extinct dinosaur" view, though creative and obviously signaling a strong feeling of being embattled, is contradicted by the fact that over 90 percent of major corporations and other major private and government organizations are currently headed by white men like our respondents.[9]

Another respondent also holds to this view that white men like himself are targets for racial discrimination today.

> I feel that I am definitely becoming discriminated against because I am white. For me, I mean, all the affirmative action things that go on make it harder for me to get a job in a governmental agency than for a Latino or an African American or any other ethnic. It's harder for me than any other group.... Quite a few years ago ... when I was applying to colleges, if a kid was black, he didn't have to get as good grades as I did because the colleges were just trying to fill the gap, so they had to fill the minority gaps. So it definitely hurt me there.... If you just watch the news, half of the news anchors, everybody, is represented.... Just look at the news anchors themselves. They always try to have a woman, a black, a Latino, Asians. They never have white males.

This man localizes his experiences, giving examples of times and places where he has felt discriminated against. He also has a sense that his competition is not only from blacks but also from Latinos and Asians. The inclusion of Latinos and Asians in some of these respondents' accounts seems to be part of a new elite consciousness of the growth and presence of groups that were more or less invisible to most whites until a decade or so ago. Like some other respondents, he cites publicly visible people of color to illustrate his point about the decline in the social position of white men. Though rarely as numerous as whites suggest, these highly visible media people seem to support the erroneous impression of many whites that black Americans and other Americans of color are doing very well across most major institutions of the society.[10]

Along with feelings of extinction or exclusion frequently comes a perception that white men are being blamed or punished for the racial wrongs of the larger society. The themes of blame and guilt repeatedly surface in these upper-income respondents' commentaries. They see blame or guilt as being unfairly pushed upon them. Thus, in response to a question about what it means to be white, a marketing professional has this to say:

> It's difficult. Sometimes I feel as though the finger is pointed at me, and I'm used as a scapegoat for a lot of the circumstances that are both artificially created and realistically the case, in terms of society. I feel as though I'm portrayed as the bad guy because of things that happened many years ago and today. Apparently, somewhere down the line, I was empowered, but nobody told me about it.

Indeed, many white men resent terms like "white privilege" because they do not feel empowered by virtue of being white or white male. In fact, they actually feel scapegoated as the "bad guys" in the society. Significantly, however, as we see in comments from other well-off respondents, these feelings seem to be based on what they feel are public images, and not on actual experiences of being excluded from particular professions or residential neighborhoods because they are white men.

In a probing comment, another respondent indicates a more nuanced concern about bearing responsibility for the country's patterns of racism.

> [In the past] I sort of felt like we had treated the blacks terribly, and I was embarrassed by that.... As I have gotten older, I've come to think, "Hey, wait a second, I don't have to pay this price forever, okay?" What more can we do? ... [I am] a member of a race who picked on

or subjugated another race, [but] in the last few years I have felt a little bit like maybe I am on the other end of that. Not truly, I really don't
believe I'm discriminated against, but I do believe that whites in general increasingly sort of pay the price of being white, okay? No matter
how much, how hard we try, there is a certain point where ... what
more can you do?

Though he personally has not been discriminated against, this concerned respondent suggests that whites in general are now paying an
excessive price for the racial discrimination of the past—which he
acknowledges was terrible. Expressing a view that is common among
white Americans, he suggests, in phrases like "no matter how hard we
try," that whites have now done everything possible to get rid of racial
discrimination.

In one of the strongest comments on white guilt made by these elite
respondents, another urban professional replies concerning the issue of
feeling guilty as the society becomes more multiracial.

Okay, I have no guilt. If anything, I have anger. And I have impatience
towards the fact that, again, the general point of view that minorities
are not responsible. And they are very, very expensive from a tax-
payer's point of view for what they demand from society—and very
little, for what they give back to society.

Much like the previous respondent who thought about his whiteness around the federal tax deadline of April 15, this well-educated professional feels that whites are paying excessively for certain unnamed
government programs that benefit minority groups. A recurring component of the racial consciousness of the white majority today seems to
be the view that black Americans and other Americans of color are making unjust demands on the society and that the latter are mostly or entirely responsible for their own problems.

POSITIVE VIEWS OF DIVERSITY

Some demographers have predicted that, sometime in the middle of the
twenty-first century, white Americans will be outnumbered by those
Americans who are not white, a trend that some have referred to as the
"browning of America." Already, the states of California, Texas, New

Mexico, and Hawaii—as well as half the country's one hundred largest cities—have majority populations that are not white and European. We have discussed previously how white fears of and exaggerations about being "taken over" by other groups often center on the growth and social mobility of African Americans. However, much of the growth that is generating the new diversification of the United States is coming from expansion in the Latino and Asian-American populations. Since the end of the racist quotas in U.S. immigration law, which targeted immigrants of color for exclusion until the late 1960s, we have seen a shift in the national origins of most immigrants, such that there are now many more entering from Latin American and Asian countries than from European countries.

Many whites, both in the elite and in the general population, view this change in population composition with skepticism or fear, and we have seen some of these concerns in the quotes of previous respondents. The prospect of whites no longer holding a majority of society's resources seems disappointing or threatening to many of our upper-income respondents. However, some of them indicate that they actually welcome such demographic changes. Some of these privileged men take a broad view and articulate the idea that the immigration of people of color is a boost to the U.S. economy and a beneficial stimulant for the country's work ethic, while others predict that whites being in the minority may possibly usher in some positive changes in U.S. racial and ethnic relations. Some adopt a variation on the traditional color-blind approach, suggesting that anyone should be able to contribute to U.S. society so long as they work hard, regardless of their racial group. Others take a more antiracist stance and focus on the possibility of the current white power structure being decentered, thereby allowing greater room for success for all people of color within a more democratic social and political system. These men do not feel threatened or angered by the reality of the white group shrinking as a percentage in the country's racial mix.

Hardworking Americans Come In All Colors

Some among these elite respondents believe that the country as a whole stands to benefit from the contributions that can be made by new Latino and Asian immigrants, and thus do not feel threatened by their inclusion in an ever more multiracial society. An insightful college professor provides one example of this view: "I'm generally pro-immigration. I really think it's been a source for revitalization of the country. And I think … people who immigrate to this country are highly motivated. They tend to be achievers [and] they tend not to be drains on society in any way." In contrast to those who feel they are "carrying a load" for people of color, this professor rejects the view that the new immigrants are a drain on society and instead views them as a revitalizing force that enhances the country's positive attribute of achievement.

Similarly, a company president holds fast to a positive view of increasing immigration, even when the interviewer offers challenges to his strong position.

> That's great. Let's get more. [Q: Why?] Because that is what makes America great. It's that good people want to come here. We're a Darwinist melting pot. [Q: What would you say if they were coming from Africa?] If they were well-educated and able to make a significant contribution to the community, I say let them come. [Q: But wouldn't you have to say that most immigrants from Latin America aren't well-educated?] I don't know that for a fact, but the immigrants with whom I come in contact are very, very, very motivated, and very productive. Very trainable, very interested in learning, good people.

Like the respondent before him, this man does not mention the racial characteristics of the current immigrants in his initial response. Viewing the matter from the position of an employer, he in effect counters the views of anti-immigration respondents with his statement that the immigrant workers he has encountered are committed to hard work and to becoming positive contributors to the society. Even when the interviewer brings up the issue of the African or Latin American origins of immigrants, this respondent does not indicate any fears but instead maintains his positive convictions about welcoming diverse groups of newcomers as part of an expanding and diversifying U.S. society.

Another respondent, a manager, rejects exclusionary views of immigration, seeing them as outdated and uninformed.

> I am really looking forward to it.... It'll be much more interesting.... Historical records show us that the work ethic productivity gains that

result from a large mix of a new ethnic population coming in has made a major contribution.... [It will be] a fabulous change in the business culture and in the diversity of the way people live.

More than just being supportive of the racial and ethnic changes brought by immigration, this man says that he is looking forward to these changes. As in the previous quotes, we see an emphasis on how the work ethic and business culture will be enriched, as well as on how everyday life will be enriched as well. These last few quotes illustrate how some explicit or implicit reference to color-blindness can be coupled with a view supportive of immigration and greater racial and ethnic diversity in the country. While in many instances asserted color-blindness is a sincere fiction masking negative beliefs and feelings about Americans of color or linking to denials of the reality of continuing racial discrimination and inequality, at times we do find it associated with views that are openly aware of these racial inequalities and that do espouse government policies favorable to Americans of color, including the recent immigrants of color.

Disrupting White Power: Some Antiracist Perspectives

Other positive views of increasing racial and ethnic diversity in the United States focus more specifically on how overturning the traditional dominance of whites in the society could benefit racial relations and improve the lives of people of color, if not all Americans. We might characterize such responses as antiracist because they explicitly acknowledge the racialized power structure at the center of U.S. society and articulate some ways to disrupt it. Although such antiracist views are clearly limited to a minority among these elite white men, they are important for us to examine in order to make it clear that not every influential white man feels threatened by the idea of having to share power with others. In fact, some welcome and work toward changes in the direction of a truly democratic, multiracial society.

In their critical responses, some of these respondents not only focus on positive changes for society at large, but also on the benefits for their own lives of a more diverse country. One corporate manager makes this penetrating comment:

I have been through a large amount of diversity training. I have been through a three-day retreat-on-diversity workshop. It was pure immersion. I have done role playing in submissive roles. I have had my eyes opened up tremendously to the plights of nonwhites. I have done in the last several years a lot of volunteer work at an inner-city, all-black school and worked for the principal and the teachers. And it has been to me a very eye-opening but rewarding and consciousness-raising experience. I have come to find out that I truly like the teachers and the principals. It has been a good experience for me.

Many companies now offer diversity workshops for their employees at all levels, but it is often unclear what effects these workshops have. In this case, however, it is clear that the workshops sensitized this man to some degree about what it is like to be oppressed. He also indicates that he has taken it upon himself to interact with people outside his racial group and class, those with whom he would not ordinarily come into interpersonal contact. These experiences with a diverse group of other people, including well-educated African Americans, have been consciousness-raising for him. Once again, we see the importance of certain types of cross-racial contacts in reshaping white thinking about racial matters. Stepping outside one's traditional reference groups opens up the possibility of new racial and ethnic understandings.

Other respondents speak less personally, but just as positively, about what an increasing population of people of color will likely mean for the society. An attorney views demographic changes in the direction of societal diversification as a beneficial development.

I believe that that will be a very good thing for our society. In recent years I have become more aware of how poorly the races relate to each other in this country. And I think that if the population numbers are such that whites do not dominate in numbers, that it might be the best chance we have for improving the divisions among the races.

This candid and perceptive response acknowledges that the root of racial problems in the society lies substantially in white domination, at least in terms of numbers. This is not an easy thing to admit when one is a member of the group that holds most of the reins of economic, political, and social power—and that thus has the greatest ability to end racial divisions.

A scientist takes a similar perspective on the country's increased diversity, informed by some thoughts about the historical background.

> I think actually it's a positive trend, in my view, because the history of racial biases [is] such [that] the minority population has been nonwhite. And being a nonwhite and being a minority is tough, it's going back to the years of slavery. We are only one hundred–plus years past the U.S. Emancipation Proclamation. So I think now it becomes more of an equilibrium, where the nonwhites equally exceed whites. I believe that this prejudice will probably subside, because the major segments of the population will now have to take leadership roles—who are nonwhite. And it will be just a matter of almost expediency that now the ... color border will essentially, I think, disappear. I think it will have to. That's what I hope happens.

While other respondents sometimes point to television broadcasters and athletes as indicators of black success, this man recognizes, insightfully, that an actual shift in the balance of power will require Americans of color to move into "leadership roles." He views racial prejudice as likely to be reduced when there are major structural changes in the society. Recent research indicates that the majority of whites believe that those problems of racial discrimination remaining in society are not major or systemic, and that, if we all could just "get along," racial tensions would subside. This majority perspective includes the idea, articulated by some of our respondents, that black Americans and other Americans of color should stop making what whites see as unreasonable demands for societal change.[11] However, as this man shows, a developed antiracist perspective means understanding racial barriers as a white problem and as built into the structure of society.

Those men who articulate strongly antiracist ideas tend to variously accent a combination of history, social structure, and individual-level factors in analyzing contemporary racism and arriving at what needs to be done to eradicate it. One professional focuses on all these levels as he responds to a question about the ongoing shift in the country's demographic composition.

> I think, actually, that may end up improving race relations. Well, for a long time, the whites were not only the majority of the population, but they were the oppressors. First they were running roughshod over the Native Americans, treating them like they were less than human,

[and] enslaving and doing horrible things to the African Americans. And ... I think the biggest problem America has is the race problem. When the numbers swing so that people of color are in the majority, then it's not going to be so easy for the whites to believe that they're somehow superior and dominant.... And the odds are that they'll have fewer positions of power ... and, well, I think then they'll have to be realistic.... Also, I'm in an interracial marriage ... and it's my personal conviction that only when we have enough intermarriage ... and we have a lot of different hues and a lot of different mixing is there really going to be an eradication to any great degree of the race problem.

As this perceptive respondent views the situation, whites have abused their power throughout history—and a numbers shift can help redress the power imbalance. Structural change, coupled with individual-level mixing across racial groups, is likely to help eliminate racism. Like the manager who has had diversity training and does volunteer work in the inner city, this professional has crossed the racial boundary in his personal life, which likely has affected his perspective on the increasing diversity of the country.

Avowedly antiracist responses like those of the last few respondents do not employ vague notions of color-blindness. These white men explicitly discuss "race" as a social construct that has generally placed whites in positions of dominance and people of color in positions of subordination. As they see it, it is not enough for everyone to stop noticing race. Rather, structural changes in the society must be made, such that whites no longer dominate and people of color are more fully included in the mainstream of society, and not just on the periphery. While in the minority in our sample, these last few elite men are on the cutting edge of contemporary thinking about issues of racism and the multiracial future of the United States.

CONCLUSION

Engaging in much symbolic effort, many whites, including many elite white men, continue to construct and reproduce an array of sincere fictions about white America and white Americans. Such fictions are taken as faithful representations of societal realities. Numerous respondents strongly assert the view that they do not see or accent racial categories in their own lives. However, behind this facade of color-blindness —a common perspective in white America today—we see that they often do, at one point or another, indicate a definite sense of their advantaged socioracial position in the society. While some hide their feelings more or less completely behind a facade of color-blindness, others note some of the ways that whiteness has benefited them. Interestingly, it is often when they undertake to compare their social or economic situations to those of Americans of color that they seem best able to articulate the meaning of whiteness in their lives. Once they discuss that meaning, it often appears as a complex mix of feeling lucky, advantaged, or entitled—and sometimes threatened or fearful. Clearly, some feel that white men are now blamed unfairly for the country's racial troubles and difficulties. It is also evident that they often have strong convictions on these racial matters, including their understandings about what the shrinking white piece of the "racial pie" means now, or will mean in the future, to them as white men. These men often hold their views on racial issues with strong conviction and some emotion.

Numerically, the majority of people in the United States fall into the lower class, the working class, and the lower-middle class. Workers and families in this sizeable group, especially those with less–skilled jobs and lower incomes, are usually the first to suffer in times of economic recession or depression. Whether they are white or not, rarely do members of this group speak of being privileged in terms of economic and other social resources.[12] In contrast, numerous men in our sample do recognize and state that they benefit, at least in a few ways, from being white and male in America. Nonetheless, however perceptive they may be about the privileges held by white men, many still hold to some sincere fictions about racial matters in the United States. Those who claim that people of color now reap at least as many of society's socioeconomic rewards as whites, or that white men are becoming "almost extinct like the dinosaur," seem rather out of touch with the reality of—or at least the data on—important societal conditions of power and privilege.

We should also keep in mind that these men are generally well-educated and well-positioned members of society. Whether based in fact or not, their perceptions about racial and related social realities have substantial power to alter the societal landscape, for better or for worse, as they help to shape important corporate, governmental, media, and other organizational policies at the local, regional, or national levels.

As we have seen, a number of these powerful men do in fact acknowledge that racial discrimination is systemic, articulating a clear understanding of the need for a significant shift in the balance of economic and political power in the United States. Sometimes passionate as well, these latter men often celebrate the positive changes in themselves and in society that might be brought about as whites share significant power with people of color. Interestingly, while they are perhaps the least likely to use vague color-blind language to indicate that they do not notice racial categories, they also show the least personal investment in their own identity as whites, and seem most hopeful about a more multiracial and more democratic future for the country.

How have these men arrived at a position not shared by the majority of whites in the United States? The accounts of their lives suggest that one critical factor, beyond their own personal openness to a counter-system view, is a greater level of equal-status or intimate contacts with Americans of color. Increasing the numbers of whites who can see beyond the facade of a vague color-blindness to an exciting new future of all Americans sharing power within a truly democratic, multiracial society may be the key to ensuring an antiracist and egalitarian future for this country. We will return to these important issues in the last chapter.

4

PERSPECTIVES ON AFRICAN AMERICANS AND OTHER AMERICANS OF COLOR

Positive images of white Americans do not stand alone. In the white mind, as in white actions, images of and feelings about the white self and white society are often associated with a range of images and feelings about the racial "others." Certainly, members of the dominant racial group differ significantly in the ways that they think about and act toward these racial others. Some may be, as sociologist Herbert Blumer suggested, openly hostile, while others may "have charitable and protective feelings, marked by a sense of piety and tinctured by benevolence; others may be condescending and reflect mild contempt; and others may be disposed to politeness and considerateness with no feelings of truculence."[1] Yet others, as we saw in the last chapter, may be strongly antiracist in their views or dispositions.

Over several centuries, whites have constructed an array of sincere fictions about the racial others. As with sincere fictions about the white self, fictional representations of racial outgroups often prevent individuals from seeing, or seeing clearly, that their society is pervaded by widespread racial prejudice and discrimination. The character of the representations often shifts over time. Interestingly, survey researchers generally report a steady decline in traditional anti-black stereotyping and prejudice among whites over the last half-century.[2] However, although whites' expressions of traditional prejudice and stereotypes in public arenas or to survey researchers have declined in number, this does not mean that anti-black stereotypes, sentiments, and discrimination are now of little consequence in the United States. Numerous researchers have noted that the contemporary forms and emphases of attitudinal expression are often different from the traditional racial stereotypes and prejudices expressed by whites, particularly those articulated prior to the 1960s civil rights movements.[3]

While traditional racial stereotyping typically branded black Americans as naturally or biologically inferior, the contemporary cultural-superiority perspective generally rejects biological notions and accents certain cultural dimensions and values that account, in the white view, for why black Americans have not done as well as white Americans in society. This cultural-deficiency perspective views white Americans as having better values (e.g., a good work ethic), families, and communities than black Americans. In some ways this perspective is no less harmful than the traditional racial views. Regularly, in the mass media, in schools, and in the statements of politicians and pundits, black Americans are reminded that they themselves are responsible for their continuing social problems. Recall the point we made in chapter 1 that black Americans, especially as a group, are often misrecognized by whites as substantially different in values and culture—even so different as to be dangerous and threatening. Continuing racial discrimination and inequality are grounded in social interactions where people are not recognized in their full humanity and do not meet as "sovereign equals."[4]

Whites who adopt some version of a blaming-the-victim point of view can accept a few black individuals who do not fit the stereotype as, more or less, exceptions. Indeed, most whites are aware that numerous African Americans have positive traits and achievements that should be respected, yet still tend to see those African Americans who are successful as somehow exceptions to their group. Social psychologist Thomas Pettigrew has noted common white reactions to the achievements of African Americans and has posited what he calls the "ultimate attribution error" on the part of whites, which includes not only blaming black

Americans for their failures, but also discounting black successes by attributing the latter to luck or unfair advantages rather than to intelligence and hard work.[5]

Often connected to the idea of cultural deficiency is the notion that there is no longer a serious problem of discrimination in U.S. society. From this perspective, it is frequently suggested that the 1960s civil rights laws and policies have taken care of most racial discrimination. Continuing racial inequality is seen as resulting primarily from weaknesses in the culture and communities of black Americans, rather than from weaknesses in the dominant, white-controlled institutions. The policy implications of this point of view are seen in survey research that finds that, while a majority of whites indicate that they believe in the innate equality of whites and blacks, they also express little support for strong public policies, such as *aggressive* affirmative action, that might bring about such equality.[6] The contemporary cultural-deficiency perspective assumes there are few racial barriers left in the society, and that the main barriers to achievement and prosperity for Americans of color are those that they create for themselves. Thus, forceful government policies aimed at reducing racial discrimination are not currently needed.

This cultural-deficiency viewpoint is also part of an atmosphere wherein certain sincere fictions of the white self and society flourish. As we see throughout this book, many whites sincerely view themselves as color-blind. Like white respondents in other research studies, our respondents often hold egalitarian views at the same time that they also espouse some negative racial views or feelings about black Americans. They have generally abandoned the old racist stereotypes and language, while at the same time they often hold views that are still racially stereotypical in regard to black culture, values, or families. We should note that this accent on cultural and family deficiencies among African Americans is not really new, for some versions of it have existed for at least two centuries in the United States. However, what is new is that it seems to have become the centerpiece of racial understandings held by a majority of white Americans.

Among other things, the now commonplace blame-the-victim perspective does not acknowledge that much racial stereotyping and discrimination are still structured into major U.S. institutions and that whites as a group continue to have substantial and distinctive social, economic, and political advantages. From this point of view, whites are open-minded, fair, hardworking, and virtuous, while the values and culture of African Americans and other Americans of color are still holding them back. This perspective relies upon the myth that the United States is a meritocracy—that is, a society that consistently and justly rewards those who are deserving, without regard for skin color, and rightly penalizes those who do not play by its allegedly meritocratic rules.

Although this viewpoint is held by whites in all social classes, we see through our interviews just how salient it is in the minds of many white men in the upper reaches of U.S. society. They, like many other whites, stress the meritocratic idea that the socioeconomic system generally rewards all those who work hard. Thus, numerous respondents view African Americans, and sometimes other Americans of color, as not working hard enough.

There are a number of likely reasons for this point of view. Because of extensive residential segregation and significant work segregation, most whites, and especially elite whites, do not have much in the way of recurring and close contacts with African Americans; we have already suggested how limited close, equal-status contacts are for many of our respondents. Most whites in the elite do not have the opportunity to observe just how hard African Americans must work to survive in U.S. society. Moreover, when they do have that opportunity, somehow socially inherited stereotypes seem to blind many of them to the reality of that hard work. Undoubtedly, African Americans generally work as hard as the typical white person.

There are a variety of perspectives found within this group of elite white men. Very few espouse elements of the older, traditional racial stereotyping and language in the interviews. Yet, numerous respondents articulate some aspects of a more contemporary blame-the-victim perspective and view the U.S. socioeconomic system as inherently fair. And, at some point in their interviews, several take an avowedly antiracist position by critiquing the structural character of U.S. racism or advocating more aggressive policy intervention, such as better enforcement of civil rights laws, to end racial discrimination.

SOME TRADITIONAL STEREOTYPING AND LANGUAGE

Even though most white Americans like to think of old-fashioned stereotyping as having disappeared among well-educated white Americans, there are still some who hold to the old racialized language and are willing to use it publicly. It is not just poorly educated whites who do so. However, in our sample, only one or two respondents made use of the traditional racialized language. For example, one respondent provides this comment:

> Well, let's look at the statistics. The Negro is about ten percent of the population and eighty percent of the crimes are committed by Negroes, so what does that tell you? What does that tell you? What does that tell us? Absolutely, of course, much more crime is committed by them. And anywhere they are, they're criminals. They're criminals here, they're criminals in Africa.

Note that this respondent uses the term "Negroes." Rare in these interviews, this usage suggests he holds to a very dated view on racial matters.

In the course of our interviews, a number of the respondents, like many other whites, cite incorrect or exaggerated statistics in discussions of contemporary social problems such as crime. In fact, African Americans do not account for such a huge share of U.S. crime as is suggested by this respondent. For several types of street crime, African Americans are in fact arrested and imprisoned in percentages that are significantly greater than their proportion in the population. However, as we will observe later in comments from a few respondents who work in the criminal justice system, such disproportion is to a significant extent the result of discrimination against African Americans within the justice system, as well as in the larger society.

Elsewhere in his interview, this respondent also strongly criticizes black Americans for citing contemporary racial oppression as a reason for their disadvantaged condition in society.

> Just look around, and see where they [black Americans] are and see where we are. And the excuses they use . . . are that they have been oppressed by the whites. Well, a lot of people were oppressed by the whites. The Jews when they came to this country were highly oppressed, the Irish were oppressed, the Italians were oppressed. They

are not sitting around sucking their thumbs, blaming society for their ills. No, they jumped up, they got ahead, they made something of themselves, while the Negro has not, by and large.

Here, oppression is only acknowledged as existing in the past. The comparisons to Jews, Irish, and Italians, who are seen as quickly moving ahead, are interesting, because they are all groups now regarded as white.

Very few respondents in the sample use such blunt language. Others who seem to hold to some of the traditional stereotypes about the natural or intellectual inferiority of black Americans use more moderate or ambiguous language. They show an awareness that such ideas and images are no longer socially desirable, with a few expressing some regret that this is the case. One respondent provides this pointed commentary:

> Well, it starts back fifteen, twenty years ago, Dr. Shockley, inventor of the transistor who did substantial sociological research, showed that, matched on a variety of variables, blacks are born differently [in intelligence], on standardized intelligence tests. . . . They attempted to adjust for socioeconomic variables such as income, nutrition, housing, educational level of parents. I'm not that familiar with the research, so I can't say, but normal research procedure would suggest that that kind of matching has to be done, otherwise you can't draw any valid conclusions. . . . It's very socially unacceptable to say blacks are not as smart as the whites, are not as smart as the Asians, but there's a lot of research pointing to the fact that it is the case. And the liberals cannot accept that, on a critical basis, because it violates the empirical philosophical ideals that everybody has to be equal and that the purpose, the reason for differences is caused by environmental and cultural factors.

It is interesting that a few of these influential respondents use the language of statistics and research to discuss or support the traditional stereotyped view that black Americans are inferior intellectually to white Americans. This respondent uses such language even though he is admittedly not familiar with the actual research. Notably, this respondent rejects the position taken by other respondents that reported racial differences in scores on so-called "intelligence" tests are due to environmental factors. Viewing himself as a conservative on these racial matters, he suggests that more "liberal" ideas dominate contemporary racial discourse and expresses some resentment about that situation.

Similarly, several other elite men either express an inclination to believe that there are some innate intelligence differences between whites and blacks, or suggest that hypotheses about such differences are reasonable and should be researched and candidly discussed in public forums. For example, one business leader put it this way:

> I believe there is some potential in the genetic trees that there could be some difference from one culture to another, or from one race to another. And it probably is something that bears some study.... I don't know whether it is right or wrong, true or false. If they really have some meaningful research done by people who really care about that area of research, are experts in that, and they've got some good empirical and rational data, then I think we should look at that and not just say, "boy, that's out of bounds, you can't look at that because it sounds racist" on the face of it.

While this respondent also indicates unfamiliarity with research on racial differences in intelligence, he does support the idea that such research should be done. Another respondent, a professional, suggests that research on intelligence has been rejected for the wrong reasons, in his response to a question about *The Bell Curve*, a book that uses paper-and-pencil test data to assert some genetically linked racial differences in intelligence.

> I think that it's an interesting concept that ... will never be answered.... But the part I found most interesting about it is that people are [saying] it's politically incorrect to even consider that.... I think it's interesting that it's caused such a big brouhaha that you could even consider that possibility.... It's politically incorrect. You're not allowed to do it.

These critical responses suggest that some elite white men are disappointed that certain traditional views of racial differences in intelligence can no longer be as freely researched, analyzed, or expressed as they once were. However, we should note that books such as *The Bell Curve* have sold hundreds of thousands of copies. Their arguments about racial differences in intelligence and related abilities have in fact received much research and media attention and more than ample public discussion after their release.

THE CONTEMPORARY BLAME-THE-VICTIM PERSPECTIVE: SOME DIMENSIONS

A large majority of these upper-income respondents do not express ideas akin to traditionally racist views accenting biology, but instead display some stereotyping and negative generalizing in more subtle or liberal ways. One thing to note in numerous comments is how the respondents change voice when talking about African Americans or other people of color. We periodically see a certain emotional and other distancing of black Americans as a clearly defined "them," which is somehow different from the equally strongly defined "us." Although these respondents frequently accept some negative stereotypes or generalizations about black Americans as a group, they attribute contemporary black problems to cultural or socialization differences, rather than to any distinctive biological or genetic factors. Either implicitly or explicitly, white families, culture, and communities are seen as superior—or at least as the standard for judging these racial matters. Those who adhere to this perspective also allow room for occasional or substantial exceptions to the stereotype, exceptions that may be seen as resulting from changes in the societal environment.

Even though they come from different occupations and areas of the country, and have been through different educational systems, these men often report broadly similar understandings of African Americans and other Americans of color. Their ideas suggest, once again, that understandings about racial matters are typically not unique to a particular person but are constructed and recalled within the social reference groups to which individuals belong.

Still, while numerous views of black America are shared, there is still considerable variability in the tone and emphases in the respondents' particular assessments. For example, the following respondent suggests his sympathetic outlook on the black family.

> So many of the black families do not have the father figure, the children go astray. It's not because they're black, it's because of the family.... I don't think the blacks are born saying, "Okay, I'm not supposed to have a father. I'm supposed to run around and do things."... There are many, many fine black families around.... We're generalizing now, and I think, unfortunately, a large part of the black

population has this family problem. . . . It's very, very difficult to generalize why some blacks work out fine while others don't, and the fact that some could work out exactly the same as anyone else leads me to believe that it's not because of the color; it's because of the environment they're brought up in. There are so many that are brought up in these urban areas that are so crummy, and the housing is bad because there is not enough money to do better, and you don't have it because there's not a regular income, and it's a vicious cycle.

Again we see some significant sympathy for the plight of black families, and an attempt to make sense out of the negative images of black families that are often communicated in the mass media. This executive feels that there are "many fine black families," but that a "large part" of the black population has major and distinctive family problems. He rejects the traditional notion that African Americans are somehow born with this problem. Although he does not mention racial discrimination, he does cite various other environmental conditions as responsible.

A common negative generalization among these elite men, as well as among whites generally, is that a very large proportion of black Americans have families that are seriously deficient, at least as measured by conventional white views of the ideal family. Indeed, as we see below, several respondents even describe black Americans as having *no* real sense of family. This common generalization is then relied on to explain problems ranging from scores on intelligence tests to incarceration rates. We should also note that such understandings typically mix facts about the problems of some African-American families with a lack of recognition of the serious role of individual and institutionalized discrimination in creating these problems—and without a realization of the many strengths of black families.

Family Background, Not Discrimination

While the contemporary white perspective on black families and communities rejects traditional racist arguments about biological inferiority, it is quite distinct from an antiracist perspective focusing on systemic and persisting discrimination as a major factor lying behind the inequalities in the lives of black Americans. Many respondents express no feelings about the painful reality of racial discrimination as it continues to affect the everyday lives of African Americans and other Americans of color. With numerous respondents, most of their negative affect is directed at what they see as the inadequate culture or problematic values of African Americans, rather than at the racial discrimination they still must face.

Indeed, as we have already seen, serious and widespread discrimination is often claimed to be a thing of the past. In discussing what he describes as a major achievement gap between whites and blacks, one professional agrees with numerous other respondents that the black family, rather than anti-black discrimination, is the likely causal factor.

> Some claim it's due to discrimination, but obviously as we ... get further and further away from the days of official discrimination, it seems to me that explanation ... is less and less believable. I think the explanation lies in different family values and family backgrounds.... [With] somebody that comes from a family where both parents are educated, education is more likely to be stressed in that home and thought of as very important.... They're going to have read to their child more, and worked with their child, taught him to learn the ABCs. Reading is going to be more important, there are going to be more books in the home.... But I think all of those things have a much more compelling explanation for the so-called gap than genetics.

Clearly, much contemporary discourse about racial matters among educated white Americans involves a significant distancing from older notions of genetic racial differences. Yet, there is often an assumption that black Americans somehow have "different family values," and, as in this last comment, that this difference includes a reduced emphasis on education. Once again, we see the accent on cultural inferiority. Such respondents may also have in mind certain class differences (between less educated, working-class black Americans and better educated, middle-class white Americans) which, in their view, involve significant differences in family values about such matters as children's education.

Though common among whites, this argument is striking because much research shows that one of the deeply held family values for black Americans, including those in the working class, is that of getting more education. Indeed, most African Americans are not as poorly educated as many whites assume. The majority now have a least a high school education, and most desire more education for themselves or their children. Moreover, several research studies have shown that black Americans have a *greater* desire for post-secondary education than whites, although they do recognize the existence of racial barriers and thus have lower expectations than whites in regard to securing that education. A comprehensive view of difficulties in regard to getting more education would incorporate the harsh reality of discriminatory barriers for black adults and children.[7]

Many whites use a cultural argument to explain not only educational differences but also the higher arrest or imprisonment rates for black Americans. For example, another professional discounts discrimination in the justice system in favor of family breakdown as the deciding factor.

> I think the reason goes back to the fundamental breakdown of the family unit within the black society. There has not been ... a value system that demanded or expected black men to stay in the traditional family unit and provide for the family in traditional ways. And, unfortunately, I think that the absence of role models for younger black males perpetuates the system.... It has to do with the absence of traditional values within the family unit. And the argument could be, if you chose to take such a position, that some of them have been put there unfairly, because the judicial system has not dealt with blacks on [an] equitable basis. I think, to use that argument, though ... it really doesn't have a lot of validity in my mind. I have no doubt that the justice [system] has not always been a fair and equitable one. I think that it is a flawed system at best, but on the other hand, to use that [as] an excuse for a third of the population sector to have been either imprisoned or on probation is to deny that there is a more significant underlying problem.

The steady repetition of this view among white Americans, including many of our elite respondents, suggests that there are group understandings on the issue of the values and character of black families—understandings that are widely shared and repeated in many white networks and associations, as well as in the mass media.

Such views generally betray a substantial lack of knowledge about the values and realities of African-American families and their arduous past and recent history. For nearly four centuries, African Americans have made aggressive efforts to maintain strong and supportive families under extremely oppressive conditions. Today, although African Americans do have fewer households headed by married couples than white Americans, for both groups the most valued and common family structure is the two-parent, married household.[8] Note, too, that there is often a patriarchal assumption in some respondents' analyses, such that the presence of a strong father figure is considered essential to a healthy family. However, social science research shows that, regardless of racial group, the most significant factor in the well-being of children in single-parent homes is not the lack of a strong father as role model, but instead the lack of economic support and stability brought about by low-wage jobs for the mother (or the absent father). Female workers earn significantly less, on the average, than male workers, generally because of various forms of gender discrimination. Black workers also earn substantially less, on the average, than white male workers, mostly because of systemic racial discrimination in the past and present.[9]

As with other respondents, this professional does not think unfair treatment in the judicial system is today a serious enough factor for it to be used as an adequate explanation for racial inequality. As we see in recent opinion surveys of white Americans, this view of discrimination is widely shared. Most well-educated whites like the men in our sample do periodically acknowledge that there are some, usually minor, flaws in U.S. institutions, yet they do not generally view such flaws as accounting for much of the racial inequality still obvious in society. Here, the respondent observes that the judicial system is imperfect, but suggests that in the case of African Americans its flaws are modest when compared to the more significant problem of the breakdown of black families. Again, these shared white understandings about the general fairness of important institutions encompass some recurring exaggerations or sincere fictions, while ignoring or downplaying other important interpretations. A significant body of social science research documents systemic racial discrimination in the criminal justice system. This can be seen, to take just one important example, in the police surveillance that often disproportionately targets neighborhoods of black Americans or other Americans of color—one major reason for the higher arrest rates there for crimes (e.g., drug crimes) that whites commit at least as often.[10] This discrimination in policing and discrimination in other aspects of the criminal justice system are clearly important factors lying behind the higher conviction and imprisonment rates for black Americans and some other Americans of color.

Blurring Sincere Fictions and Reality

Many white Americans hold strong views about black culture, families, and communities. The common white scrutiny and critique of black Americans can lead some whites to confidently advance, as if they were verified by research, other erroneous beliefs about black culture, families, and communities. For instance, this professional offers his explanation for the high black incarceration rates.

> The reason is that they have an attitude that they don't care, it's hopeless. So for them to go out and rob and mug somebody, they just don't care about the consequences. And they have no structure; they have no one to lead them. If you look at the black population fifty years ago, they had more of a family structure; they usually came from a Baptist religious [background]. Now most of them went from a Baptist religious background to a Muslim [one] in a short period of time, and at the present time, none. So they have no religious background, no family background, so they are prime candidates to commit crimes.

Once again, it is important to note that this view does not involve traditional stereotyping of black inferiority in terms of genetics. Still, there is strong cultural stereotyping. Note the imagery of black families or communities as without much structure, as well as the imagery of blacks as almost childlike ("they have no one to lead them"). Like other white commentators in the mass media and among our respondents, this man attempts to offer an informed view of these problematical issues by citing what he regards as accurate data—in this case, on changes in black family structure and religion over several decades.

However, such a common white perspective illustrates yet other sincere fictions about black Americans. There has been no dramatic shift in religious affiliations in black communities. African Americans are still Baptists (and Methodists) in large numbers, and only a small number have become Muslims. In addition, a religious perspective on life, prayer, and going to church is important for African Americans as a group, and Sundays at church and times with one's family are often significant events, at least as much as they are for white Americans as a group.[11] Why, then, do many whites come to greatly exaggerated or fictional ideas about black families and communities? As we have suggested previously, one significant reason seems to lie in the fact that the overwhelming majority of whites, including elite white men, have little in the way of sustained equal-status contacts or ongoing in-depth conversations with African Americans. Because of the racial segregation of most neighborhoods and other arenas facilitating close friendships in this society, most whites are left with the white-controlled mass media as their main—and generally inferior—source of information about the lives, families, and communities of African Americans.

In the next excerpt, one business official discusses an instance where he had to break the normal pattern of his racially segregated life to go to a Social Security office. He interprets this very limited contact with a few African Americans in this manner:

> Personally speaking, I had to go down to the Social Security office to get Social Security cards for my children. [My child] was going overseas, and needed a passport, so we didn't have her social security card. And I stood out in line. Yeah, I got there early so I could get in and out in a hurry. And I stood out in line, like out of thirteen of us there was me and twelve black people. And to listen to them talk about who are you living with this week, and ... what about that lady across the street, and it was a real eye-opener. I just sat there and kind of chuckled to myself and said, "This is what it's all about." They have no sense of family.

Interestingly, this respondent links his conclusion that blacks have no sense of healthy family life to some overheard comments while standing in a line in a setting where he may have felt out of place. His account suggests how a person can take rather small amounts of experiential information and fit them into common stereotypes of others. He does not indicate the gender of those standing in line—which might be significant, since in his interview, before telling this story, he blames the assumed breakdown of the black family unit on "disappearing" men. Elsewhere in his interview, he also makes the statement that the "black population just seems to be producing babies, babies, babies, and ba-

bies," in an assessment of why the white proportion of the U.S population is declining. This suggests another sincere fiction about black
birth-rates that is frequently held by white Americans, especially among
those most concerned about the "browning of America." Yet, in recent
years the black proportion of the U.S. population has grown only
slightly. The main reason for the declining proportion of whites in
the U.S. population, now and in coming decades, is the increase in
the Latino and Asian-American populations rather than in the black
population.[12]

In numerous respondents' accounts, as well as in national opinion
surveys, white individuals and families are generally seen as hardworking, religious, and family-focused, while black individuals and families
are often seen as having a weak work ethic, being less religious, and having poor family values. Reviewing our interviews, however, indicates
that very few of these white male respondents report any extensive or
ongoing experiences with specific black families. Even after meeting
or working with black Americans who do not fit the stereotypes, whites
often assert that such individuals are exceptions to the larger reality
of black laziness and family breakdown. In many cases, it is clear that
white generalizations about black families are largely based on the mass
media. One professional describes the familiar "no male role model"
stereotype, yet adds an interesting follow-up comment about his own
experience.

> I think that what has been presented—at least what one takes away
> from the media with regard to the black populations—is that there is
> a breakdown of the family unit. There tends to be a greater emphasis
> on mother and grandmother in raising the family, and ... I'm left
> with the impression as I read magazines and get media information
> that the father ... is often absent as a role model in the family. ... With
> that breakdown of the family unit, I think that there is a tendency to
> be less motivated in the workplace. I would have to think that cer-
> tainly this gives the impression that a large section of the black com-
> munity is not shouldering their responsibility within the workplace.
> I would have to tell you that, drawing on my own personal experi-
> ence, which is extremely limited in this geographical area ... that
> is not the situation here. But, then again, we have such a small mi-
> nority of nonwhites that ... they tend to function very much like the
> white community that swallows them up and surrounds them.

In his subsequent comments, this well-educated respondent reiterates the point made by others that the breakdown of the family is the reason for blacks being "less productive as a racial group." Yet, in the quote above, we notice the contrast between the black people that he personally observes, and his impression of blacks as a group. His conclusion about general family breakdown in the black population is mainly based, as he makes clear, on what he has taken away from numerous mass media presentations. Also note the implicit assumption here that functioning like white families—at least, ideal white families—is a viable standard for family health.

In an account that involves a distinctive elaboration of certain generalizations, an executive follows a somewhat similar line of reasoning.

> Personally, at my job, if the blacks are hired, I see no difference at all. . . . To generalize is very difficult, but if you had to take a hundred blacks from one place and a hundred whites, I would think very often the blacks aren't working as hard. And I think that goes back to the fact that the whole structure of their life. . . . Whites have a tendency more to be more concerned about keeping their job because welfare is not such a stigma to the blacks as it is to the whites. . . . I think in the black community, because there's such a high unemployment rate, that if someone should lose their job because they're not working hard, I don't think that becomes such a problem. So because of that I don't think that they very often try as hard. Once again, not all people, but if you had to look at it as an overall view, that's my opinion.

Like some others, this respondent seems sensitive to the problem involved in making generalizations, yet develops them nonetheless. The sincere fiction of whites as a distinctively hardworking racial group emerges here when they are portrayed as more likely to be concerned about job loss and going on welfare than blacks, who are assumed to find it less problematic in their communities when they lose jobs. Yet he initially admits that aspects of this opinion are unsubstantiated by his own experience with those black workers who are hired in his company.

A few respondents actually attended to this disparity between their generalizations about African Americans and their own experiences. One executive is notably insightful about his own named biases about the black work ethic, yet admittedly adheres to them nonetheless.

I've had blacks who have worked for me at various levels up to the vice president level, down to the mailroom level, and I have seen them apply themselves and work just as hard as anybody else, if not harder. I probably do share a general sense based on observations, and maybe based on bias at some level that . . . if you get the same number of black people and the same number of white people, which would likely be more productive, something intuitively tells me that the whites would really work harder and be more productive than the same population of blacks. But that is a very biased kind of [statement]. I think . . . that goes back to things that have been impounded into my head over the years . . . because when I take that apart, and I say, of the blacks that have worked for me, "Have they performed?"—generally speaking, they have. Of the Hispanics that have worked for me, "Have they performed?"—generally speaking, they have.

The distinction between the fictional imagery of a poor work ethic and the experienced reality of hardworking black Americans—who "work just as hard as anybody else, if not harder"—is unambiguously stated and assessed by this articulate respondent. Whites hold onto misinformation about black (and Latino) values and families even when their reflections and experiences tell them otherwise. Negative images of the racial "others" do seem to die hard.

Whites as Objective Analysts of Fact

Ironically, while the above quotes frequently demonstrate whites' difficulties with separating fact from exaggeration or fiction, many white Americans continue to hold to yet another fictional notion: the view that whites are considerably more rational and objective than blacks, particularly in regard to racial issues. As with numerous other interpretations of racial realities in U.S. society, this idea seems to be shared among many white Americans. It is, once again, part of the collective set of understandings developed and reinforced in white groups, networks, and communities.[13]

This view of distinctive white rationality and objectivity is evident in several of our interviews, some of which we have already examined. It is perhaps most evident when the respondents discuss the murder trial of O.J. Simpson that took place during the mid-1990s. While most whites seem to believe that they have analyzed the facts of that widely discussed criminal trial in an unbiased manner, they often argue that a majority of African Americans are unable to do so. In fact, the stereotyping of black Americans as too emotional sometimes emerges in certain white discussions of these matters.

Some skepticism about the ability of African Americans to be rational or objective comes out in this professional's remarks.

> I am absolutely convinced that O.J. Simpson was guilty; he's got to be. And I think any rational person would [think so too], except if you're a rational black person.... When all that stuff was coming out about 70 percent of whites believing he's guilty and 70 percent of blacks believing he's not guilty—and when he came back not guilty, and you saw all the blacks dancing in the streets, it was like it was a victory to their race ... it was just sad.... I really do believe this, that a higher percentage of white people look at the case rationally, examine the evidence: How could O.J. have done this ... how did the blood [get there]?—whatever it is—and came to their conclusions. I know a lot of white people who thought he was not guilty too, so they came to their conclusions upon looking at the case objectively. And ... I think somehow that black people looked at it less objectively.

This professional begins by saying a rational person would have to view Simpson as guilty on the evidence, but he later expresses the view that even the whites who decided Simpson was not guilty did so objectively. In contrast, blacks who came to the same conclusion are viewed as likely to be looking at the case with less objectivity. A research analyst agrees in this language: "I think there is a tendency to overlook the facts if you want to overlook the facts, because they [African Americans] view him as a member of their group and they don't want to believe what possibly the facts might indicate." From this general perspective, which numerous other whites expressed at the time of the verdict, most whites are fair-minded people who do not entertain stereotypes about black men that might significantly affect their own judgments in such a complex case. While seeing themselves as able to think clearly about members of their own racial group, these whites can simultaneously generalize about black citizens as unwilling to accept reality when it comes to cases involving fellow black Americans.

In some of the respondents' views of the O.J. Simpson trial, as well as in the public comments of numerous white officials and rank-and-file whites at the time, we also sense some whites' distrust of the involvement of African Americans in the fabric of American civic and political life. The jury in the Simpson trial—which was composed of two whites, a Latino, and nine blacks—represents a new and likely increasing development in urban justice systems. Under U.S. law, everyone is officially entitled to a jury of his or her peers, yet it has only been very recently in U.S. history that major juries have had African Americans and other Americans of color serving on them. For centuries, those African Americans who went to court, either as defendants or plaintiffs, almost always found not a single member of their racial group sitting as jurors (or, indeed, judges) in judgment of them. Now that there are a growing number of multiracial juries, many whites seem to feel that Americans of color cannot uphold this responsibility since they are considered to be often incapable of objectivity when it comes to their peers. Such sentiments seem to suggest that in the eyes of many whites, black Americans would rather be dishonest than see a fellow African American convicted of a serious crime.

One manager expresses a variation of this in his view of the multiracial jury that "quickly" handed down a not-guilty verdict in Simpson's criminal trial.

> To just to come out that quickly, obviously they had made their minds up right from the beginning . . . whether he was innocent or he was guilty. I don't see where anybody, with the complexity of what was going on there, could feel that there was a fair deliberation of all the facts. And obviously, knowing the ethnic background of the jury, on face value, it just seems that you were black and you were acquitted, simple as that. . . . The fact that bothers me the most [is] there was obviously no deliberation of what the facts were. . . . Me, being white, I can't understand, how could you make a decision so quickly, unless it was strictly a racial decision?

Such pointed statements suggest an element of concern or anxiety in some whites, not only about the ability of black Americans to keep an open mind about racial matters, but also about the growing involvement of black Americans in important public institutions such as juries.

Not surprisingly, perhaps, some of these respondents' opinions are similar to those expressed by many prominent whites in the mass media after the Simpson trial. For example, in a *Newsweek* column, the influential journalist Jonathan Alter expressed his views about the not-guilty verdict in the Simpson case this way:

> We assumed, unthinkingly, that we occupied some kind of demilitarized zone with moderate blacks. If it wasn't color-blind, it was at least color-farsighted, with certain common values allowed to share the foreground. Suddenly that zone was gone, at least as far as O.J. Simpson was concerned. Black moderates are familiar with the pressure to fall in line with a 'black' position. They feel it again in this case. But for many white moderates, it's jarring to find ourselves identifying not with a set of racially idealistic principles but with the so-called 'white' position. We expected more blacks to look beyond race to facts, as thousands of whites had during the Rodney King trial. When so many blacks didn't, it shocked us—and hardened us in ways that shocked us even more.[14]

A number of racial stereotypes loom large in this account. The weak reasoning abilities of "black moderates" (also a stereotype) are downplayed or even dismissed when whites like Alter believe that these blacks' decisions about guilt are based on the racial characteristics of whoever is on trial. Clearly, such white analysts have trouble seeing the social world from any viewpoint but their own, which viewpoint is often seen as idealistic and principled.

About that time, President Bill Clinton commented on the Simpson trial: "I think what has struck all Americans in the aftermath of the trial is the apparent differences of perception of the same set of facts based on the race of American citizens." He added, "I have been surprised by the depth of the divergence in so many areas, and I do think we need to work on it."[15]

In discussing U.S. justice system issues, some whites seem to believe that, if black Americans and other Americans of color gain more power in the society, they will reverse the traditional discrimination and visit miscarriages of justice upon whites similar to those that Americans of color have historically experienced. For centuries, most white Americans have shown no concern for the jury makeup or jury decisions in major cases involving black defendants. Decisions about African Americans have long been made by all-white juries, with very few whites raising questions of possible racial bias in such cases. This is true today, since trials in many state and federal courts still involve all-white juries for black defendants or plaintiffs. Knowing this discriminatory history seems to have led some whites to assume that blacks now desire to avenge these past wrongs by discriminating against whites.

In his interview, one corporate official expresses this view in regard to the black response to the Simpson trial: "Blacks tended to think that if a black jury discriminated in favor of a black defendant, that's okay to do, and ... they feel [this is] paying back for years of having it go the other way." The possibility that a multiracial jury could rationally review the facts and decide that the government prosecutors did not provide adequate proof of Simpson's guilt is not seriously considered by numerous respondents, as well as by many other white Americans.

Part of this line of thinking, that black Americans desire to right the wrongs of the past through harsh retaliatory actions, can involve an assumption that racial discrimination is mainly a thing of the past. Some whites see black Americans as so blinded by strong emotions about things that happened in the past that they cannot think rationally in the present. Reflecting upon a scene (probably on television) of black women in a nursing home who "just erupted into cheers when the verdict was announced," one respondent reasons this way: "There's a lot of parents who probably were subjected to police brutality or harassment when they were young, who still remember that [and] still have resentment." Experience of discrimination in the distant past is here viewed as clouding older black Americans' judgments about events in the contemporary criminal justice system.

Comparisons to Other Groups

One rhetorical strategy frequently used by many white Americans for minimizing the racial discrimination against African Americans involves pointing to certain other racial or ethnic groups as "model minorities." From this perspective, many whites view black culture and communities as faulty and problematic because other racial or ethnic groups have also faced some discrimination, yet are not doing as badly as African Americans in family, community, or socioeconomic terms. We saw this view in an earlier comment by one respondent about the hard work and successful upward mobility of Irish, Italian, and Jewish Americans.

Asian-American and Latino-American groups are brought up regularly by many whites when considering matters of group values, intelligence, education, and work ethic. When discussing intelligence or education, these whites mostly use Asian Americans as the model for African Americans. On the topic of the work ethic, both Asian Americans and Latino Americans are often identified as being harder workers than African Americans. This executive provides one example of this argument:

> I've seen many cases where blacks simply don't work hard. They want someone to work for them, to do it for them. I've seen many cases like that. And I've seen few cases where blacks, by brutal hard work, are willing to put in that kind of hard work to do so, compared to the Asian, the whites, and to some extent the Hispanics as well. Hispanics are often very hard workers. I don't know why that's the case, but I've seen that. I think it's because the black people have that very independent streak in them, and they tend to be more emotional than the white or these other groups. They are influenced by the whims of things more so than the other groups.

Numerous whites who make arguments like this do not view the socioeconomic differences between black Americans and other racial or ethnic groups as resulting from different historical and contemporary experiences with white-generated discrimination, but rather in terms of certain traits attributed to black personality, culture, or family—in this case, to blacks being too independent, whimsical, or emotional.

This focus on group culture rather than social structure is also evident in this executive's comments on the current situation of black Americans.

> I assume from what I read and what I see, and so forth, that that is true, that they don't [work as hard] as a group. . . . I think a perfect example of that . . . would be the Cubans moving out of Cuba and into Miami, and the conflict of blacks and Cubans in the Miami area. The way the Cubans have just taken over everything, the blacks are in ter-

rible shape down there. Here were people coming in that [had] the language barrier and everything else ... that moved themselves so that they now are ... on top of the heap. The blacks are still down at the bottom.

Here, Cuban Americans are used as a model minority, in a comparison suggesting that black Americans do not work as hard as a group. Numerous other white Americans, particularly in Florida, have articulated a similar point of view. Singling out certain Asian American or Latino groups to compare with African Americans in this manner is a common strategy among whites across the country.

One can ask why this is the case. The respondent's opening comment suggests the importance of the mainstream media. One advantage of the comparative strategy is that it leaves whites entirely out of the discussion. The media-fostered imagery provided here and in similar commentaries is of one group of color competing against another. This approach also entails the acceptance of some sincere fictions about the conditions surrounding the incorporation of Cuban immigrants into the U.S. economy. This was more than a matter of just hard work on the part of these immigrants, for the U.S. government has provided very large amounts of economic and other assistance to the Cuban immigrants, and many of them arrived (especially in the early migrations) with some monetary resources or with significant educational and occupational skills.[16]

While the previous respondent uses a Latino group as the model minority, another respondent uses two different Asian groups to make a similar type of argument.

I knew these people in [city name] who had a business [that] was labor-intensified, and for thirty years—it's a small factory—they hired mostly black people. And approximately ten years ago, they changed to Vietnamese workers. The Vietnamese have a big colony outside of [state name], where they were relocated from Vietnam. And they have all Vietnamese workers now, they like them better now, they said that they are much better workers.... Or a perfect example was in South L.A. and the Watts section, which is all black. All the businesses are owned by Koreans. And [in] the last riots, the blacks were resentful of the Koreans, and they tried to burn and rob all their stores and business down. But if you look at it deeper, how did the Koreans end up with all the business in black neighborhoods? Why didn't the blacks have these businesses? They were there for fifty years. And one of the reasons [is that at] a grocery store, or a newsstand, or these other stores, sometimes you have to put in twenty-hour workdays. And some of these Orientals will do it.

Articulating a version of the model-minority perspective, this well-educated elite respondent views the relative success of certain Asian-American workers and businesspeople as demonstrating their superior work ethic in comparison with that of black Americans. In such detailed accounts from white respondents, however, the longstanding structural barriers to black success—particularly discrimination in bank loans, education, business licenses, and employment—are usually not discussed. Note, too, that like many other whites this respondent uses the dated term, "Orientals," which many Asian Americans consider inaccurate or offensive. Because it upholds the myth of meritocracy in the U.S., this model-minority stereotype helps to justify the socioeconomic positions of white Americans, including elite white men.

Many white Americans use the model-minority stereotype to explain differences in educational achievements. In this regard, Asian Americans receive considerable attention. One executive, discussing Asians, exemplifies the conventional blaming-the-victim perspective.

Asians seem to be more successful in school [than blacks]. It has nothing to do with being lazy, or it doesn't have anything to do with being intelligent. I think it has to do ... [with what] we talked about before, that their parents push them.... It has to do with family values.... If you ask me what I [think] about an argument or a thesis that the family structure is stronger in Asian families or white families than it is in black families, there, I think that there's probably some legitimate issues.... The problem with black kids today has a lot to do with family structure. I don't know if family structure was influenced by racism, or at least recent racism ... I just don't see it.

In rejecting claims about intrinsic black laziness or lack of intelligence, this commentator distances himself from certain traditional anti-black arguments. Yet his view of the family structure as stronger for Asians and whites than for blacks is typical of the cultural-deficiencies perspective we have seen in numerous previous comments. From this point of view, family values and pressures lie behind the superior educational successes of Asian Americans. Though he wavers a bit, this respondent seems to take the view of many other whites who "just don't see" contemporary racism as being a major explanatory factor in the family problems of African Americans.

This notion of a model minority is widely shared among white (and other) Americans and continues to appear in many statements by media commentators and politicians. While particular respondents may have their own take on this issue, they generally convey ideas or use language apparently shared by many other white Americans—yet another example of how white individuals participate in collectively transmitted ideas on racial matters. Interestingly, the contemporary use of the term "model minority," as well as the strong arguments associated with it, can be traced to specific mainstream media articles and political analyses by influential white male commentators that began appearing in the mid-1960s.[17] These articles were written by white analysts at the peak of civil rights protests during the 1960s and were intentionally designed to suggest that black Americans could achieve their socioeconomic goals better by working hard and accepting their conditions just like Asian Americans supposedly did, instead of protesting actively against discrimination. Such a viewpoint not only involves negative images of black Americans, but also incorporates a distorted view of the history and socioeconomic situation of Asian Americans. The model-minority stereotype ignores serious racial discrimination and other socioeconomic barriers still faced by the diverse groups falling under the broad term "Asian American."

ANTIRACIST CRITIQUES OF PREJUDICE AND RACISM

Although a majority of our respondents fall back on some aspects of the modern blame-the-victim perspective and its associated stereotypes, some do challenge, to varying degrees, such arguments. Rather than pointing to flaws in black culture or families, these probing and often insightful respondents discuss such structural matters as restricted job opportunities, unequal education, and continuing racial discrimination in various institutions. For these men, racial discrimination is not a relic of the past. In fact, some articulate arguments about the systemic character of discrimination and trace the effects of discrimination in the past on restricted opportunities in the present.

Economic and Educational Discrimination

Like many other whites, numerous respondents agree with the stereotype that blacks do not work as hard as whites. However, others boldly challenge this common assertion. For example, a company director draws on his own work experiences when asked if he feels blacks do not work as hard.

> I think that that's incorrect. I have always worked with black people who have worked as hard and have worked sometimes harder than a white person has. And I have seen a lot of white people who are lazy, be it they're Asian, Jewish, Italian, Irish.... Growing up, [I remember] the jokes about black people taking the welfare money and drinking booze and not really caring about getting a job. [But] on the other hand, there weren't a whole lot of jobs being offered to them.

Challenging generalizations about the black work ethic, this executive cites his own experience. He explicitly notes the unfair and pejorative nature of the laziness stereotype, recalling its expression in racist joking heard since childhood. Further, he points to the critical distinction between not really caring about getting a job and not being offered a job, thereby accenting a structural explanation of racial inequality over the various blame-the-victim interpretations.

Commenting harshly about the mass media, another corporate executive explicitly rejects the conventional white view of the black work ethic.

> I think that's a stereotype. I think that, again, like the news and television and the sensationalism that goes on there. I think that for many years, blacks in this country were portrayed as not working as hard, basically lazy, weren't interested in getting a job, all of that—which I think was bunk! Everyone wants to do a little better, everyone wants to succeed, everyone wants to provide and support for a fam-

ily for themselves, or for children.... I think that it's difficult for peo-ple to succeed, [and it is] certainly difficult for people of color because of some of the stereotyping. But ... I certainly don't think it's true as a racial trait by any stretch.

While those whites holding to the dominant perspective tend to em-phasize a cycle of "broken" black families, poor values, and crime, this respondent exhibits a critical perspective that focuses on a different cy-cle, that of stereotyping by whites and consequent discrim-ination. He may be implying that stereotypical representations of black Americans in the sensationalizing media foster stereotypes in the minds of employ-ers, many of whom may discriminate as a result. His probing assessment here also rejects the stereotypical notion that black Americans have weak family values and commitments. Indeed, he suggests that they have the same family values as whites and all other Americans.

The last two comments point to the ongoing cycle of white-gen-erated prejudice and discrimination. A few respondents probe even deeper. The concept of systemic racism encompasses more than just con-temporary patterns of racial discrimination, for it acknowledges how historical exclusion is linked to racial discrimination and inequalities to-day. For example, this manager articulates such a perspective as he dis-cusses the traditional stereotype of inferior black intelligence.

Oh, I think it's obviously false.... I say "obviously." That's based on my experience over life. I don't think blacks are any less smart than whites.... Blacks in this country were held out of the professional work environment for generations. They were held out of college and university, they were held out of high schools, middle schools, and grade schools, and that cannot be made up. The gap narrows over time, and it's not a question or a function of intelligence, it's a func-tion of accumulated debt that this country created.... The blacks didn't get a vote, they got brought here as slaves. We've kept them out of the game [and] they've had 130 years slowly integrating back into it. They're not less intelligent. They've been given less opportunity, and that adds up and carries forward because if you've got parents who didn't go to school, they certainly can't help the kids. So that's a cumulative debt of experience in education that they are working diligently to reduce, and I don't believe for a heartbeat that it's a ques-tion of native intelligence.

Here, as in the last few respondents' comments, the focus is on certain structural barriers to education and employment over many generations. The rejection of more conventional white notions is clear in his statement that black Americans are "working diligently to reduce" the legacy of inequality. He goes further by looking back in history to illustrate how the pattern of past discrimination has had a strong impact on present-day racial inequalities. Using the word "cumulative," he identifies a key aspect of systemic racism missed by many of the other respondents in the sample. Indeed, he stresses the way in which opportunities denied to black parents and grandparents mean less opportunity for later generations of African Americans.

Although such a strong acknowledgment of the cumulative disadvantage stemming from systemic racism is relatively rare among elite white men, the last respondent is not alone in this view. One attorney not only identifies the cumulative impact of systemic racism on racial inequalities, but also advocates significant social change. When asked about the traditional notion that black Americans are less intelligent than whites, he replies:

> It really is a way of excusing the failure of American society to educate and lift up its black, African Americans. There's no question that, historically, African Americans suffered tremendous cruelty and deprivation. And . . . how you can think that [about] a group of people who were basically treated . . . as aliens, and who weren't allowed to even read! . . . They used to cut off peoples' hands if they read a book, with the slaves; they used to lynch them and kill them, if they . . . violated [rules against reading,] because knowledge is power. . . . So that went on for generations and generations. They couldn't vote, didn't have any representation. We consigned them, by discriminating against them in employment, living conditions, to areas where the schools are inferior. And so how convenient to say, "Oh, it's not our [fault], we didn't do anything wrong, they're just genetically inferior." It's just a bunch of malarkey. . . . I think it's just a way of excusing historically what whites have done to blacks and what we're still doing. And it's a way of avoiding rectifying the wrongs, and doing the right thing. I think we ought to just do the right thing.

This man is clearly knowledgeable about past and current anti-black discrimination. In contrast, not being aware of this history or discounting its seamy reality, those ascribing to the white-majority perspective can readily reject important policies that would likely curtail persisting racial discrimination. Whereas the dominant white perspective says that "we've done enough" in terms of antidiscrimination policies, this strongly antiracist position calls for accelerated policy intervention to effectively rectify ongoing racial wrongs. Indeed, the last two respondents make arguments that are similar in substance and language to those long made by black Americans in regard to the need for a government policy of substantial reparations for centuries of racial oppression. This way of framing racial matters suggests how new perspectives are born in any group—by understanding better or drawing upon the ideas and experiences of those who lie outside one's own group.

Injustice in the Justice System

Discussing discrimination in the criminal justice system, several of our respondents are specific about the ways in which the system's structure unfairly targets or discriminates against African Americans. Recall that a conventional white outlook perceives high incarceration rates as indicating that black Americans are significantly more prone to crime than others, and often links that idea to an alleged lack of proper family values.

A few respondents question whether such statistics indicate that black people actually commit more crimes, or whether they are really indicative of how unfairly the police and justice systems operate. One manager offers this response in regard to what he thinks about the reported statistic that one-third of black men are in jail or on probation:

> I am suspicious of the one-third number. If the real question is, "Are there a lot of blacks in jail?" you say, "Well, show me facts." Show me a percentage of the jail population, yes, it's high. Show me a percentage of the U.S. population, yes, it's high. Why is that? Is it because blacks commit more crime, or because they're prosecuted more vigorously, or because they lack the economic resources to get the Park Avenue lawyers to get them out of jail and beat raps? Is it because they are involved in the kinds of crimes, drug-related for example, that the country is sensitive to in mandating strict punishments on? I have yet to see Congress vote a death sentence for Wall Street finagling.

Many whites think of racism as involving only blatant prejudice and willful acts of discrimination, such as cases of overt police brutality. Yet, revealing a mind that questions conventional wisdom in white communities, this respondent points to the more systemic ways in which discrimination operates against black Americans. He makes the point, uncommon in these interviews, that prosecution may be less vigorous when a defendant is represented by prominent Manhattan lawyers or is accused of white-collar crimes. In the justice system, upper-middle-class and upper-class whites usually get strong defenses or more lenient punishment. Thus, the workings of systemic racism can be seen as much in the high-level privileges that whites accord to one another as in blatant white-against-black discrimination.

One business owner gives a poignant explanation of how institutional racism can be seen in the routine operation of the criminal justice system, even in the absence of personal prejudice.

> If there was ten black guys and ten white guys, and all twenty of them did the same crime, they would prosecute all ten of the black guys, and they would prosecute two of the white guys. And then of ten black guys that they prosecuted, they all would be convicted. And of the two white guys, only one would be convicted. . . . You're the prosecutor, right? The prosecutor says, "I'm not going to prosecute anybody I'm sure I can't get a conviction [for]." He's in front of the voters, and [can] say, "Ninety-seven percent of my cases, I convicted." Okay, so right after, he knows that if he can get a white jury, and it's a black crime, half the battle is over. The other thing he knows about is the guy is poor—he's not going to have a proper representation. It's going to be court-appointed, and that guy isn't going to do a good job for him. So the prosecutor might not be looking at it as prejudice to a black guy; he's looking at it from [the standpoint,] "The only cases I'm going to prosecute [are] those cases that I can win."

This respondent suggests that many prosecutors, like many police officers, are rewarded politically or in other ways for good arrest-to-conviction ratios. Although not necessarily prejudiced themselves, these central figures in the justice system can capitalize on the racism already institutionalized there to make their prosecutions easier. The respondent's alternative perspective involves not only acknowledging the reality of current discrimination, but also being insightful about the ways in which the justice system's routine functioning perpetuates inequalities through its racial and class biases.

This is not to say that overt prejudice and blatant discrimination are not present in the justice system. Some white attorneys who observe the system and participate in it firsthand willingly acknowledge the ways in which it is stacked against African Americans. In contemplating the O.J. Simpson trial, one lawyer highlights such bias: "I know firsthand, from representing blacks, that blacks don't get an even shake in the criminal justice system, and particularly out in L.A. [Los Angeles] has one of the worst discriminatory police forces, and it's because it has a huge minority population, and [has had] problems for years and years and years." He then comments that African Americans are indeed knowledgeable about the realities of the justice system.

Another legal professional relates similar observations of racial discrimination, not only in regard to the actions of the police but also in regard to practices at other levels of the justice system.

> I think that the system is still white-run, and there is a bias against blacks.... They are perceived to live in high-crime neighborhoods, so there are police [in those neighborhoods], so there's more likelihood that they're going to get apprehended. There's more sense of a need to prosecute.... The natural consequence of all of that is there're going to be more black people in jail. I also think that judges and juries are racist.... I think we're guilty of not [doing] enough to ensure that justice is fair and equal and that people of all colors are treated equally.... I don't think the issue is availability. I [think] there [are] sufficient lawyers available, I just don't think they're being [as] conscientious about justice as they should be.

Several racially biased misuses of the justice system are highlighted here, including excessive police surveillance and the greater tendency to prosecute black defendants coming from certain areas, a point also made by a previous respondent. This attorney also implicates judges, juries, and the legal profession in the dynamic of injustice that he has personally observed. His view provides a more compelling explanation for why more African Americans are incarcerated than the popular black-criminality stereotypes that some other elite respondents have cited. This portrait of white advantages structured into the justice system, coupled with individual acts of discrimination within it, captures the complexity of systemic racism that is not grasped by most white Americans.

CONCLUSION

Reviewing the comments and assessments in this chapter and in chapters 2 and 3, as well as other data on the views of white Americans in the literature, one finds different emphases in white assessments of the racial conditions of U.S. society. A majority of whites now seem to acknowledge in one fashion or another that black Americans have a tough life, but often view that reality as having little or nothing to do with them or with whiteness per se. Some in this group have a greater sense than others of the difficulties that black Americans face, as is indicated by the fact that they seem glad that they are not black. Some also show sympathy for the black poor having to face difficult problems. For these whites, nonetheless, to be white is not to be black, and blackness remains the focal point in much of their thinking about racial issues. The prevailing viewpoint situates racial problems in black culture and communities rather than recognizing the reality of serious anti-black discrimination and major white privileges. A minority of whites, such as those quoted in the last section, see whiteness as a distinct part of the racial problem in the United States; they are more likely to understand that racism is systemic, and that it is fundamentally a system of white privileges that are often invisible to most whites.[18]

Many of our respondents seem to mirror, in one respect or another, the larger white society's focus on blackness and the shortcomings in black individuals, families, and communities. There is in much white thought and discourse an array of sincere fictions about black Americans, including the notion that they have inferior values, customs, or behavioral propensities. These prevailing images indicate that many whites generalize, as though black America consisted of just the troubled low-income black neighborhoods often stereotyped in the mass media. Missing in the typical white view of black America is the knowledge that many black neighborhoods are substantially working class or middle class, and that the majority of black Americans hold values in regard to work, family, and life success that are similar to those of the majority of white Americans. The common racial-cultural stereotypes are usually part of a white mind-set that generally fails to recognize black men, women, and children as who they really are—human beings who are just like whites in many fundamental ways.

The cultural-deficiency point of view can serve to rationalize a dismantling of civil rights initiatives, such as affirmative action and the vigorous enforcement of civil rights laws, because it relies on a range of sincere fictions, including notions about a meritocratic social system that is thought to be unbiased and fair. Individual black families are frequently viewed as the appropriate focus for social change. Black men and women are called on to make personal changes. A few respondents even applauded the Nation of Islam's minister Louis Farrakhan, who received such attention from the media as a leader of the 1995 Million Man March, because he had called for black men to take more responsibility for their families. Whites holding to the dominant perspective prefer a focus on troubled families, values, and culture as sources of black problems, rather than confronting persisting discrimination and systemic racism. Today, many white Americans indicate that they are tired of hearing accounts from black Americans about discrimination, and in national surveys many prefer to emphasize the personal responsibility of black Americans, rather than aggressive government intervention to eliminate continuing discrimination. It is particularly significant when so many white elite men subscribe to this point of view, since it is they who wield the most influence in the social, economic, legal, and political sectors of this society. We will return to these policy issues in a later chapter.

Many of these well-educated and influential white men hold complex or inconsistent views on important racial issues. They often seem to be juggling contradictory ideas about African Americans, other Americans of color, and social policy issues. In this regard, they are like most white Americans. Sometimes, they will start a comment in a more liberal direction, then move toward some more conventional stereotyping. At other times, they will back off a stereotyped statement, to some degree, with a few qualifying words. They are often of a "mixed mind" about contemporary racial issues.

Meanwhile, their own personal experiences may or may not have a greater effect on their views than outside influences such as the mass media. Although their comments often minimize the current extent of discrimination against African Americans or other Americans of color, in line with common media portraits, they do sometimes give firsthand accounts of encountering racist jokes and other overt prejudice or discrimination on the part of other whites (see also chapter 6). In addition, it is likely that numerous respondents have at least brief contacts at work with one or two African-American employees for whom their "no family, no religion" stereotypes do not hold true. It would seem that, even when whites know hard-working, family-oriented, and religious African Americans, they often adhere to the notion of a fictional mass of problematic black people who resemble the negative media images that they consume daily. Indeed, as they sometimes note, their own experiential evidence stands in contrast to what they glean about various racial matters from the media. Still, because many of these men are generally isolated from sustained, equal-status contacts with African Americans —particularly in residential neighborhoods, social clubs, and churches —the limited contacts that they have do not seem to provide enough evidence to challenge fundamentally their ingrained cultural-deficiency point of view.

Like the majority of whites, these men often do not see accurately across the color line and view men and women of color as they really are. Their stereotyping of African Americans and other Americans of color operates to alienate them from whole groups of people who are seen as socially inferior or lacking. Indeed, in the commentaries of the majority of the respondents, we sense the impact of spatial segregation not only in their cognitive misunderstandings and fictions, but also in a missing affective component. We note in these commentaries how numerous respondents periodically change voice and distance black Americans as a "them," in contrast to a fundamentally different "us." Many respondents express no empathetic feelings about the present reality and painful impact of the discrimination still faced by African Americans and other Americans of color. Strong identification across the color line seems to be difficult for most whites, as it entails deep understandings, an ability to reject stereotypes, and a sustained capacity to feel some of the pain of the racialized others.[19]

Negative stereotypes of African Americans are generally well-known among most white Americans. For that reason, an encounter

with a black person often calls forth a stereotype that may be unconsciously held, even by those who are relatively unprejudiced.[20] However,
those with less in the way of racial animus are more likely to *counter* the
triggering of a stereotype by conscious processing that stops them from
thinking or acting on the recalled stereotype. This countering is difficult
and must be constantly reproduced, since stereotypes learned in childhood often reside deeply in the mind.[21] As we see in the last section
above, several of these influential white men take a more consistently antiracist tack on these matters, one often close to that of many African
Americans on key racial issues.

We can return briefly to an issue raised at the end of the last chapter:
What has enabled these latter men to break free from the dominant
white discourse, to be able to see systemic racism, or to advocate for
aggressive public policies to end discrimination? In addition to some
factors we have suggested in chapter 3—such as their own personal
openness to a countersystem view and their greater level of close equal-
status contacts with Americans of color—we can add an additional factor that can be seen in the accounts above. What stands out for some of
these respondents is that, by some means, they have gained a more critical knowledge of the racist history of the United States than most whites
have, as well as an ability to see more accurately how that history has
shaped continuing discrimination in present-day societal institutions.
They likely came to these views from their own reading, educational in-
volvements, diversity training, or other efforts, for such a critical perspective is rarely represented in the mainstream media. Their historical
knowledge seems to have helped them to understand discrimination today and to advocate for antidiscrimination policies, whereas most whites
feel personal or family changes on the part of black Americans will
suffice to alter ongoing racial inequalities. We also sense, as we did in the
last chapter, that for some of these men the commitment to the old egalitarian values of U.S. society is very deep and has more than counterbal-
anced the racial stereotypes and other white-centered views that they,
like the other respondents, have inherited from their reference groups
and the larger society.

5

ISSUES OF INTERRACIAL DATING AND MARRIAGE

Interracial dating and interracial marriage are difficult issues for most white Americans. This is especially true when those involved in such dating and marriages are white and black Americans. Thus, one national survey found two-thirds of white respondents saying that they would have a negative reaction if a close relative of theirs married a black person.[1] This negative reaction generally signals how deeply rooted certain anti-black attitudes are. Indeed, attitudes toward interracial dating and marriage reveal that many otherwise liberal whites are less liberal when it comes to issues of mates, marriages, and families. This seems to be as true for elite white men as for the general white population.

Recall our interpretive theme that understandings about life and society do not grow in isolated, individual minds, but rather are recalled, used, and reinforced in social interaction and social networks. Undoubtedly, "our most private thoughts and feelings arise out of a constant feedback and flow-through of the thoughts and feelings of others who have influenced us. Our individuality is decidedly a part of a collective movement."[2] Once key social ideas and feelings are developed, they are often not reflected upon very much, at least until someone questions or challenges them. Moreover, judging from the commentaries throughout this book, it is evident that the ways that whites think and feel about racial matters are frequently shaped by family, friendship, and school contexts in which they grew up, as well as current social networks, including family and neighborhood contexts. Positive or negative understandings about black Americans or other Americans of color are likely handed down from one white generation to the next, or from one friend or neighbor to another. Through a lifetime socialization process, a person typically adopts inherited ways of understanding racial issues, yet may rework some of the views for his or her own purposes. As in previous chapters, the racial understandings that are espoused in these commentaries are often localized, situated, learned, or called forth in particular family or other informal social settings.

NEGATIVE REACTIONS: INTERRACIAL DATING AND MARRIAGE

Preserving Whiteness

Only a few of these elite respondents explicitly accent racial concerns in response to questions about interracial dating or marriage. In one such instance, one professional gives this candid reply when asked about these issues in regard to his children:

> To be perfectly frank, I would rather that my grandchildren be white. I have a tremendous amount invested in my identity as a white person, and I would prefer—and I have a tremendous amount of emotional energy and psychic energy invested in being a white person. I prefer that my lineage, my descendants remain white.

Wishing to have people in one's family who are like oneself in terms of values may be parochial, but it is not necessarily racially biased. Yet this respondent's concern goes beyond having people who are like him in the values they hold. Underscoring the emotional energy he has invested in being white, he clearly indicates his desire for this whiteness to be preserved in coming generations.

It is relatively rare for whites, including these elite white men, to openly discuss in any detail their investment in being white, since, for most, the experience of whiteness is like a being a fish in water—that is, it is usually lived without much reflection. We should note that this man's strongly racialized view on interracial intimacy is not the dominant view in these interviews. Instead, the majority of these elite respondents generally adopt other strategies in assessing or resisting intimate interracial arrangements.

Citing Obstacles for Interracial Relationships

Like the man just quoted, most of the elite male respondents are opposed to interracial dating or marriage, or have mixed feelings about these issues, at least in regard to there being such relationships among their own close relatives. Yet they mostly cite factors other than explicitly racial ones for their opposition to such relationships. For example, when asked how he would feel if he had a teenager dating a black person, one well-placed respondent expresses his opposition this way:

> Certainly, I would be opposed to it. I would have a lot of difficulty accepting that on many, many different grounds, simply because, first, I think that their lives would be extremely difficult, and no matter how my answers may have evolved, or I may have answered my questions previously, something like that would still come down to the quality of their lives together. Regardless of how I feel or they feel, it would be something that would detract dramatically from what they could do together. So, yeah, I would not favor it whatsoever.

He minces no words about his opposition, yet bases his view on the obstacles and difficulties he thinks the couple will face. His primary concerns are about practical matters. In reply to a follow-up question asking, "Even if you knew this person personally, even if this black person was a great person, you would still oppose it on grounds of other problems?" the respondent amplifies the reasons for his opposition.

> I think that it can work out. I think that the people, the individuals can be happy. I think there are, there is no question that it can be done and should be done in a lot of cases. But you are asking me how I would feel, not how they would be. I would feel that their lives would be very, very difficult, and the individual could be a great individual and likewise his family might feel the very same way about my child.

> But having experienced different positions in this limited world that
> I live in, I guess it's just a better place when you are starting out with
> a more common ground.

While many of these men do not object in principle to interracial relationships, they often qualify this apparently liberal viewpoint with
comments indicating that they wish to seem practical in their assessments. In this man's commentary, as in numerous other commentaries
by these respondents, two general themes recur. One is the pervasive
concern about such interracial couples needing common ground, which
usually seems to mean shared backgrounds, values, or behavioral patterns. The idea seems to be that homogeneity in values and customs re-
duces marital and family problems in daily life. On the surface, certainly,
such a view appears to be nonracial. However, there often seems to be an
underlying assumption that people who are racially different do in fact
have significantly different values or cultures.

A second recurring theme is the worry expressed over the quality of
the lives of interracial couples in the larger society. As many whites view
such interracial relationships, by choosing dating or marriage partners
from a different racial group, people risk a life troubled with more social
barriers and obstacles than they might otherwise face. They may list a variety of such barriers in their assessments. Once again, this appears to be
a nonracial reason. Yet, beneath the surface, racially linked understandings seem to be involved, for there is a certain fatalism—or lack of concern—about the possibility of overcoming the discriminatory barriers
in society. Yet these barriers to interracial relationships are substantially
generated by members of these whites' own racial group.

Another successful professional is very forceful and candid about
his likely reactions, in reply to a question about his child dating a black
person.

> I would be very unhappy. . . . I don't think it's healthy for either party.
> I don't think anything is gained. I think they have a greater likelihood
> of being ostracized by their own friends. And it's difficult today just
> to be a teenager, just to grow up, and just to learn male-female rela-
> tionships—and I think that if you complicate it with interracial rela-
> tionships, it makes it much more difficult. . . . It would be extremely
> difficult for me to keep my mouth shut and not express my feelings.

On the next question, about a close relative marrying a black person, he expresses this point of view:

> I would probably not be quite so concerned as I would be with my own child, but I think that they complicate what is a difficult relationship anyway by introducing racial issues, peer issues, and society's issues towards the black population. If asked, I would discourage it. If not asked, I would keep my mouth shut. I would not keep my mouth shut with my own children.

Once again we see a worry about the quality of life, the well-being, of the two parties to an interracial relationship. One of the specific obstacles envisioned here is the likelihood of being socially ostracized by friends, a recurring apprehension of these men. Such social exclusion can indeed make life more difficult, especially for younger people in white communities. Judging from the last part of this commentary, as well as from those of other respondents, the greater the closeness of the particular interracial relationship to a white person, the greater the likelihood of a strong objection to it.

Commenting on the interracial dating question, an executive is also opposed to the idea for his children, yet indicates he would allow them some freedom.

> I probably would not like it at all. I don't think I could forbid my teenager, you know, not to do it, but I just don't feel that would be a very healthy situation for either one, you know, as they grow up, because . . . I still do believe that there are prejudices out there. . . . There are black people who are much better as human beings in quality and character than whites and just because you are black doesn't mean you're a bad person, and there are some extremely fine black people out there who would be better or too good for certain white teenagers or white people. There are many of them that are phenomenal, phenomenal. But I think my feeling would be more of a—from a sensitive side, that my child or my grandchildren would be the object of prejudice and, you know, some persecution. It would be a very tough life for them, but that's the way I would feel if they were having a tough time getting a job or didn't do as well as I did.

Once again we see the theme of questioning how "healthy" such a situation would be for these teenagers, in this case because of the way they would be treated by the prejudiced people around them. From this perspective, interracial coupling should be discouraged, because many people in the larger society are prejudiced and would cause them difficulty.

Given such recurring comments on the racial and related societal barriers faced by interracial couples, it is significant that not one of the respondents expressing such views then goes on to strongly condemn such racial barriers and suggest that, as influential white men, they (or the government) should work aggressively to eradicate them as potential hurdles in the lives of interracial couples. They do not argue strongly for eradicating these widespread racial barriers to love and marriage—which are family values, after all.

Replying next to a question about a close relative marrying a black person, this very articulate respondent admits that he may have some deeper fears, fears that are likely shared by many other white men.

> I would react—if it were my brother, it wouldn't bother me. If it were my sister, it would bother me. I'll tell you the truth, as I think of it now, I'd probably be more bothered by it if it was a daughter than if it was a son.... So I think you might see a little, in my case, a little bit more of a male/female thing, actually, than rather a black/white situation, now, talking about it now. [Q: Do you think {you would} be able to talk easier with a black female than a black male of your family?] Yeah. I would feel, yes, absolutely, I would. I don't know where it comes from, maybe it comes from the fact that ... a black male to me is much more intimidating than a black female. I could easily converse with a black female who was married to a brother or a cousin.... I think if you go back in time, you would have to say that I was probably intimidated, somewhat afraid of blacks growing up. Therefore, that that still carries forth in my thinking about a black male. And also, you know, the fact that it appears, or, you know, more headlines are shown that black men beat up their wives and are abusive.

Undoubtedly expressing a view common among many whites, this respondent is candid in stating that his concern is much more with interracial relationships that involve white women and black men than with the reverse situation. Several respondents indicate that they would have fewer problems with black women marrying into the family. They usually do not provide much information as to why this is the case, but it appears that black women are imaged as less threatening and, perhaps, as stereotypically more nurturing by these (and other) whites. This respondent admits he is more afraid of black men, which apparently began under the influence of those who raised him and continues to the present day because of media images. He goes on in his interview (not quoted here) to question the mass media's imaging of black men, which he notes is distorted and influential in shaping white thinking. Yet, even with liberal views on racial matters, such as this questioning of media, manifested in several of his responses, he still admits to having trouble with the idea of his child or his sister marrying a black person. Such a reaction suggests how deeply held certain racial images or feelings are among white Americans.

In another interesting explanation, another executive assesses how he feels about marriages and dating across the color line. After explaining that in general he does not mind interracial dating and marriage, he adds, "However, I would rather see the neighbor's daughter dating a black person than my own daughter dating a black person." When asked about how he would react if a close relative married a black person, he makes this comment, which again is candid in questioning his own tolerance.

> I think it would be how the marriage would be viewed by friends, associates, and how my peers would feel about this. I don't think they would be as tolerant of [interracial] dating or marriage as I would be. And, in that, I'm saying that I wouldn't favor it for my own daughter, maybe I'm not as tolerant of it as I think I am.

While, generally speaking, interracial marriages and dating are acceptable to him, he does not want his daughter engaging in such relationship. And he would also have concerns about any close relative marrying a black person because of the reaction of that couple's associates. Once again, a respondent's concern for how other whites might react is in evidence.

This mixed, often complex, view of interracial marriages and dating seems to be widespread among white Americans today. Sometimes, positive views, usually at the abstract level, are mixed with negative reactions to personal family situations. Interestingly, recent research on three major university campuses has found that the attitudes expressed by white students on short-answer survey items about interracial marriages are

often different, and more positive, than those they express in longer interviews. Thus, on a brief multiple-choice survey item, 80 percent of 451
students at these universities indicated approval of marriages between
whites and blacks. Yet, when a smaller group of comparable students
was interviewed at greater length, consistent approval of interracial marriages dropped significantly, to just 30 percent. When given time to explain their views, the majority of the students now expressed a range of
reservations generally similar to those of many of these elite respondents. The majority of white students often used a variety of qualifying
or hedging phrases (for example, "I agree and I disagree") to explain
their views in opposition to interracial marriages.[3]

As we have already observed, some of these upper-class men recognize the challenge of trying to get children to adhere to their own views
on certain issues, including these racial matters. For example, one respondent indicates that he is willing to be open-minded about his
daughter being involved in an interracial dating relationship, but with
qualifications.

> I would allow my daughter to make her own choices of what she did.
> I would not feel particularly good about it. As a matter of fact, I would
> probably feel even unhappy about it. But I also know that the way to
> deal with it is not to force rules or opinions, but to present informa-
> tion and allow my intelligent and wonderful daughter to make her
> own good-sense choices. And I would encourage her in order to do
> so. [Q: Why would you be unhappy?] Because I don't believe that it is
> a publicly, socially accepted pattern. . . . I don't think I would be par-
> ticularly happy if my daughter were dating someone who was re-
> tarded, or someone that was so wealthy and extravagant that it would
> cause her to have a distorted view of life. There are a lot of—not just
> black—that I don't think would be good for my daughter.

There are limitations in contemporary America as to how much parents
can pressure their children to act in certain ways, a point that a number
of these respondents reiterate. In this answer to a key question, the respondent shows the persistent concern among whites with interracial relationships not being socially accepted, which would have an impact on
an interracial couple's quality of life. It is significant that he compares the

choice of a black mate to that of a retarded person or an extravagant person. Blackness often seems to be intrinsically negative or associated with other social categories seen as problematic.

When asked about a close relative marrying a black person, this respondent indicates his somewhat contradictory views.

> I would accept whatever it was that my close relative did, and it's their own business, and basically support them in whatever they did.... Not so much my own feeling, but in deference to my wife's feelings, we probably would not attend. And it just simply wouldn't happen. There would be no extended family dinner under those circumstances.

While he would basically support the decision of this hypothetical relative, he notes that his wife's negative feelings about the matter would mean he would likely not attend the wedding or socialize with the interracial couple. This comment underscores the point that racial views and propensities are not just individual matters, but are localized and contextualized in terms of immediate families and other informal social groups that are recurrently important in the lives of white Americans.

"Thinking Twice"

Like the white college students in the previously discussed study, numerous respondents choose subdued language like being "concerned," "thinking twice," or "needing to think through" matters in assessing their reactions to interracial dating and marriage. They use this language both for those involved and for the respondents themselves. One of these influential men uses this more subdued terminology, and not terms like "opposed," in discussing the hypothetical possibility of an interracial marriage within his family.

> I think today I would still be very concerned about it.... I just don't think society as a whole generally accepts these interracial marriages at this time.... I have a feeling it still continues to work hardships on the children. I still wonder, at the adult level, if, over the years and all, certain jealousies and so forth build in because of cultural differences, which you know can either result in an increased tension or divorce or domestic violence and this type of thing. I still, in our society

today, could be very concerned about it. [Q: But would you as an individual, excluding society's reaction, would you be opposed to such a relationship?] Probably so, still today.... That is not one I am sure I can definitely explain.... I would worry about the cultural differences, mainly whether younger adults and all have thought through the various issues in all that they may face from such mixed marriages. And whether, when those issues would eventually ... arise, are they going to be capable and mature enough to handle it?

This expressive respondent also draws on the theme of an interracial couple's lack of social acceptance and believes such a couple needs to reflect carefully on the problems they would likely face. Like numerous other men in our sample, he emphasizes what he views as the problem of cultural differences between the partners in interracial marriages.

Throughout the interviews, as we see here and in other chapters, numerous white men view skin color as a distinctive marker of significant differences in values and customs, including in this case, apparently, a greater propensity for serious domestic problems. This idea of white Americans and black Americans as having substantially different cultural approaches to such social relationships as dating, marriage, family, and children seems to be assumed by many white Americans, yet there is no evidence for such significant divisions across the color line in regard to the more basic family values, views of work and success, or, indeed, most ordinary life issues. There is agreement among whites and blacks on the value of friends and family and on hard work, education, and other values that facilitate achievement and mobility.[4] Thus, more or less stereotyped racial-cultural understandings and interpretations often creep into white commentaries on interracial dating and marriage.

The Importance of the Family Context

These men are often forthright in speaking about their discomfort, ambivalence, or confusion about interracial dating and marital relationships, especially those closer to home. The context of the family and the network of relatives is either explicitly indicated or implicit in most of these comments from the respondents. One professional is quite honest about his negative feelings about a child who engaged in interracial dating.

> I wouldn't be that happy, to be honest with you. But only because I've been shown in the long run, having been in interracial relationships, it helps to have people with similar upbringings as you. Because it makes things a lot more comfortable and a lot more sturdy in our own relationship as well in others. It's like someone I know, a friend of my mom's, had this whole story where she implored her daughter to date a nice Jewish boy. "Make sure you bring a nice Jewish boy home with you. It's very important. It's good, it makes sense, it makes life easier. Everyone is happy. You'll have more in common."

His opposition to a child dating across the color line is clear, and here again there seems to be an underlying assumption that interracial differences mean cultural differences. He continues with an explanation for his questioning of interracial dating.

> I think a lot of my opinion on it comes from my parents and my grandparents, who would really have a problem with me were I to date someone of a different race. I'm perfectly accepting of people I know dating interracially. Whether or not I had a child who did it, would that make me happy? I would, honestly, have to say "no." Simply because I've been taught that it isn't the smoothest and the easiest way to go through life. If it's what makes you happy, I think that's what matters most. But at the same time, if you know it's going to make the people around you that care about you uncomfortable, then you have to take that into consideration as well.

Note the emphasis here on doing what is easiest, not necessarily what he might think is the loving or the right thing to do, though he seems to be aware of what that is. In response to the next question, about a close relative marrying a black person, he conditions his reaction this way:

> It depends. For the most part—well, no, it doesn't even depend. I would do everything in my power to support the move because what matters to me is the continued happiness of those around me. If someone were truly happy with someone of a different race, then, you know, that's fine. I know, particularly, if someone were to marry someone who wasn't Jewish, then I would try and support that. However, it does create all sorts of difficulties as you go down the line: Where are you going to live, how are you going to raise your children, what values you instill in them, what you believe in, is, for the most part, entirely different. And there have to be a lot of common grounds

that are met before any kind of union should go ahead and be forged, because you don't know necessarily what you're in for. If you can comfortably work all of those out, then so be it. Go ahead and create the next pluralistic, racially harmonized society.

Note here the complex and interesting blend of interracial concerns that characterizes the positions of many reflective whites. This respondent seems to have mixed feelings about interracial dating and marriage, apparently having had some experience himself with such relationships. He would be unhappy if a child engaged in dating, but would likely support a marriage involving other relatives. Like the previous respondents, and many whites in other research studies, he worries greatly about an array of sociocultural obstacles, including the lack of similar upbringings, problems in finding a residence, and challenges in childrearing. In responses to both questions, there is some fretting about the lack of cultural similarities between white and black partners. There also seems to be an implicit generalization about black family values being different from those of whites. We see, too, the critical importance of family context for judgments about interracial alliances. Conforming, at least in part, to what others in one's family and friendship networks think and do on racial matters is central to much white experience.

Other respondents also accentuate what they see as cultural differences between black and white Americans. We can see the concern with religious dissimilarity again in this professional's response to the question about a child possibly dating a black person. He says that he

> wouldn't feel too comfortable about it because it's hard enough to develop relationships with people who have had a similar childhood and home life, and it's just an added complication. I don't think I would be comfortable. [Q: What if {the} only thing that was different about them was their color?] Well, they might certainly be of a different religion from us, and I don't think I would be too comfortable with that.

Then, when asked about a close relative marrying a black person, he adds:

> I don't think I'd be too comfortable with that. Well, just like I said, we certainly would be of different religion, and we, we have a tradition of religion that we would like to see upheld and continued into the next

generations, and that would ensure that it wouldn't happen. So it's not a pleasant thought. Also, I think that with all the discrimination that there is in this world, it isn't easy, it's harder to be a black person or a Hispanic person than it is to be a white person in most experiences. And I think that nobody wants to see somebody he loves having anything in life harder than it need be.

In both his responses, this respondent clearly worries about the lack of similarities between the hypothetical white and black partners. As with previous respondents, he assumes that there might be a problem of dissimilar childhood, home life, and religious upbringing. He distinguishes himself somewhat by making a clear point about an issue that some other respondents have only implied, noting that blacks and Hispanics face much discrimination and offering this as an explicit reason to discourage relatives from interracial relationships. This comment has a fatalistic ring to it; it does not suggest that working to end this discriminatory reality might make interpersonal relationships easier. It is significant that, while many respondents often play down the continuing importance of racial discrimination in U.S. society in other parts of their interviews, some do note, if not accent, its importance when commenting on interracial dating and marriage.

Many whites seem to have received comparable lessons about interracial dating and marriage matters from their families and other networks of relatives or friends. Indeed, they often use rather similar language in describing their understandings and apprehensions. In the following comment, for example, we again see the cautious concern about "thinking carefully," this time from another professional answering a question about an older child dating a black person.

> I would say to the child that they should think carefully before, let's say, getting married to someone who's of a different race, because customs are different, outlooks are different, common friends are different, living patterns are different. Therefore ... they should think carefully about it before getting married, because they would have these things to overcome, that they would not have were they dating somebody who was the same race.

Once again, certain obstacles are cited, including the presumably different customs, outlooks, living patterns, and friends. Then he adds that people are all the same and, and everyone is just as capable of loving or being loved as anyone else. And people—human beings' needs and wants and fears are all the same, but behavioral patterns and customs are still different. And so, if one of my kids was seriously involved with, with someone who was of a different racial group, I would say the same thing. And it's not just racial. What if my kid was seriously involved with a white person who came from a totally different economic situation as ours, their family lived differently and had different outlooks on things, and their patterns and customs were different—I would say the same thing for the same reasons.

There is the stated ethic of a common humanity here, for all people are said to have similar needs and wants. It is of course legitimate to be concerned with the company that one's child keeps. Still, there is again an assumption here that certain important behavioral patterns and customs of the black Americans who are, or might become, involved in relationships with whites are significantly different from those of whites. In these interviews, the matter of skin color is repeatedly attached to a range of hidden and expressed assumptions about value and custom differences across racial groups in family, culture, or community.

The importance of family context in the fostering and drawing forth of an array of negative racial attitudes probably cannot be stressed too much. Indeed, some elite men express their fears and concerns in this regard in even stronger language than the foregoing respondents. For example, a previous research study includes this provocative interview with a white father, an influential employer who owns his own business. He responds to a hypothetical question about an adult child dating a black person with this intense observation:

I'd be sick to my stomach. I would feel like, that I failed along the way.... I'd feel like I probably failed as a father, if that was to happen. And it's something that I could never accept.... It would truly be a problem in my family because I could never handle that, and I don't know what would happen, because I couldn't handle that, ever.[5]

Negative images of the black outgroup do not stand alone, but are evidently linked closely to his views not only of his white self and but also of fatherhood. As in other accounts, we see that views of interracial dating and marriage are often much more than matters of cognition and thought, for they have significant emotional roots. Again, too, we observe how such an interracial relationship is immediately and strongly evaluated against the backdrop of a strong family context. Always in the background, if not explicitly noted, are the reference-group frameworks of racial understandings, interpretations, and emotions.

WILLING TO CONSIDER IT, BUT...

A number of the respondents seem a bit more willing to consider the possibility of interracial dating and marriage specifically for themselves or their relatives, yet still may put something like a qualifying "but" into their analyses. They often seem to agonize a bit more over the issues than most of the preceding respondents. They vacillate and seem ambivalent, often citing the same hurdles and impediments remarked upon by those who are more strongly opposed to intimate interracial relationships. For instance, one professional notes that, though he would try to support his child, an interracial coupling would create difficulties.

> I think that would be really difficult. And I don't care how much you say that it's okay, I don't [think] you're being quite honest. Particularly anybody who grew up in the South.... But, you know, I'd have to cope. I love my children and I respect my children, and I'd have to support them in what they did. I think I would be very concerned about how my child and their friend would be treated by all their other constituents. And I guess in that sense, you know, I think that would even be the hardest part, because you know they're going to suffer, and you know there's going to be a lot of pain and trouble.... I would be real concerned for all the possibilities.... And then they, you know, have mixed-race children and stuff like that, you know. I think unless they moved somewhere else it would be a difficult time for those kids to grow up here and not really belong in any other place. I mean, society is divided.

Unlike numerous other respondents, this man is clearly willing to support his children in their choices. Yet he, too, brings up the problem—and in much the same language—of the suffering they might well face at the hands of their peers. The language of obstacles appears anew, this time with an important emphasis on the racially "divided society." When asked about a close relative marrying a black person, he continues:

I mean, I don't have the same concerns as I have about a kid that—you know, [are] you sure you know what you're getting into, with all the other pressure? I think, I hope, I would be very accepting of them—if you're a good decent person, regardless, and if I felt like they were going to treat my relative appropriately. Probably five or six years ago, I might have said—well, it could have been a real problem—but now having had some relatives marry some pretty crummy people otherwise, I might welcome it.... Again, the quality of the person still matters a lot more than their racial background.

Again we see some emphasis in his answers on how interracial couples face recurring obstacles from certain others in society, although he is less concerned when it comes to other close relatives. Interestingly, this respondent is one of just a few respondents who specifically acknowledge in their responses to these questions the point that whites may also have character flaws that impede successful marital relationships. Indeed, he indicates that in the last few years he has changed his views on the matter in a positive direction, because of a clearer understanding of this reality.

Another interviewee also begins with an apparently liberal response, but goes on to discuss his mixed feelings in regard to dating and marriage across the color line.

Having a black son-in-law or daughter-in-law, I can't envision a problem. I mean they would come here, and I wouldn't see a problem. They would have dinner or, you know, have a grandchild that.... I don't know if there would entail ... in this small community, any problems. But ... then again it starts getting complicated. Just a simple thing [like] your son marrying a black girl, that's no big deal. Then when you start taking into consideration her fame if your son marries a black.... I'm not one of these people that, you know, that thinks my daughter should go out of her way to marry a black man because ... that's the liberal thing to do, you know.

Ambivalence about interracial relationships creeps into the discussion of the complications of living interracially in a smaller community. He agonizes a bit over his answer and seems to want to say the right thing. Small, predominantly white communities may indeed be difficult places for interracial relationships, though this likely varies by region across the

United States. Moreover, in a few of the interviews we find statements similar to the one in his last sentence, indicating opposition to the social pressures to be very liberal and condone interracial relationships. This is a puzzling comment, and it is hard to know what has generated this concern, for where in white communities does one find such social pressure for interracial marriages?

Only a few of the respondents reported actual interracial relationships among their children or other relatives. Noting that his children have dated across racial lines, one respondent initially asserts that this does not bother him.

> They have. [Daughter's name] has. I mean, in fact, the joke in our house is that I don't think [daughter's name] has ever, ever dated a white boy . . . a Caucasian, anyway. . . . It doesn't bother me. I have to admit that if it came to marriage, it wouldn't bother me, except that I want to make sure that they understood what they were getting themselves into—not together, but how society faces it. I mean that . . . I'd just want to make sure that they understood all that because I do believe that that is still a hassle . . . less so than it was ten years ago. But I mean, listen, that's their choice. And we're going to love whoever they pick. Such is life. My mother, she'd go nuts, but you know, she's . . . [of a] different generation.

Even with his relatively positive attitude, he makes it clear that he would make sure that his children came to understand the possible social hassles that come with interracial relationships. The teaching mode that a number of the respondents enter into when discussing younger whites, including their own children, is interesting because young people involved in interracial relationships are likely to already know much more about the social hassles than their parents or other whites seeking to instruct them. Note, too, that for this respondent family of origin comes into the analysis, for he mentions that his mother has a quite different and negative view of intermarriage. To the follow-up question about intermarriage by a relative, he also indicates that he would have no problem. Then, in response to the interviewer's question, "What if your mother did?" he replies:

> That would be a real shock. It wouldn't bother me. I—it wouldn't bother me. I mean, I would think—the interesting thing about that

is that that is similar to a Jewish-Christian marriage, where values—
it depends on where your values are. I mean, the cultural values are
different and I don't know how people would cope with that as a couple. It's not an issue, but all of the friends that go along with the couple that [have] different values and have grown up in different
cultural situations....

Like several others among these influential respondents, this man brings
up the analogous situation of religious differences between people considering dating or marriage. Even those with relatively liberal views of
dating and marriage across racial lines appear to have certain underlying presumptions about the different cultural values and traditions of
African Americans.

SOME POSITIVE VIEWS OF INTERRACIAL RELATIONSHIPS

Some of these powerful men, albeit a modest minority, are strongly positive in their views of interracial dating and marriage, although they, too,
will sometimes qualify their responses a bit, perhaps by expressing a desire to know the black person in the relationship well. As we have seen, a
few of these respondents note that their children have already dated
across the color line. This real-world experience can affect the general
view of interracial dating or marriage. Witness this interesting account
from another influential respondent, who is commenting on his daughter's interracial relationship.

> I didn't have a real problem with it. I, we sat down with my daughter
> and said this is fine if you're doing it for the right reasons.... It was
> early teenage, you know, if you call it, dating. They call each other on
> the phone and what-have-you. So, these things last about a week, any-
> way, and this is what happened.... None of them have ever gone out
> on a "date" date, you know, a movie date or a dinner date or what-
> have-you with a minority person. I think they needed to test the wa-
> ters at the early age to see what would happen.... No, I wouldn't have
> a problem with that. [Q: Do you think that's because of your back-
> ground, the way you were raised?] I think so, and like I said, I think I
> would—I might have to qualify my answer, in that if it were, I would
> want to know the person, get to meet him. And if I didn't think much
> of him, then regardless if he was black or white, I would draw the line.

Viewing this early interracial dating as a temporary fling, he indicates that he had no problem with it. Yet even he qualifies his view by noting that he made sure she was doing it "for the right reasons." This comment seems reminiscent of a previous respondent's about the social pressures to get into interracial relationships. He also states what might seem to be obvious: that any father would want to meet the person dating a daughter, no matter who he is. He does seem to be rather cautious about interracial relationships that have developed, or might develop, within his immediate family.

One of the strongest positive statements in the interviews is this professional's noteworthy and probing answer to the question about his reactions to intermarriage by a close relative.

> I think intermarriage is a great thing. I like to see an eradication of ethnic distinctions. The more intermarriage there is, including in my own family, I think the better off society is.... I'm hoping that, first of all, intermarriage is proceeding. The greatest amount of intermarriage is of other ethnic groups.... For all ethnic groups, intermarriage is increasing. And, generally, when members of other ethnic groups intermarry—Italian marries an Irish person, a Jew marries a non-Jew—the children of those kinds of marriages think of themselves as being half of this, and half of that, or a quarter of this or that. It's a very odd thing that with blacks we still have this certain notion that, if any member of your family is black, you're black. I think that is going to change.... There are very, very few ethnic pure-blooded people in the United States these days. The whites, who may think of themselves as predominantly white, still are very much aware of their different national origins. Very few whites think of themselves as white. They think of themselves as Polish Americans, Italian Americans, et cetera, but very few people are completely Polish-American, Italian-American.

In this atypical statement for these elite white men, this professional views racial intermarriage as a great thing because it helps to build a society that is more fully integrated across divisive racial and ethnic lines. He is correct in stating that the number of interethnic and interracial marriages is increasing across the United States. More than one million marriages occur each year across various racial lines, and many more across traditionally difficult ethnic lines. It is also true that most white

Americans already have a mixed ethnic or racial ancestry. Indeed, they are themselves a rather hybrid human population, though this fact is not often noted when racial blending is being discussed.[6]

A significant level of interethnic and interracial blending has been taking place for more than four centuries in North America. Yet it is mainly in the case of black Americans blending with white Americans, as the last respondent notes, that the so-called "one drop of blood" rule comes into play. This white-generated societal norm, now centuries old, stipulates that a little black American ancestry—for example, one great-grandmother—makes a person "black."

One well-educated professional gives this strong and favorable answer to the question on a child dating a black person.

> Well, we did. [Gives name] did for a while.... Actually, what I really think is the—what's going to eventually be the solution to this [racism], if we give it enough time, is for more interracial marriage. Because the thing is, that if it's "those people," they're different. But if, well, that's your daughter-in-law, or your son-in-law, or your aunt or your uncle. I remember, you know, when I was growing up, the real biases were against people who were Polish or Italian or, you know, things like that, and that the real breakdown of it came when my parents' brothers and sisters started marrying people like that.... And [you] find out that they're also like everybody else. You know, they've got some different dances and stuff, but ... they're nice people too.... The other thing is, it's eventually got to break down this ridiculous thing that ... if somehow two people get married ... of different races, they become, that their offspring is automatically...black or Hispanic.

In his broadly accepting view, interracial marriages will eventually mean that many, if not most, white Americans will have to learn about people in other racial groups and come to recognize and accept them as people very much like themselves. These close personal relationships across racial lines will break down much racial bias and eventually destroy the color line.

That "race" is socially constructed can be seen in the fact that a light-skinned person, perhaps of one-eighth or less African ancestry (and the rest white European), is often regarded as "black" by many whites, because one of his or her ancestors is known to be of African ancestry. This is in part a legacy of many former state laws that defined who was black in terms of a similarly small proportion of black ancestry. Yet in most Caribbean, Latin American, and African nations, a person who is one-eighth African in ancestry and seven-eighths European would usually be considered "white." Significantly, growing numbers of Americans of mixed ancestry are putting pressure on this traditional white understanding of racial categories. Consider, for example, the case of Tiger Woods, one of the world's premier golfers. In the late 1990s, at the age of 21, Woods became the center of media attention when he won several major golf tournaments, including the Masters. Woods has described his ancestry as one-eighth white, one-eighth Native American, one-fourth African American, one-fourth Thai American, and one-fourth Chinese American, and has even coined the combinatorial term "Cablinasian" to describe himself. However, in spite of the fact that his ancestry is mostly not African, the mass media (and his family) have generally portrayed him as an African American.[7]

CONCLUSION

White Americans have long exhibited fears of interracial relationships that involve any contact between the sexes. In the past, these views often involved crude and blatant racial stereotyping. This stereotyping was not limited to lower- or middle-class whites, for members of the white male elite have long played a key role in maintaining highly stereotyped images of the sexuality of black Americans. As recently as the 1950s, President Dwight D. Eisenhower was reported (by Earl Warren, then Chief Justice of the Supreme Court) as having made this pointed comment about white Southerners opposed to school desegregation at a private dinner in 1954. They were, he said, "not bad people. All they are concerned about is to see that their sweet little girls are not required to sit in school alongside some big overgrown Negroes."[8] None of our respondents comes close to expressing such a highly racialized view in the interviews, which likely indicates significant progress since the 1950s in white thinking about these matters.

Still, there is much concern, uneasiness, and opposition among white Americans, including many elite white men, about issues of interracial dating and marriage. A certain tentativeness or fearfulness can be seen in various places in the society. For example, on television and in the movies, interracial dating and marriage have been taboo topics until very recently. While there were a few scattered attempts to break this taboo in television shows (and the movies) prior to the late 1990s, it was only about the year 2000 that more than one or two major television series had the courage to show significant interracial dating and marriage relationships even as temporary plot lines. In March 2000, the NBC White House series *The West Wing* showed such a story, in this case about the president's teenage daughter dating a black man. Nonetheless, even with a number of such series now showing interracial relationships, almost all such relationships have not been mature and long-lasting, but have been portrayed as seriously problematic or have abruptly ended. As yet, no series producers have been willing to put such an ongoing story line at the center of a major television series.[9] It is also the case that only rarely have the movies been willing to portray such relationships. Clearly, interracial dating and marriage issues are still matters of debate and deep concern throughout white America.

We can see some of the reasons for this continuing sensitivity in the comments of the elite men in this chapter. While these men are well-educated and hold influential positions in society, many of them still express opposition, concern, or unease in regard to interracial dating or marriage, views that are likely similar to those of whites in various classes throughout the society. In their interviews, we see the majority exhibiting a certain cautiousness in their assessments, for they often seem aware that injudicious comments on these matters can make them appear racist in their perspective. There is much talk about having to carefully think through issues surrounding interracial relationships, should they arise, and about discussing such issues fully with their children or other relatives who might be involved in such relationships. Conspicuous in the answers given by numerous men is the extent to which their objections are couched in what seem to be nonracial terms. In many cases, these men, like other whites, provide reasons for their differentiating attitudes, explanations, propensities, and actions that seem to ignore or downplay the racial dimensions of these matters. In some cases, nonracial assessments citing social obstacles or cautions may subtly hide a critique of the culture or values of black Americans.

Certain themes recur in their answers to questions about interracial dating and marriage. One is a concern or anxiety about the everyday difficulties and suffering, the poor quality of life, thought to be faced by interracial couples. Included among these obstacles are the negative attitudes and reactions of other people in the couple's social environment, the probability that the couple will be social outcasts, the difficulty such a couple will have in finding a good home or neighborhood, and the projected problems they will face in raising their children. These concerns are portrayed as being about what various other people will think or how they will react, whether they be other family members or people in the larger society. The respondents who make such assessments mostly seem to have in mind the reactions of other whites to these interracial relationships. Even those who exhibit opposition to or significant discomfort about these interracial relationships usually do not seem to include themselves in the list of those whites who would react to the interracial relationships in racially hostile ways.

Another major theme is concern, phrased in different ways, about the presumed lack of common ground for partners in such interracial relationships. As they indicate in other contexts, numerous respondents are concerned about what they misperceive as significantly different family values, social customs, or personal behaviors across the color line. They sometimes draw on analogies with religious differences, although most whites and blacks in the United States have Protestant backgrounds. In talking about interracial relationships, these men often do not spell out what contradictory values or customs they have in mind. They may be thinking that there are certain black cultural values—perhaps the allegedly weak work ethic or lack of emphasis on education they bring up in other contexts—or certain problematic family customs and behavior that they think may create difficulties for the white partner in an interracial relationship, if not for the relationship itself.

Among these respondents—including those who are relatively liberal in principle concerning interracial relationships—there often seems to be more concern, unease, or qualification in their comments as the hypothetical relationships get closer to them personally, especially in the case of their own children. Several men seem especially concerned about interracial relationships involving daughters, sisters, mothers, or other close female relatives, more so than about those involving the men in their families. Here we see an intersection of racial and gender issues.

These attitudes may signal patriarchal concern for the girls and women in immediate families, or stereotyped assessments of the character of black men as a group.

Recall the comments of the black protagonist in Ralph Ellison's novel *Invisible Man,* about how whites often view him: "I am an invisible man. . . . I am a man of substance, of flesh and bone, fiber and liquids —and I might even be said to possess a mind. I am invisible, understand, simply because people refuse to see me."[10] Numerous comments in this chapter signal again that black Americans as a group are often misunderstood by whites as being significantly different in terms of family values, ordinary customs, and personal or family goals. In this regard, they seem much like the majority of white Americans, who still have difficulty, perhaps great difficulty, recognizing black men, women, and children as typically much like white men, women, and children in their values, orientations, and lives.

6

SITUATIONS OF POSSIBLE DISCRIMINATION: ACTION AND INACTION

Racial attitudes are important in upholding the U.S. system of racism, but it is discriminatory actions carried out by whites that form the central component of this system. Discrimination against African Americans and other Americans of color is much more extensive than most whites believe it to be. While television and other media reports suggest that it is largely uneducated or working-class whites who engage in whatever overt discrimination remains in the society, it is actually middle- and upper-class white Americans who carry out much of this discrimination, for they are usually the people with the power and resources to do so.

The decision to discriminate, or to not discriminate, involves a complex set of factors and considerations. It is made by individuals, yet these individuals are again influenced greatly by other whites in the social groups that are important in their lives. The social contexts of actions that are discriminatory—or of actions that oppose discrimination—are of great consequence. The role of others, particularly other whites, is usually critical not only to the immediate situation of discrimination itself, but also to the long-term build-up to the situation. This build-up includes the continuing socialization of the white individuals involved in regard to racial images, racial stereotypes, and related matters. Thus, a white person's own views and values, as well as those of relevant others, can make a difference not only in the character of the social setting, but also in the discriminatory actions considered, actually carried out, sometimes abandoned, openly questioned, or actively opposed.

We can consider the generally recurring rituals of discrimination in U.S. society as involving an array of potential players, who vary in their contributions to the discrimination and its persistence. In a particular setting where discrimination takes place, there are typically "officiants," those whites who make the key decision and do the actual discrimination. Often there are also "acolytes," those whites who provide varying support for the officiants. In addition, and most significant for many contemporary settings, there are the "passive supporters" or "bystanders," those whites whose passive agreement or inaction more or less allows the performance of discriminatory actions.[1] There is yet another category as well, the "opponents" of discrimination, those whites who are willing to take at least some, or perhaps considerable, action in a given setting to resist or act against discrimination by other whites. To varying degrees, these latter whites often have to resist tendencies toward racialized thinking or discrimination on their own part as well.

The power held by upper-middle-class and upper-class whites, especially white men, places them in individual or institutional contexts where they can be officiants, acolytes, bystanders, and opponents in regard to an array of racialized actions and discriminatory practices. They may be employers who hire and fire, storeowners who control the actions of their clerks, or leading politicians who are architects of public policies on the creation or enforcement of antidiscrimination laws. White men of higher class standing can give active or passive support to, or counter and block, the discriminatory actions of others, such as those below them in organizational positions.

Our respondents generally do not discuss the discrimination in which they themselves might have engaged, but they do discuss their reactions to the racialized behavior or discrimination by other whites, including their views of a white person in a hypothetical discriminatory situation presented to them in the interview. As a group, these men are often among those whites who have substantial power to fight racial prejudice and to usher in important changes in the patterns of discrimination against Americans of color, within their own organizational bailiwicks and in the larger society, if they so choose. Whether or not they express or enact their disagreement with discrimination when they see it happen, whether or not they actually take (or might take) a proactive role in combating discrimination, most of these men do indeed have access to sociocultural resources and power that the majority of Americans do not have. Thus, they can, and sometimes do, play a central role in active antidiscrimination efforts. They have the power, as well, to take such action in the future. Aggressive actions that routinely challenge the discriminatory patterns associated with systemic racism may not be a priority for many of the powerful white men in this country, but, given their resources and spheres of influence, it is noteworthy when they make use of their power against discrimination. Their reactions to discrimination, hypothetical and otherwise, can provide us with deep insights into the character, meaning, and future of racial hostility and discrimination in the contemporary United States.

EMPLOYMENT SITUATIONS: ACTION AND INACTION

The executives, administrators, entrepreneurs, and professionals in this sample are often in positions of influence and power over many other people. When asked to recall a situation where they had to make a difficult decision involving racial issues, one common setting for such incidents was the workplace. Indeed, they infrequently cite other social settings such as neighborhoods and churches. This is not surprising, given the relatively segregated nature of white lives outside the workplace. Places of employment are one of the few arenas where many elite white men come into contact with at least a few black Americans or other people of color on a basis that is more equal in status than their contacts with domestic workers and other service workers.

Many of these men have the ability to decide who will be hired or fired. Recalling a difficult decision, one insightful executive details the criteria he took into account when making one promotion decision. Research on the "glass ceiling" for employees of color documents the reality that they are often passed over for promotions, even when they are more qualified than the white men who get the advancement.[2] In a less common case, this respondent goes against the prevailing pattern as he makes this decision.

> There was a promotion that was up, and it was narrowed down between this black individual and this white male. And I was almost, I was probably at an impasse. Even though I felt that the white male was more qualified than the black male, but not by much, I was sort of at an impasse, it took me about two weeks, but I decided to give the black guy a shot, and give him a chance ... That was a tough decision. It took me a couple of weeks to wrestle with that thing, but I gave it to the black guy.... And everything turned out fine. In fact, he's still with me today. So everything worked out well ... That and the fact that he was there a couple years more, although I felt that the white man was more qualified, was better qualified is what I should say. I gave the shot to the black guy because he was with me for a few years.

This man uses the phrase "more qualified," but he does not spell out what he had in mind. His caveat "but not by much" indicates the somewhat arbitrary nature of such decisions when candidates are comparably qualified. In fact, each candidate here had fairly comparable merit for the promotion, which is likely why the respondent agonized over the choice. Indeed, we do learn that the black candidate was better qualified in one way, in that he had been at the company for a longer period. This employer takes a proactive role in helping to shatter the glass ceiling for African Americans, a step that seems to be seldom taken in many areas of corporate America today.

To act thus in opposition to the racial status quo generally means challenging business as usual, a situation where most whites have the ability to act because they have inherited and garnered white privileges, including socioeconomic resources. Now that the old-fashioned, door-slamming exclusion has declined in significance, racial inequality is reproduced instead through the normal operations of society. Just by "living in a segregated neighborhood, sending their children to segregated schools, interacting fundamentally with their racial peers, working in a mostly segregated job or if in an integrated setting, maintaining superficial relations with nonwhites, etc., [whites] help reproduce the racial status quo."[3] Every major part of a white (or other) person's life is shaped by the racial inequalities systemic in the United States.

In the above case, the usual decision of preferring a white employee with a little better credentials in this case was not taken, and this respondent provides one example of how the legacies of past discrimination can be overcome. Similarly, another powerful manager discusses how he went against the grain by acknowledging and dealing with racial discrimination in his training program.

> The first time I was confronted with [a racial situation] where I didn't know what to do is when I was training hardcore unemployables, so called . . . mostly black and Hispanic kids in [names city]. . . . I was training them to go to work for [names company], to upgrade their basic skills so they could become [company] trainees. And one of the program elements was discrimination and how they could deal with discrimination. And I really didn't quite know how to handle it until I finally glommed onto the great idea of telling the kids, "What do I know, I'm a white male, why don't you tell me about discrimination and such?" So that seemed to work reasonably well.

As we have seen in previous chapters, many white Americans accent color-blindness in their thinking about racial matters today. One aspect of this view, seen in numerous respondents' comments, is a minimizing of the impact of racial discrimination, such as by claiming that it is now relatively rare in the United States. By acknowledging discrimination and, as important, the ability of the trainees of color to identify and describe it, this man thereby challenged the racial status quo and likely advanced the cause of cross-racial understanding and economic justice to some degree through his innovative actions.

In many cases, however, whites with authority regarding employment do not wish to intervene in the racial status quo. In some cases, they may downplay the reality of a negative racial climate at work, either by not doing much about it or by taking the view that employees of color bring their workplace troubles on themselves. While the option of not intervening in a negative racial climate created by other white employees may seem rather passive and benign, in fact it can become problematic when the person who is not intervening has the power to do something about it.

Recalling a workplace situation, another respondent provides this example of a difficult decision:

> [A black] candidate just left us because they felt uncomfortable in the workplace. I didn't tell their supervisor. Maybe someday, but I didn't tell his supervisor.... I don't know. The timing isn't right, maybe. Maybe the supervisor would wake up if he knew, be a little more sensitive. I don't think the one I'm thinking of is real receptive to it [racial sensitivity], so I haven't said anything to the person. I think when the time is right, I'll say something about it, but there is no rush.

Clearly, this respondent did not create the problem described. A black employee made a decision to leave his job because of some type of insensitive attitude on the part of a white supervisor. Yet this was evidently a much more serious matter for the black employee, since it prompted such a drastic response on his part, than for this respondent, who reports seeing no need to have taken countering action, at least not in the immediate situation.

One way many whites, including employers, view an array of racial issues in the workplace is to see many of them as fallacious, as brought up by employees of color when they are trying to use as an excuse for their own shortcomings and inadequacies. One assumption implicit in this viewpoint is that whites rarely discriminate anymore in the workplace. These whites take the position that problems with racial discrimination arise mainly, or only, when people of color "make race an issue." This concern about what black employees might do can affect the decisions of white employers who are struggling with hiring-and-firing matters. They may come to view black employees, or potential employees, as possible instigators of racial tension in a workplace where there is now, they assume, no racial problem.

Unlike a respondent discussed above, another indicates that he chose a white candidate for a job over a black candidate when qualifications were apparently similar.

> I had ... a candidate for a job in my organization, and I just didn't know if he was going to work out ... and I knew if I picked the white candidate I could transfer him, I could demote him, I could fire him if he couldn't do the job, [but] if I chose the black candidate he was mine forever.... I wouldn't be able to fire him with all the pressure of

affirmative action—he would just be mine forever. I took the white candidate. I agonized over that one not only when I made it, but later. And I would do it again ... because all I know about that person is where he graduated from, and that could have been a standard much lower than that school normally has. I know I am not going to be able to get rid of him if he doesn't do the job because I know he is going to have an employment history. And I can't lie to people who are in my peer group about what kind of person he is. They will find out quickly enough anyway and ruin my reputation. So I know I am not the only one who does this. I may be the only one [who] agonized over it more than most.

Here the respondent seems very concerned about what would happen if a black candidate's work was not up to par. He creates hypothetical scenarios that include some misconceptions about affirmative action and schooling. He assumes that affirmative action would keep him from firing a black person and that the black candidate may have been held to a lower standard while in school. Underlying these speculations is his view that hiring black employees can bring unnecessary problems, which can apparently be avoided by not hiring them. Interestingly, in this case the potential problems are blamed on schools and affirmative action, rather than on the lack of ability of the potential black employee.

In the minds of many whites, the government policies set in place in the past to help remedy discrimination, such as modest programs of affirmative action (usually put into place by liberal white officials), become the causes of today's racial difficulties and tensions. Those holding this view often ignore the pervasive anti-black discrimination that is the real racial problem in workplaces, as it is in the society. The millions of black targets of societal discrimination are thus not made real in the mind's eye of these whites. Instead, they perceive a major contemporary racial problem in the fact that white men in power are seemingly inconvenienced by affirmative action or unfounded antidiscrimination complaints and lawsuits.

INFORMAL SOCIAL SETTINGS: ACTION AND INACTION

White Americans, including elite white men, periodically encounter opportunities in social settings and situations outside the workplace where they can influence others by opposing discrimination, by ignoring it, or by discriminating themselves. Many upper-middle-class and upper-class white men have active social lives, participating in clubs and engaging in other social activities where there are very limited numbers of (or no) people of color involved. According to numerous respondents, in all-white, or almost all-white, settings they periodically hear anti-black statements, such as racist epithets or racialized joking, or they witness the discomfort of other whites with the inclusion of even a few people of color in these social environments.

Interestingly, in contrast to some accounts of work-related situations, where the significance of racial characteristics is minimized or discounted, in the following accounts of incidents in social settings the racial dimension is consistently recognized. The accounts are often followed by some justification for why they happened or why the given action or inaction was deemed necessary. The sociologist Eduardo Bonilla-Silva describes some of the framing of such events as the "naturalization of racial matters."[4] Many whites justify contemporary racial arrangements by statements to the effect that human beings "naturally" gravitate to their "own kind," whether the topic is residential segregation, informal socializing, or marriage. Such rationalization may be accompanied by a minimizing of the reality of discrimination or an apparent assumption that social segregation occurs in the absence of any stereotyped thinking or racial exclusion on the part of whites. Statements like "that's just the way things are" serve to naturalize the racial status quo and reduce the possibilities for redress.

These elite men have been part of many social settings, both formal and informal, and they were asked how they had responded to other whites who engaged in racial comments or discriminatory action. Several respondents discussed why they did not take countering action in the face of racial slurs, humor, or exclusion perpetrated by white associates or acquaintances. For instance, this executive identifies some reasons why he may not confront racist humor if it comes up in a given situation.

> You could argue that's a bit of a cop-out, but I would probably tend
> to ignore it [a racial slur or joke].... I think all of us—I don't care if
> you're white, black, red, yellow, whatever ... there is a degree of racial

> prejudice in each one of us, without question.... I can tell you that I
> would be one who probably would not do [anything about] it unless
> it was just absolutely blatant. In front of members of a minority race,
> I think I would probably step forward that time because I think that's
> just stripping someone of their dignity, which I don't ever believe in.
> But if it was done among a group of white males, for example, I'm not
> sure I would want to embarrass that person publicly.... I don't think
> on most occasions ... [the remark is] made in as serious a vein as
> some might think.... I'm not saying anything of that's right, but it's
> part of our society.

This executive indicates very clearly that in his view such racial slurs
and jokes are not right, but explains his likely inaction in the face of
such comments in terms of not wanting to embarrass the white person
involved. He does make an exception for the situation when a person
of color is present, in which he would probably step forward—thereby
indicating a sense of social justice. We see here some of the explanatory
language used by many whites to account for continuing racial prejudice among whites—that "there is a degree of racial prejudice in each
one of us." This somewhat fatalistic type of commentary tends to take
the focus off eradicating the prejudiced behavior of whites, who as a
group generally have the most power to change the system of racial prejudice and discrimination in the United States.

Similarly, another influential respondent recalls a time when his
college fraternity chose to exclude a black member, and offers his view on
creating discomfort for those who were involved.

> Our fraternity had no blacks and a black was brought up, had come
> to rush, and there was a decision on what to do.... [Q: And can you
> tell me what happened?] Well, he was denied. He was rejected and not
> offered a bid for several reasons, but obviously it was because of his
> color.... I still think it was a good decision, I think from my perspec-
> tive, I think everybody would have felt uncomfortable.

Again there is an acknowledgment of the racial bias in the incident, coupled with a justification of why it occurred. Preservation of an all-white
social space is here viewed, at least in part, as a matter of comfort and
harmony. His view is that "everybody" would be uncomfortable, includ-

ing the black man, so the exclusion was for the latter's own good. In such decisions, the power to define what is or is not comfortable is taken out of the hands of the black student and put solely in the hands of white students. The segregated social space is more or less naturalized as a healthy way of living and relating, while integration is seen as introducing an unnecessary and unhealthy disruption of the status quo.

Another executive recounts his experience in an exclusionary fraternity.

> I was in a fraternity, white males, Jews and Christians, not all Christians—but we had a black guy come through . . . who I thought was terrific and so did ninety percent of us. And I was really ticked because in those days it only took one person to blackball somebody. . . . But I had no decision to make other than I guess I could have left, but that wasn't the decision that I was going to do. . . . There's nothing you can do about it. . . . You can argue or change the rules and all that. That just wasn't where I was at that point in my life. I mean, I was struggling to stay in school, I didn't care about anything else.

Unlike the previous respondent, this man did not think the fraternity members made the right decision in excluding a black man. However, the end result was the same in that the fraternity remained all-white, and the exclusionary actions apparently went unchallenged. Like the executive who views racist comments as "part of our society," this man accepts discrimination more or less fatalistically because "there's nothing you can do." Although later in his interview he suggests that something might have been done, his reaction as a youth exemplifies how preoccupation with one's own comfort in such social interaction frequently precludes whites from intervening against discriminatory actions. Noticeably, in such cases, there is a type of informal group intimacy, sharing, and support that makes responses critical of the group's actions difficult.

From time to time, these elite white men indicate that they do break out of the role of passive observer and take assertive actions to challenge racial bias or exclusion in certain types of social settings, including important informal ones. For example, one banker says that he wrote a letter of support for the "first black to ever join our golf club." Another important business leader recalls an incident from college when he rebuked a white friend's use of a racial slur.

I was a freshman at [college name] … and I had roomed with two black individuals and another white male. It was four of us all together.… Apparently the white male, my roommate, came in fairly intoxicated … and the two black males that were sleeping awoke because we were apparently too loud. Anyway, my roommate proceeded to sit on the couch and start babbling. Apparently the couch was wet and he said, "Why is the couch wet? I'll tell you why this couch is wet: Because a bunch of niggers were sitting on it!" And I was shocked to tell you the truth, and I didn't know what to do.… My first reaction was, "Shhh, stop, like, you can't talk like that.… You can't do that." And that's what I did. But the next morning I was in a little dilemma because I enjoyed their company, these two black males, and I liked them a lot.… Do I stick by my buddy, because he was, like, my close friend, he was my roommate and close friend? Or do I confront him right now in front of them, or do I go up to them and say, "Hey, listen, he was a little bit drunk"? [Q: So, what did you end up doing?] I went up to them, and I apologized for being loud and I mentioned to them that [student's name] was way out of line in what he said, and he had a little too much to drink, he shouldn't talk like that.

This man's detailed account reveals some of the difficulty that many whites have in interrupting the flow of their own social interactions and relationships with other whites. He wanted to act against the racist intrusion, yet he also wanted to remain friends with all his roommates after this incident, so his dilemma concerned how to do that. His comments center on the point that two black roommates had heard the racist epithet, and what to do about that, and not on whether he wanted to remain friends in the future with a white person who would act and think in those overtly racist terms. Like the executive quoted previously, he seems to believe that racist slurs should be confronted when people of color are around, but it is less clear whether he would react the same way if only whites were present. Here the racially derogatory comment was directly challenged, but in a limited manner that accented the perpetrator's temporary state of drunkenness and not the larger implications of what he had said. Interestingly, it is common for many whites to explain the overtly racist behavior of other whites by such statements as "they were drunk" or "they were just joking."

The actions of a respondent active in civic affairs further illustrate this point. He indicates that when he saw some racial joking being aimed at a person of color on the team that he coached, his choice was not to ignore it but to intervene.

> I had really only one minority on my team. I found that for his acceptance into the group he would allow other peers to use his racial background as a teasing zone which gave him acceptability. And I cared so much for this young person, I had a conversation with him about it, that he should have more self-respect. . . . He would almost invite the fact that, well . . . he'll pick up the balls or he'll pick up this because he's the only black person on the team and stuff like that. . . . He would almost volunteer because it was his way of being accepted into the group. [Q: Like admitting to other people that he realizes that he's black?] Well, that he's different. And then he changed a great deal from eighth grade until he graduated. . . . I think he grew out of it. I think he just grew, he increased his self-confidence. [Q: Then did he take a leadership role?] Absolutely. Because he earned it.

In this account a black person is experiencing racialized teasing and joking, so there seems to be more motivation for a concerned white person to intervene. Interestingly, this respondent focuses on the fact that the young black man allowed the racial teasing by whites to take place. Apparently, he did not clearly define the white teammates' racial attitudes as the problem to be dealt with in the immediate situation. Like many other liberal whites, when speaking out against discrimination, this white man opts to connect with the person of color and express his disapproval. He does not mention directly challenging the young whites doing the harassing. Although the racial harassment apparently stopped because of this commendable intervention, such an approach does less to stop future harassment of other black Americans than more active intervention with the whites might have.

Even in accounts by those respondents who have challenged the racist actions of other whites, we often see a tendency among these more liberal men to deal with anti-black actions or exclusion in ways that do not significantly disrupt the flow of their own interactions with the other whites. White social spaces seem to be valorized as zones where the comfort and harmony among whites have to be preserved with as little disruption as is possible under the circumstances. In addition, the focus is generally on the immediate discriminatory events, rather than on the underlying causes, which are rooted in continuing systemic racism. While racially hostile or exclusionary actions are certainly not praised as proper or moral, they are often not seen as events of enough seriousness to warrant abandoning or significantly endangering important social relationships and networks with other whites.

Many of our respondents indicate to their interviewers that racial prejudice and discriminatory actions by whites are "not right." To varying degrees, they indicate that they are aware of the moral dilemma facing U.S. society in regard to racial discrimination and inequality. Much less often, however, do these men interpret the racist events they have witnessed as reasons for taking aggressive action against all anti-black discrimination, in the immediate social settings or in the larger society. Whether it is the mistreatment by other whites of black Americans in various social settings, or other whites' commenting on or to black Americans in derogatory ways, even the majority of liberal whites seem to be willing to allow these discriminatory patterns to more or less continue, with situational or modest counters at best.

Sociologist Lawrence Bobo has noted that most whites today adhere to what he calls an "ideology of bounded racial change."[5] In this view, the support of the majority of whites for government and other action to bring changes in continuing patterns of racial discrimination and inequality generally ends when actual or proposed changes might significantly endanger whites' socioeconomic positions and privileges. We can add to this important analysis the additional point that white support for action against discrimination, especially in immediate social settings, is often limited by whites' concerns about the impact of such action on their relationships to and interaction with other whites. Most whites have difficulty seeing these critical everyday situations of discrimination *from the point of view* of the people of color who are forced to be the central targets in them.

PUBLIC PLACES: ACTION OR INACTION

In addition to workplaces and informal social networks, many whites do encounter black Americans or other people of color in the streets. These encounters are usually brief, and often result in some type of defensive or fearful reaction on the part of the whites involved. The elite respondents are sometimes quite forthcoming in discussing the racial stereotyping or bias that has appeared in their thoughts and actions in these public places. They also offer insight into how they justified their actions and reactions. One prominent respondent provides this succinct commentary:

> [When I see] a group of blacks on a street corner, teenage blacks, [I may find myself] making a decision whether I should walk in that direction or not. [My] decision [was to] go into a store, turn around and go out of the store, go in the opposite direction. No problem.... In other words, he who lives to run away lives to run another day.

When the interviewer then asks if he would react the same way to young whites on a street corner, he responds candidly, "possibly not." Many whites would likely be less candid than this man in response to such a question. In his actions he is responding like many white Americans, whose often defensive or withdrawal reactions are well-described in interviews with black Americans—including working-class and middle-class black Americans—about their everyday experiences with whites in the streets and other public places such as shopping malls.[6] This respondent recognizes the stereotyping behind his actions, yet a better-safe-than-sorry rationale is used to justify his response.

Whites may frequently use the term "blacks" when discussing such defensive reactions in various public places, but they likely have in mind black men and not black women when they reflect on hypothetical or real situations. Thus, one reason for the often excessively defensive reactions of whites to black men—and not to otherwise similar white men—in a variety of public places is the constant emphasis on the negative image of black men that is circulated by prominent whites in a variety of political, educational, and mass media settings. As a few of the respondents suggest, the fearful image of "criminal black men" has continued to be exaggerated and emphasized in recent years, and many whites pick it up from, and use it within, important reference groups. For example, in the 1990s Ron Paul, a former member of the U.S. Congress, made this assertion in one of his publications about black men in Washington, D.C.: "I think we can safely assume that 95 percent of the black males are semi-criminal or entirely criminal."[7] Using the mass media in this way, white commentators often circulate and reinforce stereotyped mental images of black Americans. As one recent analyst has put it, "For countless Americans, fears of Black violence stem from, among other things, the complex interaction of cultural stereotypes, racial antagonism, and unremitting overrepresentations of Black violence in the mass media."[8]

In our interviews, one powerful manager acknowledges struggling with the irrationality of some stereotyped responses to black people on the street.

> I think I have some deep-seated fears that I try to overcome. For example, if I am walking down a street, and it is dark and some blacks approach me, then I will probably cross over to the other side of the street. These blacks may be very professional and outstanding citizens, but my mental model on a deserted street is to be very careful. Those are issues that I must rise and face, and I mean no offense to the blacks when I do that, but I do it anyway.

This manager is articulate and perceptive about a problematic "mental model" of black people, which he is trying to overcome. Unlike some other respondents, moreover, he does recognize the offense he causes to African Americans with this type of defensive behavior in public places. Indeed, other research studies do show that such actions as whites' crossing the street in obvious avoidance maneuvers do often give pain and offense to black Americans.[9] This man justifies his defensive response in terms of caution and safety, a rationale that is common among white Americans. Many people would argue that it is realistic for most people to be cautious in regard to strangers in public places, whatever the racial or ethnic characteristics of those encountered. However, as we have seen, these respondents sometimes explicitly acknowledge that their fears of black men usually do not translate into similar avoidance reactions to comparable white strangers.

Another respondent gives a complex account of his likely and actual reactions to strangers with different racial characteristics encountered in public places.

> I remember being asked for money recently. . . . It was a black person on a dark street, probably eleven-thirty or twelve o'clock at night. . . . [And I asked myself] how I would have felt if it were a white person. Would I be less threatened? I usually respond negatively when that

happens, meaning . . . I don't immediately turn around and say, "Yes, you can have what you want." I don't remember ever doing that. I did that at the time because my first fear was, [since he was] black, maybe the next minute I was going to have very little control over the situation. So I gave him just what he was looking for, not to question whether this was going to accelerate into something beyond this simple request for money. . . . If it was a white person of equal severity in his posture, it probably wouldn't have been different. If it was a white person such as myself who was asking for money. . . . [For example, recently there was] . . . a guy who just simply expressed the fact that he was from [city name] and needed train fare and basically told me these things which may or may not have been true. I treated that differently, yes.

This reflective commentary illustrates how a white person's general response in justifying fear of strangers in public places may be to say that he or she would react in the same cautious way, regardless of the strangers' racial characteristics. Yet this type of statement is usually an abstraction, divorced from real life. Although this respondent first indicates that his response to assertive strangers would probably have been consistent and equally concerned regardless of racial characteristics, at the end of his comment he uses an instance from his recent experience to acknowledge that a "white person such as myself" did elicit a different, apparently less fearful and concerned, reaction from him. In his account, we also sense some linkage of the racial and class characteristics of the strangers encountered.

Another professional is quite articulate about his own double standard regarding fear of strangers. Like some of the other respondents, he, too, views his stereotyping as problematic.

Part of me tenses up whenever I'm on a subway, for example, in [city name], or walking down the street, and I see someone, usually of a different race, but not always, scragglier looking than myself, walking toward me or sitting near me or eyeing me funny. I would be lying to tell you . . . it's not because of their skin, because in a large part it is. Because, for better or for worse, what you see in TV and in the papers and on the radio is things that happened by, to, or because of blacks and minorities just because [of] the way society has laid out its cards. . . . You wind up keeping an eye on your wallet more when you see a black man who hasn't shaved in a few days, who's wearing ratty clothes. Whereas, if I saw a white man in ratty clothes I would think, "Oh, he's looking for money." Whereas a black man, I might think, "Oh, he might be dangerous".... Yes, I can't deny it. It's nothing that I'm proud of and it's nothing that I like to have in me, but it's something that I definitely have experienced at length.

Unlike many other white Americans, this insightful observer does not try to justify his fearful reactions to blacks who are walking or sitting nearby by making those reactions seem natural and normal. While there are varying levels of awareness among these men as to whether their stereotype-generated reactions are seen as justified, deplorable, or somewhere in between, the end result of the stereotyping in street situations is probably going to be roughly the same. Even when they notice their racial stereotyping or bias, either in themselves or in other whites, they seldom take the difficult additional step of recasting the usual patterns of differential reactions to racialized strangers.

This perceptive interviewee brings up an issue that is seldom so strongly noted in other respondents' discussions of interracial interactions in public places. He locates the source of his admittedly stereotyped fears in television, radio, and newspaper portrayals of black Americans; later in the interview, he refers to old myths created by his "forefathers." His point about the media perpetuating racial stereotypes is important, for it helps to explain the widespread negative reactions of whites to the presence of black men, not only on the street but in other social settings. His understanding about the media is accurate in regard to widespread imaging of black men as dangerous and criminal. For example, crime stories make up about a third of all local television news programming. One recent study of such programming in a large metropolitan area found that violent crimes received almost all the crime coverage on local news, with accounts of violent crime featuring blacks in much higher proportion than their arrest rate indicates would be an accurate portrayal.[10] Other studies show that white Americans are usually overrepresented as victims of crime, while black Americans are overrepresented among those said to be perpetrators.[11] When pervasive and influential media greatly exaggerate the crimes of black Americans, not surprisingly, these acts come to be linked in the white mind with many or all black Americans. Moreover, at least as serious in the media distortions is the failure of news shows to present black Americans in the favorable light that most deserve. In one study of Chicago news programs, whites got much more positive coverage (a ratio of 14 to 1) as "good Samaritans" than blacks, even though the latter make up a percentage of the local population only a little less than that of whites.[12]

A HYPOTHETICAL SITUATION: WHAT WOULD YOU DO?

To probe some of these issues further, we consider now an interactive scenario that was posed to our respondents in order to examine how they would react if witnessing an event where a white clerk gives preferential treatment to a white person in a commercial place:

> You walk into a jewelry store in downtown Washington, D.C. There are already two black customers waiting. The only salesperson, who is white, looks at you and seems relieved. He comes over to help you first, ignoring the black customers who are waiting for help. What do you think of this salesperson's special treatment of you?[13]

This question gave the respondents one common situation to respond to, which allows us to examine some interesting contrasts in their responses. We should note that their responses to this question may possibly be more decisive or optimistic than were their responses to the real-world situations already discussed, because this situation is hypothetical and carries an imagined social risk, versus the real social risk they face in confronting whites with whom they share important social bonds.

Drawing on Images and Stereotypes

The respondents give diverse responses to this hypothetical scenario. Some of these men say that they would indicate their disapproval of the clerk's differential treatment in some way, but then often go on to offer possible defenses of his actions. Numerous others see nothing wrong with the clerk's response. However they interpret the clerk's response, many indicate that they ultimately would speak out or otherwise intervene. Some note that they simply would not want to cause a scene, pointing to the existence of a comfort zone for white-on-white interactions, while others use the stereotype of black criminality to justify the white store clerk's actions. This latter interpretation both justifies the likely racial preference and minimizes its reality in this commercial situation. According to this line of thinking, it is, once again, the deficient values or behavior of black Americans that are cited as likely creating the problem.

One respondent provides an interesting example of how whites might react in this real-life situation. First, he says that "it's wrong," that he would confront the white clerk, and, if the clerk said it was because they were black, he would walk out of the store. Then he offers further reflective analysis of the situation:

> Maybe . . . he's worried about them shoplifting. I guess if five guys carrying guns walked into the store, and I was working in the store, I might be a little inclined to stay away from them, too. And in many respects, blacks, because of where they find themselves in the societal situation—[a black man] is effectively wearing that gun at his side. He's got hanging on him the moniker of likely being someone . . . that's a criminal. Also there is another reason, and another angle that could be. And that is . . . because most black people don't make much money, maybe . . . he doesn't figure there's any money in the sale . . . he's trying to do his job. If he doesn't sell stuff and he spends all his time being racially harmonious and correct, his boss . . . isn't going to evaluate him on his racial harmoniousness. Did he sell ten thousand dollars' worth of jewelry this week or didn't he? So . . . I'm not exactly sure how directly racially motivated it is, and I think . . . there's a lot of other things that can go into this.

In an intriguing discussion that includes his own expansion of the scenario to include more than two black people in the store, this man attempts to sort through the possible thinking of a white clerk who engages in preferential treatment. One of his key assumptions is revealing, for he, like numerous other respondents, assumes that the black customers are men, though no mention of their gender is made in the scenario. He first suggests that a clerk in such a scenario may have worried about certain traits that whites tend to link to black men, the stereotypical notions that they are very likely to be criminal or violent. In his view, given that belief, the actions of the clerk could have been justified. In his account, as in numerous others, it is also unclear how the white clerk's not serving the black customers and serving the white man first would have reduced the likelihood of criminal action in the situation, had that actually been a possibility.

In his reflections, the respondent implies a statistical-discrimination argument that is advanced by numerous whites to account for white actions in response to black men. There is a common argument that, since a greater proportion of black men than white men are arrested for certain crimes, it is rational for whites to take actions that may violate the rights of black Americans, such as by refusing to serve them.[14]

We have previously discussed black-criminality imagery, but let us add a few additional points, since this is a major issue in many white minds. Although very few of the respondents did so, there are some things they could have taken into consideration in evaluating the hypothetical scenario. The black customers may not have been men, so one could well take that possibility into account in assessing the scenario. There is no hint of a crime in progress or threatened, so no cue to the respondents was provided for going in that direction. Moreover, even if one does take one's thinking in the direction of crime imagery, then certain realities concerning crime should be considered. In any given year, fewer than 2 percent of black men are arrested for violent crimes of any type, which suggests that there is a very low probability that a given black man in a store or elsewhere is likely to engage in a violent crime like robbery.[15] In addition, the substantial majority of those arrested for shoplifting are white—which is an interesting fact in light of the opening comment above in regard to the white clerk's situation.

In his interpretive comment, the last respondent also suggests that the white clerk may have considered the point that blacks on the whole have less money than whites. However, black families engage in a relatively high level of consumer spending relative to their incomes, so it would probably be imprudent for a clerk to assume that the blacks there would not be paying customers.[16] Note, too, his significant phrase, "because of where they find themselves in the societal situation." In his interesting speculation, black men are viewed as criminal because of sociocultural conditions, not because of biological tendencies. A sociocultural interpretation serves as a rationale in thinking through the clerk's motivation. It is particularly interesting that this lengthy assessment and justification of the clerk's reaction follows a brief statement by the respondent that the hypothetical actions of the clerk were wrong and that in protest he might walk out of the store.

Conventional assumptions about black criminality can be seen in numerous interviews. Sometimes, such assumptions come into play after a general statement about how it was inappropriate for the white person to get waited on first, when the black customers were there first. Thus, a statement rejecting racially motivated behavior serves as preface to the more or less racially framed comments that follow. One respondent begins with disapproval of the unfairness, but concludes with a justification suggesting the criminality stereotype.

> That's not necessarily right, but ... I couldn't throw a lot of stones at those people, either, if they are trying to be safe. I think it would be inappropriate to choose me over them.... But for them to be cautious about somebody they did not know—and if you think about it, you're getting ready to plop out there some piece of jewelry, maybe worth several thousand dollars, and it could be scooped up and run out the door with pretty quick. You've got to be careful.... But I wouldn't be bothered if they came to me, when it comes down to it.

Although he feels that the clerk's actions were not necessarily right, this respondent also envisions a possible robbery and later admits he "wouldn't be bothered" by witnessing this type of preferential treatment by a white clerk acting in his favor.

Another respondent says that he would indeed tell the clerk the black shoppers were there first, but then follows that positive statement with a hint at the possible criminality of the black customers, when he states, "One of the reasons that I would probably say that they were there first is so that I would remain in the store until they left." Yet another of these elite men also indicates that it is inappropriate for the clerk to serve him first, and then adds the following comment:

> I don't know why the salesperson would come to me and not go to them and help them. It would seem to me that she should help them first, and I'm second in line and then they help me. But if she comes over to me and she looks relieved and acts relieved and if they have had problems in the past, if their store's been robbed, yeah, I can understand what's going on.

A racial consideration is not explicitly mentioned in this commentary. The respondent views the reaction of the white clerk as unfair, yet then states that the clerk's action was justified if the store had been robbed. The respondent thereby seems to address the situation in a color-blind way without using explicit racial terms. Yet the common imagery of black robbers is implied nonetheless, and it seems to be taken for granted that the interviewer will follow the respondent's logic without his having to make that more explicit. This line of thinking also posits that a robbery may have occurred, a commentary that tends to minimize the reality of the preferential treatment.

In the interviews, numerous respondents attempt to justify the clerk's actions by using certain stereotyped images that they seem to view as defensible, nonracial, or unbiased. Thus, the clerk is seen not as racially motivated, but rather as concerned about such seemingly racially neutral issues as the likelihood of a robbery or the possibility of a greater sales commission. One interesting attempt at making the criminality stereotype seem defensible or nonracial can be seen in the interviews of a few respondents who bring up a comment once made by the civil rights leader Jesse Jackson in their justification of certain stereotyping on the part of whites. The comment, made by Jackson in the mid-1990s, was as follows: "There is nothing more painful to me at this stage in my life than to walk down the street and hear footsteps and start thinking about robbery, then look around and see somebody white and feel relieved."[17] After white commentators started frequently citing his brief comment, Jackson explained that his statement was regrettable and had been taken out of context. Significantly, Jackson's comment is most often cited in conservative white publications. It also illustrates how the steady doses of negative imagery about African Americans, especially in the media, are sometimes so powerful that they even infect some blacks themselves. This type of passing comment has sometimes been used by whites as justification for racial profiling and statistical discrimination on the part of merchants, police, and various other white discriminators. In this manner, the fear of black people becomes universal and therefore defensible, rather than being just a rationalization for continuing racial discrimination by whites.

Referring to the Jackson comment in regard to the hypothetical example of the white clerk, one professional follows the pattern discussed above by citing a color-blind ethic of fairness, and then adding a justification using stereotypes.

> I don't think much of it. I would say, "Well, these people were here ahead of me, you ought to wait on them first." . . . I would be offended by that. . . . And I would not let the salesperson get away with it. [Q: Would you maybe leave and take your business elsewhere? Or would you stay at the store?] I don't know. I might. . . . If they were the only store in town with what I wanted, I might not. . . . well, I was thinking if you had asked, "If you were walking down the street late at night and saw two black teenagers on the other side of the street trailing you, what would your reaction be?" And I remember somebody asking Jesse Jackson that same question, he said he would be very concerned, he would cross over to the other side of the street, and I guess my reaction would probably be the same.

He indicates first that he would be offended by the discriminatory behavior of the clerk and thus intervene. Then he indicates that his consumer needs might in certain situations take precedence over his challenging of the likely injustice. Finally, like several other respondents, he moves from discussing the black customers to other issues, in this case to black teenagers behind him on the street, apparently a situation that brings up some fearful imagery for him. At the end, he justifies these fears by pointing out that Jesse Jackson has indicated he would be fearful in such a situation. As with numerous other respondents, no specific attention is given to the problematic character of white stereotyping of black Americans, especially in terms of conventional images of criminality.

The Jackson comment was brought up by another professional who uses a version of the statistical discrimination argument to justify the white clerk's behavior.

> Jesse Jackson said one time that he was walking down the street in the middle of the night [in] Washington, D.C., and he heard footsteps coming across the street, and when he looked around he saw three men coming at him fast. When he saw that they were white, he said that he was relieved. That tells me that the reason why he was relieved was that the chances of getting mugged by three white men is a lot less than [of] getting mugged by three black men, because of the statistics. . . . The chances are greater that you will be robbed by a black person than a white person, and especially in certain areas.

By drawing on the words of Jackson, somewhat embellished, and by his statistical-discrimination interpretation, this man concludes that the clerk's behavior is not misguided and discriminatory but prudent. After the statement above, this respondent adds that the clerk "would have a better chance of making a sale with me, probably, and ... I'm not going to rob nothing [laughs]." Drawing on the conventional notion about blacks likely being criminal, some of these white managers and professionals—who are probably knowledgeable about civil rights—see little wrong with this differential treatment by a white clerk in such a jewelry store situation.

Other respondents do not agree with this line of argument. One professor brings up the statistical-discrimination issue, but offers the following critique:

> There has been a lot of stuff written on this so-called justifiable suspicion.... People say there are a lot of black perpetrators, so the chances of a cab driver picking up a mugger if he's black [are good. So] if he randomly assesses his customers, and maybe just statistically, owners of jewelry stores are most statistically likely to be robbed by a black person. It goes back to the fact that you can't base social relations on statistical probabilities. If you operate a jewelry store in Washington, D.C., you have to be able to take customers in the order they come in. If you are fearful of black customers, then you are probably doing business in the wrong place.

This professor asserts that even if blacks statistically were somewhat more likely to rob a store than whites, that does not justify the clerk's discriminatory action against ordinary black customers. Significantly, this respondent was in the minority among these elite interviewees in explicitly thinking through the problematic logic of the statistical-discrimination arguments or assumptions and in understanding how they can perpetuate racial discrimination and lead to violations of civil rights in regard to black citizens.

Responding to the Clerk's Actions

We see in our interviews a diverse array of responses to the hypothetical scenario. Numerous respondents feel that the sales clerk's reaction can be more or less justified, often in terms of some version of a black male criminality stereotype, and indicate that they would probably or certainly take no action in the situation. Yet other respondents, who generally see unfairness in the situation, indicate that they would at least consider the possibility of intervening in the situation.

Numerous respondents agonize over whether bringing up the racial issue with another white person in such a situation would be overreacting, be unhelpful, or involve making a scene. Thus, in an interesting example, one professional makes an argument concerning credibility.

> There are certain times when there's nothing you can do about it.... You can't fight a crusade on every issue, on every experience, or you lose credibility. You become irrelevant.... First of all, I don't know if it's my function in that setting to create a scene, which is what would happen. I don't think that's going to help anybody.

"There's nothing you can do about it" suggests a type of fatalism about responding to likely discriminatory incidents, at least in certain settings, that we have encountered before. Such justifications for inaction generally operate to preserve the status quo. The respondent also notes that he feels it is probably not his function to "create a scene." This position perhaps signals the concern among many whites to preserve social harmony, especially in most white-to-white relations. Interestingly, just before the statements quoted, when asked how he felt about the hypothetical incident, this respondent replied, "I don't have any feeling about it because I'm not black."

Other respondents indicate that they might take some action, but not with regard to the likely racial aspects of the scenario. When the interviewer asks whether the clerk's reaction seems to be a "racial thing," one executive responds, "My tendency would be not to initially think it was that case.... It sounds more like it's just somebody being not sensitive to the particular customers, that's all.... I would say, 'I believe these people were before me.' I would turn and make it that simple. I wouldn't necessarily need to turn it into a great and vast occasion." This respondent would take some action, yet he still prefers to view the incident in nonracial terms, as a case of an employee's insensitivity rather than intentional discrimination.

Similarly, another respondent, who is highly placed in his company, indicates that he would not stand by idly but would take some action to remind the sales clerk of who was there first.

> I think I would say, "These other people are here first, why don't you serve them?" Would I then lecture to him about race relations? I don't think so.... I don't think I'd pick up on the fact that it was racist. I'd be most likely to assume they're looking at stuff . . . and while they're looking at it, he's going to get me started looking at stuff. I'm not sure I would glom onto the fact that it was a racist thing.

Again, a sensitive executive prefers to respond to the incident without confronting the clerk in a way that indicates the latter's actions might be racially discriminatory. While some of these elite men suggest that the differential treatment may have been racially motivated, they generally say that they would not call attention to that racial reality. They are reluctant to deal with other whites in that way. Numerous respondents do not seem to mind speaking out, but stress that their resistance would likely be to the unfair order of service. Their feeling about the hypothetical scenario is that it is no different than if two white customers were being served out of order. For instance, this respondent succinctly states: "I think it's ridiculous. I think that it's inappropriate. Why? Because I wasn't there first. There are three human beings waiting to be waited on and I was there third, so I should be waited on third. If a black comes in after me as a fourth, then he should be waited on fourth." It is significant that this respondent would speak out at the clerk's action, yet he implies a color-blind interpretation that does not touch on the possibility of discrimination.

Another respondent articulates a somewhat similar view, this time in relation to the clerk's boss.

> If I were her employer, okay, I would say to [the] white clerk, "That wasn't right." . . . There are certain situations when people take preference. But it has nothing to do with color. It would have to do with a real good customer.... Whether I was waited on in front of two other white people, I would have no difference in feeling.... Just as a customer, that's a . . . normal response. I think what you are trying to ask, if it was great that I beat out two blacks. No, I wouldn't put any color on those other people.... Maybe [it was] the way I looked. Or

maybe she thought I was going to spend more or whatever.... So, when the black guy is in first, and I wait on him first, it's not because I am some liberal and thinking that I'm trying to do something to raise my fellow man. It's just because ... that's the fair thing, the fair way to treat him.

This commentator loosely strings together a number of ideas about the hypothetical situation. While his observations begin and end by referring to what is fair or not right, most of what is in between those statements more or less ignores the probable racial injustice in the clerk's actions. He ponders the hypothetical incident in part in nonracial terms—such as in terms of judgments about the clerk's singling out preferred customers. If white salespersons stand to benefit economically, then they may prefer one customer over another, and this makes sense to him.

We should also note that in most of these respondents' assessments there is no concern expressed for the negative impact of such commonplace differential treatment on black customers. Black shoppers often report recurring problems with discrimination by white clerks in an array of commercial settings.

ACTIVELY ANTIRACIST RESPONSES

Numerous respondents initially say something like, "I would tell the clerk that other customers were here first," but then they often go on to say that the sales clerk was probably justified in his or her racial stereotyping or that his or her actions were not really racially motivated. While the first justification here can be characterized as racialized, the latter position might be described as nonracial or perhaps as part of the color-blind ideology.

One analyst of systemic racism in the United States, Joe Barndt, has distinguished between "nonracist" thinking and action, and antiracist thinking and action.[18] Numerous respondents who do not draw on racial stereotypes and who state that they would object to a sales clerk's differential treatment of customers no matter what their racial characteristics might be said to generally represent a nonracist or nonracial interpretation of the situation. A number of these respondents unmistakably object to the differential treatment of the black customers, yet seem to see little or no possibility of racial discrimination in this hypothetical account. Yet others see the possibility of discrimination, but do not see it as a major issue. However, as we will see in some of the respondents' comments that follow, a perspective ignoring the likely racial character of the mistreatment of black customers is itself problematical. Drawing on Barndt's concepts, one might view whites who adopt an explicitly antiracist perspective as not only acknowledging the likelihood of racial discrimination in such situations, but also seeing that as something serious which they must openly confront.

There are several examples of such actively antiracist thought and action in the interviews. What is striking about some of those who object to the clerk's differential treatment of the African-American customers from an antiracist perspective is not only that they acknowledge the likely reality of racial discrimination, but that they also refer to situations where they themselves have witnessed similar behavior and have actually done something about it.

Take the example of this health professional commenting on what he would say to the white clerk in such a situation.

> What I would say is, "I think they're ahead of me. In fact, I know they're ahead of me." ... I think it would be terrible to be walking around life so scared of dealing with other people. And also, the other thing I would think is that, I would find it offensive that they would be seeing me as like them. You know, "Oh, here's one of us!" I haven't done it very often, but a couple of times I've claimed to have either a Jewish or black mother. With the black, I've actually said it was my stepmother. But one time I was [at a meeting in a predominantly Jewish area]. So it was, you know, a middle-level manager ... who heard my name and said, "Oh, it's nice to—my name's [gives non-Jewish name]," or something like that. "It's nice to see somebody else among all these...." He was saying ... "It's nice to see one of us amidst all these Jews." So I said, "Well, my mother's Jewish."

This perceptive respondent reports that he has, in a specific situation, *intentionally* disrupted the flow of white-on-white interactions when they involve racial or ethnic stereotyping or discrimination on the part of other whites. This is not a common report in the interviews, for only a few of the respondents who acknowledge the reality of racial discrimination in the scenario and suggest they would take action also indicate that they are willing to take such a personal risk in real-life situations. In their interviews, several men indicate that, in theory, they should object to racist slurs and discriminatory actions by other whites, yet when they touch on examples from their own lives, or the hypothetical scenario we provided, they suggest that their tendency would likely be to take no such action. In contrast, when other respondents like this health professional point to a time and place where they have actually taken action against racial discrimination, their antidiscrimination statements seem more grounded.

Relating the hypothetical scenario to personal experiences of having confronted racial discrimination, a senior executive makes this comment:

> I think it stinks, and I've seen that before. . . . I would at that point say, "I think you have other customers first." And I have done that in the past, years ago with the same thing, so I've actually had that happen. . . . I've been in stores where they definitely go to the white people first even when the blacks are waiting. And I've directed them back to them: "Wait till you take care of those other customers." . . . I don't think I could sit and deal . . . I think that that does nothing but continue the racist policies that we've been trying to get rid of. . . . I think it happens a lot. . . . I think that there are some businesses, for instance Denny's, it's a restaurant chain, has been found guilty of, in many, many of their restaurants, of promoting racist policies where the black people aren't served [and] are made to wait for extended periods of time, to the point now where Denny's has to put up signs saying that they are equal opportunity restaurants and that everybody is welcome into their restaurant, that kind of thing. They paid millions of dollars in fines . . . but I think it's also in the other businesses.

This well-spoken executive not only suggests that he would take action in such a hypothetical situation, but also indicates that he has indeed done so—and that he does it assertively and within the framework of an antiracist perspective on the matter. Unlike other whites who try to ignore or minimize racial discrimination, or who try to suggest nonracial motives on the part of white employees in situations like the hypothetical scenario, this executive acknowledges the reality of everyday discrimination against black customers by citing examples from his life and from a celebrated restaurant case that made the national news. He also suggests that he knows the problem goes on in other business arenas. The option of inaction is described as impossible for him. This example includes a definite recognition of the character and extent of the discrimination in commercial settings that is often reported by black customers. The hypothetical scenario becomes much more than an abstraction, as respondents like this one refer to times when they have seen it happen and have actually taken action to redress the situation.

In contrast to the respondents who excuse the clerk's behavior, this legal professional also adopts an antiracist position. He indicates that this is more than a hypothetical for him.

> I think it is wrong, and I think I would say to him that these people are first. I've actually said that on occasion in similar situations. . . . As my own personal philosophy, I try to take little steps every day to try to overcome whatever racism I see around me, and I try not to let it seep into my own life. I can't say that I'm perfect, because I've come to where I am through my own experiences and prejudices, but I do try to do whatever steps I can to try to help things.

This respondent, too, reports having actually taken countering action against discrimination in similar situations.

Whites who work actively against persisting racism often use recovering from alcoholism as a metaphor in regard to those whites who are "recovering from racism." Thus, these whites are aware of the potential to relapse into racially stereotyped ways of thinking and acting. This professional suggests such a position by saying that he takes "little steps every day," that he's not perfect, and that he still carries the baggage of his prejudices. This distinguishes him from those whites who adopt what they think is a nonracial perspective—those who, often sincerely yet usually naively, profess to see what is in fact an often highly racialized social world in color-blind terms. A color-blind perspective in a racialized world can serve as a basis for not seeing and confronting racial discrimination. This man's viewpoint also distinguishes him from those who say "everyone is prejudiced" as a way of justifying the related view that "there's nothing one can do." Instead, this respondent tries to do something to reduce the omnipresent prejudice within himself and in the world around him. Although there are only a modest number of respondents who articulate a strong antiracist perspective in this sample, their presence could conceivably have important ripple effects as they keep disrupting the racialized spaces around them.

CONCLUSION

Recall from chapter 1 the ethnographic study that found that ordinary whites who are unlikely to make racially barbed or stereotypical comments in public about black Americans or other Americans of color often do make such comments in private. That study, and another now under way, have found that when many whites discuss racial matters out of the public eye, especially with white acquaintances or relatives, Americans of color are targets of openly stereotypical or hostile racial commentary.[19] Significantly, the racialized spaces of some elite white men are also periodically unmasked in the mass media, and the discrimination and exclusion within them are made public. For example, recent reports of corporation executives, white sports officials, and police chiefs using racist language or making racist judgments—in what they thought were private spaces, or other situations among supportive whites—have appeared in the media. Periodically, one sees or hears accounts of well-educated, well-positioned white men being officiants, acolytes, or passive observers in various racist rituals.

However, the elite white respondents quoted in this book virtually never describe themselves as using such racial slurs, making racial jokes, or engaging in discrimination. When they do comment on discriminatory or other racialized situations, the majority describe themselves as more or less bystanders to the racial comments and practices that they see others engage in. They do refer to witnessing discrimination carried out by other whites, whether it is white employees who create a hostile work environment for employees of color, an acquaintance using racist language, some friends excluding a black person from an organization, or a white clerk ignoring black shoppers. In most cases, they see this behavior as at least inappropriate if not troubling, yet the majority do not report having directly challenged such incidents for their racial content.

Indeed, in numerous cases they try to provide what they view as a non-racial justification for why whites acted the way they did in these situations, or in similar hypothetical situations.

Thus, numerous respondents react to the scenario in the jewelry store by more or less justifying the clerk's likely discriminatory actions, such as by citing certain black stereotypes. One such image suggested as being in the mind of the clerk is that of the criminal black man. This is significant, since the only information given about the hypothetical shoppers is a racial designation, and not their gender. Some respondents seem to envision only the possibility of black male shoppers in such a scenario of differential treatment. There is also no hint in the scenario that a crime might take place—an interpretation often suggested by the respondents.

While they frequently note a certain injustice in the white sales clerk's action, these men often move on to justifying that action in a variety of apparently nonracial ways. Notice that many of them state or imply that they would indicate somehow that the black customers were there first—but what follows that statement often moves in a different direction. Numerous respondents seem to sense the publicly desirable response, but then draw on some racially stereotyped images or views in interpreting the white clerk's response by the end of their remarks. Their views are often presented as based in terms of reputed statistics, or simply as color-blind. However, to say, "I would tell them they were here first, but I can understand or empathize with the white sales clerk's reaction," is problematic.

Moreover, one reason given by some elite white men, as well as by other whites, for not openly challenging the racial comments or discrimination that they have witnessed (or might witness) has to do with making the other whites involved feel comfortable. Here we see the importance of group views and understandings. Recall our point that perspectives on racial matters in this society do not arise or remain in the isolated nooks of individual minds but rather are remembered, used, and reinforced in social interaction and social networks. This is true for white Americans not only in regard to important informal groups, such as those of family and friends, but often in regard to more impersonal social settings.

Interestingly, in response to the hypothetical example, some respondents who say they are confident enough to intervene in the situation choose a way of intervening that in effect involves some excusing of the clerk's likely discriminatory actions, or perhaps some sympathizing with the black customers, rather than challenging the white perpetrator directly about the discrimination. It is almost as if many important social spaces shared among whites are sacred spaces where harmony has to be preserved, except in extreme situations. When they reflect on the actions of a white clerk they do not know, there is reluctance on the part of many to "make a scene." We should remember that it may also be easier for these men to imagine confronting a fictional discriminator than a real one, and that a sales clerk is probably not perceived as a peer by a member of the white elite. The idea of interrupting the flow of differential treatment may seem more realistic when that interruption means confronting a stranger outside of their social circles, rather than a peer with whom they come into regular contact or on whom they depend for social esteem.

In their thinking about real-life and hypothetical situations, many respondents indicate or imply that at some level they are aware of certain of the racial inequities in society. Yet, in their recounted experiences and their commentaries we often see a minimization of discrimination's reality or importance. A likely racial interpretation may be played down in favor of what they view as nonracial explanations. Racist comments and discriminatory practices on the part of other whites are frequently seen as not very important—and, clearly, as something one should not make a big deal over. This viewpoint is problematic for several reasons, not the least of which is that most of these men are in powerful positions in the society.

One consequence of the minimization or rationalizing of discrimination in these accounts, as elsewhere among white Americans, is that the humanity that whites share with Americans of color is usually not clearly recognized. In communicating that the comfort and stability of white social spaces are more important than speaking out about racial hostility or discrimination, many whites convey the impression that they value the feelings of other whites above those of the targeted people of color. In effect, they are allowing a black person to suffer pain and indignity from the dehumanizing comments or actions of other whites, rather than make those other whites uncomfortable from encountering criticism of their dehumanizing behavior. Weighing one person's modest discomfort against another person's often substantial pain and agony, and finding the former more important, sends a troubling message about the latter's worth as a human being.

In the cases where whites are able to step out of their comfort zones to interrupt racial discrimination, such actions sometimes involve making sympathetic statements to the targeted people of color, rather than taking direct action to deal with the white perpetrators. Such a mode of response indicates not a neglect of the discrimination, but some minimization of its significance. Those who offer this limited form of active response to discrimination likely view such discriminatory incidents as isolated rather than systemic. As a result, there is typically no recognition of the need to strongly challenge the white perpetrators so as to reduce the likelihood of a recurrence of that type of racial discrimination.

The ethnographic studies mentioned above found that numerous whites who were not actively engaged in openly racist talk, but who were passive bystanders to such talk, only occasionally took enough offense at the racist remarks of other whites to intervene in the situation. Although they do not portray themselves in any way as officiants of discrimination, numerous elite respondents in our study admit they have stood by—or might stand by—more or less in silence when other whites make racial comments or take what are likely discriminatory actions. This silence or inaction is troubling given the powerful and influential positions that these men hold. In many settings, something as seemingly benign as just not saying or doing anything about others' actions can have a significant impact. Antidiscrimination laws depend on people in powerful positions to advocate and enforce them.

7

VIEWS ON PUBLIC POLICY: AFFIRMATIVE ACTION AND "REVERSE DISCRIMINATION"

For many generations now, powerful white men have ensured that their views were represented in actual government policies dealing with the racial realities of U.S. society. This was true under the systems of legal slavery and segregation, and it remains true today. Elite white men have historically played the central role not only in creating the economic, legal, and political institutions that imbed racial antagonism and discrimination, but also in crafting some changes in these systems when resistance to them from African Americans and other Americans of color has built to a high point. When protests from the oppressed increase, it is usually elite white men who put most of the viable policy programs into place, if only to forestall more social upheaval.

This was clearly the case in the response to the civil rights movement of the 1950s and 1960s. During that period, the country's white male elite responded to the protests of African Americans and other Americans with new civil rights laws and with remedial programs such as those called "affirmative action." Most affirmative action policies are generally the result of presidential executive orders of the 1960s, some court orders, and later independent efforts in the private and public sectors aimed at increasing opportunities for people of color and white women.

When President John F. Kennedy issued his Executive Order 10925 in the early 1960s, he was the first leading white official to use the then uncontroversial term "affirmative action," which referred to positive action by government aimed at creating better opportunities for workers of color and white women in the hiring processes of government contractors. Later executive orders issued by President Lyndon Johnson in the mid-1960s were much more extensive and required government contractors to act affirmatively to desegregate the formerly all-white, or all-white-male, job categories in their workplaces.

Significantly, at the *top level* of government policymaking, virtually none of the major affirmative action programs were inaugurated by Americans of color. Some elite white men, typically those with a more liberal view, did most of the initial constructing of affirmative action policies in the public and private sectors. These men often viewed strategies like affirmative action and civil rights laws as strategies for dealing with the protests against discrimination that took place from the 1950s to the 1970s. Not surprisingly, considering who initiated them, most affirmative action plans have historically involved relatively limited remedies for past and present discrimination. Put into initial operation by primarily white and male government and corporate officials, affirmative action plans have typically involved efforts to bring modest numbers of people of color and white women into corporate, small business, educational, legal, and political institutions where these groups have been historically segregated or excluded. Only in a few institutional sectors, such as some branches of the U.S. military, have those efforts resulted in large-scale restructuring of middle- to-upper-level positions in an array of departments or agencies.

Support for these remedial programs among the majority of white men in higher-income groups was, from the beginning, often critical, grudging, and tenuous. Indeed, a majority did not share the view of the more liberal members of the leadership class who supported aggressive affirmative action. Thus, a 1977 survey of mostly white and male local and national leaders in business, farming, unions, the media, and academia found that most were overwhelmingly opposed to affirmative action quotas and timetables for black Americans in education and jobs.[1] These opposing views were expressed just a decade after affirmative action was inaugurated.

Opposition to aggressive affirmative action has continued among the elite over the intervening decades. In recent years, numerous U.S. judges and legislatures have cut back or eradicated a variety of affirmative action programs. Private and government-fostered affirmative action programs have been widely condemned in white America. Influential whites have made speeches or written books downplaying racial discrimination and the need for affirmative action and similar remedies for discrimination.

Conservative white politicians and academics have been the most aggressive in openly criticizing affirmative action. Thus, one prominent white analyst and sometime presidential candidate, Patrick Buchanan, has recently written that the civil rights movement brought fully equal rights for black Americans, and that as a result the latter have had to "invent" unreasonable causes, such as calling for affirmative action. Buchanan concedes that there is "truth in the indictment of America's past. Our fathers did participate in slavery. We did practice segregation." Yet, like many other white Americans at all class levels, he argues that "the time for apologies is past."[2] More moderate white analysts have made similar arguments. In a recent book, historian Elisabeth Lasch-Quinn mocks those working in diversity training programs as seeing a social "world of endless slights." Using terms like "slights" plays down the significance of continuing racial discrimination. While Lasch-Quinn admits that the history of discrimination should be remembered, such discrimination is viewed as largely a matter of past evils. Diversity trainers and their materials "exploit this looming presence of racism's legacy to make their rendering of current slights seem more pressing than common sense would have it."[3] Nowhere in either book do these prominent analysts examine the extensive social science literature documenting the widespread discrimination still faced by African Americans and other Americans of color.

We now turn to our respondents' understandings of affirmative action programs—including both the rejection of, and positive support for, such programs. It is important to underscore the point that these respondents are similar in a number of ways to the white men who originally created, and often thereafter have maintained, government and private affirmative action programs.

OPPOSITION TO AFFIRMATIVE ACTION

The majority of our respondents express negative, or mixed negative and positive, reactions to U.S. affirmative action programs. Once again, in the language and metaphors that many of these men use, as well as in many of their interpretations, we see a collective white consciousness—a more or less shared understanding of affirmative action programs and of how they should be analyzed. While many of these respondents do understand or articulate the original need for such remedial programs to deal with past discrimination, the majority now seem to think that all or most of these programs are no longer needed. Indeed, a common theme among many white Americans, including those in this upper-income group, is that there is no way to fully redress the "sins of the past." After a modest period of special remedies, the majority of whites seem to believe that we as a country should "let bygones be bygones," which means keeping more or less in place substantial racial inequalities inherited from the past.

One sign of a widely shared perspective and set of understandings can be seen in the recurring use by numerous respondents of versions of the cultural-deficiency perspective in regard to a variety of racial matters, including affirmative action and related programs. Recall that in earlier eras of U.S. history, the racial attitudes of the overwhelming majority of whites were grounded in the view that black Americans and other darker-skinned Americans are very different from whites in biological and genetic terms. As we have noted previously, this view is now much less important and has generally been replaced by a cultural-deficiency perspective. The strong emphasis on the cultural deficiencies of Americans of color becomes a means of evading the issue of the discrimination still practiced by many white Americans. A color-blind view is often linked to cultural-deficiency theories that put the blame for continuing problems on the victims of discrimination. This is an often contradictory viewpoint: Its advocates say they "do not see color," yet in practice they usually do think and act in terms revealing color-associated understandings and stereotypes.[4]

Contemporary opposition to affirmative action is generally buttressed by the mass media and by white politicians and other influential leaders who often misinform the public about what affirmative action programs have typically involved. For the majority of white Americans today, "affirmative action" usually means something like rigid "quotas" for "unqualified minorities." Here again, there is much that is common and recurring in the language and thinking of a majority of whites about affirmative action, including many of our respondents. Yet there are, in fact, several major types of program that receive the label "affirmative action." (We will focus here on such programs for people of color, though white women are also covered by many affirmative action programs.)

According to legal scholar David Oppenheimer, affirmative action programs using fixed quotas are the *least* common.[5] Model I, or the quota model for affirmative action, is usually imposed by the courts or a government agency as a punitive measure—such as a program imposed on a company or governmental employer that has flagrantly discriminated against underrepresented groups as a matter of course. These programs typically require that these discriminating employers must fill certain quotas with formerly excluded workers as a means of rectifying their long histories of discrimination. This type of affirmative action program has become increasingly rare in the last decade. Oppenheimer's Model II might be termed the preference type of affirmative action. Using this model, an affirmative action program is set up for an organization where there has been a history of racial restriction or exclusion. Although these preferential programs are commonly misunderstood as forcing the hiring of much less qualified people of color or as admitting much less qualified students of color, typically they involve giving some limited preference to members of underrepresented groups who have met essential and reasonable qualifications.

Two other types of affirmative action programs, called by Oppenheimer Models III and IV, represent the most common ways that affirmative action has actually been implemented in various organizations. They typically involve setting some type of broad goals, as opposed to rigid quotas, for hiring or student admissions. They involve an organization conducting an examination of its own history of excluding or restricting people of color (Model III), or making additional, often more aggressive, outreach efforts to bring people of color into consideration for hiring or admission by a company, educational institution, or other organization (Model IV). Significantly, therefore, the least used form of affirmative action is often misrepresented by many whites as the typical form.

In assessing the comments that follow, we will see that these elite white male respondents refer to different models or types of affirmative action. While many focus on quota programs and the hiring of much less qualified individuals, others bring up outreach programs and other, less emphasized but more typical, programs. Furthermore, some emphasize the impact of affirmative action in employment or business contracting, while others discuss affirmative action in education.

Questioning and Opposing Affirmative Action

Some of the respondents are strongly negative and relatively unequivocal in their appraisal of affirmative action and similar redress programs. For example, one professional articulates his view of the desirability of a color-blind society:

> We have an affirmative obligation to aggressively tell ourselves that opportunity is color-blind, opportunity is available—and insist that it be color-blind, that merit be the sole basis to determine what one is to get or what rewards one is to receive. To do otherwise is first of all to demean the individual. . . . No, because affirmative action will just justify the perception of injustice when people think they're being deprived of what is their due because someone else, because they happen to be black or brown or red or yellow, gets something.

In this brief commentary, the respondent links three important ideas: the idea of color-blindness, merit, and a sense of injustice among whites. These important ideas are often found together in discussions of affirmative action among influential whites, as well as among whites in less powerful social groups. Seen from this widely shared perspective, affirmative action programs violate principles of merit and color-blindness, thereby creating a sense of injustice among whites who are not the beneficiaries.

Note here the common color language—"black or brown or red or yellow"—that is used in many discussions of U.S. racial relations. Here the colors are those often employed to denote African Americans, Latinos (Hispanics), Native Americans, and Asian Americans. In some contexts, this color language is extended by those critical of affirmative action to include certain mythical color groups, as is the case in this commentary:

> I frankly believe that we all should be held to the same standard, and that we all should be compared to each other on equal footing, and the best person, whether they be purple, white, or black, gets that job.... While I will not sit here and whine about it, I will say that I am at that point where I am fed up with having the finger pointed at me for the problems. I am sick of being the scapegoat, I am sick of being offered up as an excuse to why people have it that much more difficult.

Expressing irritation over being singled out, as a white man, as responsible for continuing inequality, he uses the phrase "purple, white, or black" to accent a color-blind point of view. Similarly, a partner in one company notes, "You'd never know the difference from when it was black, white, or, or green, you know, we deal with everyone exactly the same." As we suggested in a previous chapter, this seems an odd way of putting things. Why are these mythical color groups often included when whites assert that all people should be treated the same? Perhaps this common listing of colors that do not represent real groups of people is a subtle way of deflecting attention from the serious animosity and discrimination that still targets Americans of color, particularly *black* Americans.

Another respondent also uses strong words in criticizing affirmative action in hiring and admissions in higher education.

> Within academics, I think it's been a horrible program. I think that it's created racial division. It's made [people] even more racially conscious. It's caused a strife where it need not be there. I think that there's really no need whatsoever to have goals quoted, as they pretty much amount to ... discrimination against whites. And ... I think that if we had no [affirmative] action program, I think that we'd be much more likely to hire simply on the basis of merit; there would be less self-consciousness. As far as admissions go ... I think we'd have ... students ... better matched to their institution. I think we'd have

a much more harmonious situation. I think that's why you see Asians blending in very easily and comfortably, because they're not admitted to any special programs. You're quite comfortable, there's very little racial tension or ethnic tension there.

As he describes the situation in academia, affirmative action programs in hiring and admissions have created unnecessary divisions because of the violation of the merit principle. Important here is the strong adjective "horrible," which hints that his view involves more than a cognitive appraisal of the college situation. In numerous interviews, various racial issues often spark strong reactions from some respondents, as from many other white Americans.

In the last two quotes, the respondents in effect reflect white interests and concerns, yet envision these as universal, thereby neglecting the discriminatory realities faced by Americans of color in the past and the present. The first respondent asserts that he opposes affirmative action because "we all" should be viewed equally, yet most affirmative action programs have actually helped an inegalitarian society move in the direction of treating formerly excluded or restricted Americans of color more equally. That is one reason why they are supported by African Americans and other Americans of color. Similarly, the last respondent asserts that affirmative action has made people more racially conscious and caused racial division that would not have existed without it. While most whites may not have been very conscious of these racial matters prior to affirmative action programs, people of color certainly were, because racial discrimination has long been the ongoing reality for them.

Yet another important aspect of the last respondent's argument is the reference to Asian Americans, who are viewed as a group facing few, or no, problems with discrimination. This comment is not exceptional, for many whites in all social classes seem to hold such a view of Asian Americans. Recall from chapter 3 that, since the 1960s, influential white leaders and opinion makers, as well as many other whites, have frequently cited Asian Americans as a "model minority." This "model minority" image, however, is at base a sophisticated stereotype, originally created in the 1960s by members of the elite seeking to condemn black (and sometimes Latino) Americans for their organized protests against institutionalized racism. Interestingly, numerous affirmative action programs in employment and education *have* indeed included Asian Americans, thereby indicating that they too have faced discrimination.

Concern about the qualifications of employees or students of color is common in many white discussions of private and government programs designed as remedies for past discrimination. For example, when asked about his view of affirmative action programs, one professional answers with this critical assessment:

> I don't like affirmative action, because I wouldn't like to have a physician taking care of me who didn't have the appropriate background, nor would I want to be defended by a lawyer who ... did not have the educational background to really have earned his way into law school, nor would I want my accountant to be someone who passed his accountancy examination because he got an extra ten points because he was a black person or a green person or a purple person. I want my accountant to be able to do the numbers because he's competent and capable, my lawyer to defend me because he got into law school because he had the appropriate grades and LSAT score, and I want my doctor to have graduated from medical school.

Here we see the familiar notion that affirmative action policies place unqualified employees of color into important occupational settings. Given that social science data indicate that in most job categories the employees of color are basically as qualified, on the average, as the white employees,[6] one has to wonder why this view concerning "unqualified minorities" has surfaced so strongly in white America. One reason may be that white politicians and media analysts have often misrepresented the preference type of affirmative action (Model II) as requiring the selection of unqualified minority candidates, for the purpose of conjuring up white outrage over the alleged injustice. Yet preference programs usually select people of color who are qualified for the positions involved.

Speaking on the same topic of employment and qualifications, one corporate manager argues that affirmative action programs are only appropriate if they give "the most qualified person the job, regardless of sex or color." He later adds a comment about the importance of efficiency in making this judgment:

> If it's in a governmental job, then you want to maximize the efficiency of the person in that job and have the best person there. In industry, you want to do the same thing, plus you want to maximize the profits generated by a particular individual as a function of their performance. So, again, I don't have any first-hand experience with it, but my general feeling is, I guess I am opposed to giving opportunities to less qualified people.

Here again, in assessing programs of redress, the focus is not on those who have been the victims of discrimination, but rather on employers and their needs for efficiency and profits, which are the normal concerns of corporate managers.

Turning his attention to institutions of higher education, one professional also feels that affirmative action programs have been problematic. When asked if he thought such programs were still necessary, he replies:

> I am very much ambivalent about that issue. I voted for Proposition 209 in California, in, in part because it doesn't seem fair to me that somebody who's white, or, in California, Hispanic or Asian, ought to be, ought to lose a job, or a spot in a university or a state college, because somebody else gets preferential treatment.... I have a daughter and I have a son who both applied to schools. They didn't have anything to do with slavery; they didn't create it. They are not racist kids. And it just seems to me that it's not fair that they should lose a spot in school, or ... competing against somebody hiring for a job, because we are trying to do something to benefit someone of a different class.

A key element of this commentary, like numerous others, is breaking the connection with the racist past. We see the denial of a connection between slavery and the benefits and privileges inherited by younger people in his family.[7] Moreover, this respondent does not really seem to be ambivalent about the affirmative action issue in education, at least in practice, for he voted for the initiative (Proposition 209) ending many affirmative action programs in higher education in California.

Perhaps what he means about being ambivalent is evident in what he says next. In this statement he underscores the need to increase educational opportunities for those from disadvantaged backgrounds.

> Now, having said that, I think, at the same time, that we do have a tremendous obligation to make sure that every group gets adequate schooling and an adequate opportunity to compete.... So I guess where, where I've come out, is that I don't think it's fair to give people preferential treatment, but at the same time, we are not doing nearly as much as we should, especially in terms of educational means, [to] make sure kids who come from disadvantaged economic backgrounds get the education they should, so that they can compete.

In stating his philosophy that everyone should have a chance to compete, this man seems to support the sort of aggressive outreach and upgrading program that, interestingly enough, is created within some types of affirmative action programs (Model IV). He recognizes that such a program is one way of trying to provide more equality of access to schooling and other resources. The distorted views of affirmative action presented in the media may prevent many white Americans from realizing that they might actually support in practice certain commonly implemented models of affirmative action.

Note, too, in the last quote and in other comments from these respondents, the recurring emphasis on education and educational reform. Most Americans of all social backgrounds propose education as a major solution to a broad range of societal problems, including racial inequality. This emphasis on education is not new, but has been made now for many decades in all regions of the United States. While there is certainly strong evidence for the view that better schooling improves individual opportunities, sometimes this heavy stress on education can be a way of deflecting attention away from the disabling structural realities of racial, class, or gender discrimination.

Once Necessary, but No More

A recurring theme in numerous assessments of affirmative action is that such programs can now be cut back significantly or abandoned. While many respondents feel that it may have once been appropriate to use affirmative action programs and related efforts to deal with patterns of racial or other discrimination in society, they now perceive such private and government policies as no longer needed. One manager explains his concerns.

> At this point, I think they have run their course. I can understand the necessary—the need for them years ago in changing the course of [what] the country was making available to people, whether it was education or jobs, to better themselves economically. There was a need for it, but ... I think that any ethnic group, whether they were Irish, or German, or Hispanic, Latino, or Black, at a certain point after so many generations.... I see more improvement with certain ethnic groups who have pulled themselves up by the bootstraps and worked together within their communities, improved their economic lot, and have gone to, you know, to have much better standards of living than to just constantly rely on a numbers game....

While this questioning respondent does recognize the need for affirmative action some time back, he suggests that after "many generations" of efforts the country should now abandon it. Like many other whites, this man exaggerates the time frame of efforts to remediate discrimination, for affirmative action programs were put in place just a little more than a generation prior to his statement. He also articulates another critical view of such redress programs, in his idea that some (perhaps white) ethnic groups have pulled themselves up by their own bootstraps and have not had to resort to the "numbers game" of affirmative action programs.

Another topic that appears periodically in the interviews with these powerful men is the idea that white attitudes have changed so much that affirmative action programs can be phased out. Thus, one corporate executive justifies his growing opposition to these programs.

> I believe they are inherently unfair. I'd like to believe that over the last thirty years of having those kinds of programs, however, that attitudes have changed dramatically enough that maybe those programs aren't as necessary as they were before. So I'd like to see them ... phased out. I'm actually very pleased to see the courts now starting to review some, some of these cases and viewing them as being reverse discriminatory. I think the legal system is starting to wake up to the fact that these programs may have gone overboard.

Many public commentators and analysts share with this respondent the opinion that there has been much change in recent decades in white attitudes about racial matters. In earlier chapters, we noted data that indicate that such a view is warranted for certain blatantly racist attitudes once held by whites. Yet white attitudes about cultural-deficiency issues or about the aggressive enforcement of civil rights laws remain negative and problematical. His statement that he would "like to believe" that white attitudes have changed enough to warrant ending these programs is perhaps telling, for it may indicate that at some level he recognizes the reality of some continuing negative views of Americans of color.

Interestingly, a few historically minded respondents compared affirmative action programs to labor unions. One executive explains how in his view both types of programs for working Americans have outlived their usefulness.

> I think they've served their purpose. Our company is non-union, so I think the unions have served their purpose.... They've helped establish better working conditions for people over the years. When you go back to the miners and the auto workers and what-have-you. But I firmly believe that unions have outlived their use for us. And I think affirmative action has served its purpose, at least as far as I've been exposed to minorities in business and industry and what-have-you. Do I feel we still need it? No. I hear too many cases of either in the, as I mentioned, in the college application process or in business where, as I mentioned, the Kodaks and the Xeroxes and the Bausch and Lombs require a certain percentage of their business to be with minorities, and it's dictating. And I've heard more than one tale where they've been forced to do business with a minority group that just cannot perform to, you know, their expectations and specifications.

As he views the situation, at one time in U.S. history, both workers' unions and affirmative action programs had a purpose in helping improve workplace conditions for disadvantaged Americans in various groups, yet now should be eliminated. Like other white executives, he justifies this elimination with reference to a few cases of people of color who, according to other sources (not apparently from his own experience, interestingly), have been unable to perform to business expectations. This lack of performance is again framed from the point of view of white officials, with no reference to the very serious racial barriers that are often faced today by businesses run by Americans of color.

This professional also compares affirmative action programs to unions in order to make a similar point.

Before they had unions, the sweatshops predominated and treated the workforce ... without compassion and really as slaves. Unions were necessary. But now with all the rights conferred on the workforce, you question sometimes as to whether the unions have served their purpose. Affirmative action has now gotten to that point. As far as I'm concerned, I feel that it is an effrontery to qualified African Americans to have an outside source place them in a position over those who are superior.... I think that there are enough now qualified African Americans in almost every area of our society that you don't need that crutch. I think it does them a disservice and certainly is unfair to the majority.... Everyone is cognizant in their hiring or their enrollments of having representatives from every area of our society. So I think it's taken care of itself, and I think affirmative action per se is past its time.

From this perspective, affirmative action programs have now increased the number of "qualified" African Americans to the point that they no longer need the "crutch"—yet another metaphor sometimes used to censure antidiscrimination programs. The argument that affirmative action is harmful to its beneficiaries is frequently made by many white analysts in the media, by a few conservative analysts of color, and by many in the white public. In contrast, opinion polls of African Americans find that the majority of them feel that affirmative action and similar redress plans are still essential for dealing with ongoing racial discrimination in society and are, on the whole, positive in their effects.[8]

Concern with "Reverse Discrimination"

A major concern of numerous elite respondents is the situation that has come to be called by the contradictory term "reverse discrimination." For example, one leading executive reports more negative than positive feelings about affirmative action programs: "I do and I don't believe in them. I do believe in fairness, I believe in giving everybody an equal opportunity...." Then he adds this thought about affirmative action becoming something else:

I think it borders on reverse discrimination.... I think it creates more of a gap between the races. Because now you have.... Well, you have a white male, let's say, who feels he has been discriminated against because he is not a minority. Right or wrong, he feels his credentials are superior in terms of being hired for that job or promoted into that job, and let's say a minority candidate—and let's say for the moment he's right and that does happen, a minority candidate gets the job. I think that widens the gap between the races. Because the white male feels as if he doesn't have a chance now.... You know, to me, I don't buy the fact that, that "we have been suppressed for years." I mean, if people are worthy of the position, if their character, their credentials, et cetera, make them the best candidate for the job, I don't think a company is going to do anything other than put the best candidate in the job, simply because companies, I think, go out of their way to search for quality minority candidates.

As is often the case in interviews with white men and women, the concerns of whites are the predominant focus. Like some previous respondents, this executive invokes the traditional view of merit and views affirmative action as angering white men and creating a serious racial gap, which seems to be new in his view. Note, too, the rather optimistic portrait of the business sector, seen in his idea that employers consistently seek out the best candidates for positions in their companies. Yet numerous research studies show that many white executives and managers do not in fact act in this nondiscriminatory fashion.[9]

In corporate and other institutional settings there are many positions that have traditionally been filled only by white men, from which employees of color and women were entirely excluded until the late 1960s and 1970s. In such settings, there is sometimes pressure from internal or external forces to hire at least one person from the formerly excluded groups in order to break down old patterns of exclusion. One professional responds to an interviewer's question asking if there are a lot of cases of less-qualified blacks getting job preferences over better-qualified whites:

> I think that to a certain extent that is true. Black people get extra points on certain civil service exams, people bend over backwards to let a black person have a better chance at a position. To a certain extent they deserve it, but on the other hand, it's not me or my father or grandfather who gave these black people a bad start in life. That goes back for two hundred years and . . . I don't feel responsible for what happened two hundred years ago, even if it hasn't been totally cured.

> I wouldn't want to give up my position in life so that somebody who, whose great-great-grandfather came over and was a slave—I think people should succeed because they have the innate capability and they do the hard work that's necessary to get ahead, and there certainly are black and Hispanic and Oriental people who have worked hard and accomplished a lot and I think that they get a lot of credit.

He continues, relating how his own ancestors made it because of their merit.

> When my grandparents came to this country they worked hard in menial jobs so that their children could get educated, and they didn't get affirmative action. As a matter of fact they got quotas against them. Nonetheless, by dint of their hard work they did improve themselves and their children became well educated and their grandchildren became very well educated, and that's why you are interviewing me as a high-class white person or whatever the term is.

He recognizes that to some extent black Americans deserve consideration under affirmative action programs, yet he does not think his family's privileges are related to the situation faced by those black Americans. Here we see the important and recurring theme that the most severe racial oppression, particularly slavery, took place centuries prior to the time of the interview. Actually, the legal enslavement of African Americans ended less than 140 years prior to the date of the interview. We observe here a tendency that many white Americans demonstrate in assessing their privileges and advantaged situations, as well as in assessing the disadvantages of African Americans—the tendency to push the reality of the most severe racial oppression as far back into history as possible. In making such assessments, most whites also tend to overlook the reality of the severe oppression of legal segregation, which did not end until the late 1960s.

Interestingly, many in the white elite now articulate the idea that affirmative action is a problem because of the new discrimination that is thought to be hurting many whites, especially white (or white male) employees and students. The recent discussion of affirmative action and similar redress programs in terms of "reverse discrimination" is not a matter of linguistic chance, for this phrase came into common usage soon after affirmative action programs were put in operation. This term and concept have been emphasized as part of a counterattack by conservative white scholars and popular commentators. They have argued vigorously that white men suffer seriously from programs set up to redress discrimination against women and Americans of color. Yet the term "reverse discrimination" is contradictory. In social science research and public discussions prior to the emergence of that term, the word *discrimination* was used mainly to refer to what members of the dominant group, such as whites, were doing to harm those in subordinate groups. Thus, a true reversal of that traditional white-generated discrimination would mean that the once racially subordinate groups now discriminate on a large scale against whites. While individual members of subordinate racial groups can be prejudiced, and a few do discriminate against whites, this is relatively uncommon compared to the widespread discrimination carried out in the past and in the present by whites against African Americans and other people of color. There has never been society-wide, institutionalized discrimination against white Americans as a group—a condition that might reasonably be termed "reverse discrimination."[10]

Qualified Support for Affirmative Action

Numerous respondents report both negative and positive views of private or governmental affirmative action efforts to improve the opportunities of people of color and white women. These respondents are generally more candid than the previous respondents in discussing and deploring the racial oppression of Americans of color. They sometimes link the severity of the oppressive treatment of African Americans in the past to the necessity for remedial policies in more recent decades. For example, one observant respondent, whom we cited in an earlier chapter, feels affirmative action programs were once essential to deal with racism, but questions their continuation in the present and future. After noting the serious racism that African Americans faced in the past, he adds:

> In the last few years I have felt a little bit like maybe I am on the other end of that. Not truly, I really don't believe ... I'm discriminated against, but I do believe that whites in general increasingly sort of pay the price of being white, okay? I mean, no matter how much, how hard we try, there is a certain point where ... what more can you do?

Interestingly, this concerned respondent strongly acknowledges the white subjugation of black Americans, even to the present. He also rejects the idea that he as a white man is now suffering discrimination, a view contrary to that of some of the previous respondents. In his intriguing and probing commentary, he then adds:

> I think they probably were necessary, unfortunately.... I think that there are probably places where they are appropriate and places where they aren't appropriate. But unfortunately this is sort of [an] either everything or nothing environment we are in. I mean, the fact of the matter is ... I think that we definitely need to bend over backwards to help black people get a fair shake. Is that affirmative action? Yeah, well, but I think it got carried too far, I think it got to be exploited and that sort of thing. And I think that's absurd, okay? ... And bureaucrats don't know how to deal with that sort of thing. They create formulas, okay? As opposed to trying to answer the right question or the wrong question.

Strong affirmative action programs, while once needed to deal with racist realities for black Americans, have been distorted by "bureaucrats." Among the important villains in the recent history of affirmative action are those government officials who have constructed what are seen as inappropriate rules and rigid formulas. This emphasis, once again, suggests a critical evaluation of affirmative action that accents only one factor in a complex remedial picture. Nonetheless, he recognizes that affirmative action programs may still be appropriate in some areas.

As we have already seen, numerous respondents brought up or alluded to the issue of "quotas" for women employees or employees of color. This is another theme in the assessments that many whites make of various programs of affirmative action. While viewing remedial action for discrimination as perhaps necessary today, one business analyst rejects the idea of quotas.

> They may be, they may be in some degree necessary, but I think that they cause their own set of problems by discriminating against other people.... I feel, and strongly, in the equality of opportunity, but not in specific quotas.... The beauty of this country is that the opportunity is there at a variety of levels for everyone to start from basically

nothing and make whatever they want out of their lives, and it's one of the few areas in the, in the world where there is no caste system, where there is no class system.

Evidently, he has in mind the minority of affirmative action and similar remedial (Model I) programs that do in fact have such quotas. Note, too, that central to the value system of a majority of Americans of many different backgrounds is this sincerely expressed view of the United States as a classless society. In spite of much data to the contrary,[11] even many well-educated Americans insist on holding strongly to the individualistic idea that any person, no matter how little they have to start with, has real equality of opportunity.

Speaking from a similar point of view, a manager in a major firm views affirmative action programs as appropriate if they do not use "extreme" tools such as quotas.

> I think that affirmative action is appropriate if it is not carried to an extreme. I think it is important for employers or whoever to dig out, to include minorities and to bring a better diversity to the programs. I think to do it on a quota system is a mistake.... I think quotas are an extreme episode, the way the federal government took it to, a while back.

Beginning in the late 1960s, in response to actions such as presidential executive orders mandating desegregation of traditionally segregated workforces of government contractors, federal agencies have pressed firms doing government business to develop self-studies of their hiring practices. Such studies are often followed by the establishment of goals and timetables for hiring previously excluded employees. This approach to past discrimination involves the self-examination hinted at in this comment, as opposed to the rigid quota system that this respondent also points to. Significantly, over the decades since the presidential executive orders put this pressure on government contractors, the latter have often ignored the obligation to self-examine or to implement hiring and outreach goals.

RECOGNIZING NETWORKS AND OTHER SOCIAL BARRIERS

While they, too, are frequently critical of contemporary affirmative action programs, some respondents do note certain important social and
geographical barriers that impede workers of color, often with some
recognition of how these barriers have led to the implementation of such
remedial programs. Thus, some describe the ways in which whites tend
to prefer to hire and promote other whites, those whom they are most
comfortable dealing or working with. Several are articulate in regard to
how traditional social networks that favor whites provide some justification for the outreach model of affirmative action.

For example, one manager first states, "To be honest with you, I
don't like affirmative action." However, he then develops his view by
adding a considered judgment about why such remedial policies have
been necessary.

> The problem is, I suppose, if you're white, you have a tendency to hire
> the people you feel most comfortable with. And I believe you are most
> comfortable with people that are, that have the same background as
> you—maybe look the same as you, have the nationality background.
> So I guess in those instances, I mean that's what they are trying to do.
> I think they are trying to break down those barriers. Do I think that
> the blacks or any other nationalities need affirmative action? Proba-
> bly do, in certain cases. It's just that it's such a . . . difficult thing to do
> and . . . people get so upset over it and so angry over it.

This man's explicit point about the comfort that whites feel with other
white employees is reminiscent of our discussion of the hypothetical
store scenario in a previous chapter. In this case, however, it is workplace
settings that conjure up images of white zones of interpersonal comfort.
Notice how often in the interviews of these elite men that words like
"comfort" and "comfortable" appear in describing these issues. It seems
evident that there are numerous zones and places throughout the society that a great many whites would prefer to remain white in composition and, thus, more socially comfortable. These social spaces seem to be
valorized as those where the ease and comfort of whites are to be con-
served with as little disturbance as possible.

In response to a question on affirmative action at his place of employment, a firm with few black employees, another respondent in management provides these observations on the impact of traditional hiring procedures:

> And that is just, pure and simple, a function of when we advertise for jobs, who shows up. We don't have very many blue-collar kinds of jobs, and the business is sited in the ... suburbs of [names a city], so the pool of employees that we draw upon is predominantly white. So at this point we've got an affirmative action program in terms of the people who are there, but we don't actively go out and seek black employees.... To back up, looking at affirmative action, which says we are actively going out and pursuing the hiring of black people to raise our numbers in our work pool, we don't do that. The ownership of the business is just not set up to do that. If a black person comes in the door, who is qualified and so on, yeah, we would hire that person without any misgivings or any second thoughts, but we don't actively go out and seek black applicants.

His company has an affirmative action program for those who are already hired, but not in terms of special outreach for recruitment of nontraditional employees. Many U.S. companies follow this laid-back approach, which tends to limit those employed to applicants from nearby geographical areas or who come in through the networks of existing (often mostly or all white) employees. Such an approach tends to result in patterns of employment segregation that parallel the existing patterns of residential segregation.

This same respondent then comments on affirmative action programs for people of color in a more general context.

> I think we have to do something to give them a head start, to give them maybe a little bit of a leg up. And that's really the infrastructure of business and industry, it's so predominantly white. And I think it is a relatively natural thing for people to seek people like themselves in job placement and career enhancement and those kinds of things, so I think the people of color in America have a problem getting ahead because of the way our business infrastructure is set up, so I think affirmative action and those kinds of things are important. I think they are abused and I don't think they are terribly well run, but conceptually, they're important.

He, too, problematizes the widespread tendency in hiring practices for whites to seek those who are like themselves—the interpersonal comfort factor, once again. In his considered view, this propensity of like-seeking-like reinforces the white-dominated infrastructure in the substantially segregated economy. The concept of affirmative action is acceptable, but he questions how it has been implemented. Subsequently, this man broadens his critique of affirmative action to include other government programs.

> The problem with all these government entitlements, it seems to me, is that they are set up to be abused, and they are, over time. The money that is set aside to perform a specific good doesn't always perform that good because they are abused and people use the money for reasons not necessarily originally intended, so I think there is a problem with the delivery system. But I don't know what the solution is. We've been struggling with that for a long time, and we have spent, as a country, I don't know what, you know, a trillion dollars on affirmative action and entitlement kinds of programs and we are no better off today than we were in 1950 in terms of, I think, the penetration of black America, talking specifically about the black America, the penetration of black America into the mainstream of life in America.

Including various entitlement programs in an appraisal of affirmative action, this respondent views all such government programs as likely to be too bureaucratic and often abused. This seems to be a view shared by many Americans. Yet affirmative action programs are not general entitlement programs like Social Security, for they are limited to groups that have been targets of widespread discrimination. Here, too, is suggested another sincerely held, yet exaggerated, view that is common among white Americans—that a "trillion dollars" have been spent on programs for affirmative action and certain related entitlements for the poor and disadvantaged in recent decades.[12]

Like some previous respondents, another executive views affirmative action programs as appropriate, depending on their timing and placement.

> I think they have a place based on trying to move people with diverse backgrounds and minorities, diverse people into higher positions in

business. Eventually, I don't think it's a perfect world, and . . . eventually people should just be put in jobs based on their merit and skills, not based on the fact that they're any particular color.

In another context in his interview, this expressive respondent adds that affirmative action is required because whites naturally prefer their own kind.

> Diverse placement of people in mid-to-higher-level jobs in the company has to be monitored to some extent, or it won't happen. I think that there is a glass ceiling, still, and that people basically are most comfortable with people who look like themselves, whether that be a color or language. And they don't always realize that. It's not that they are prejudiced, but they just don't think . . . as much about it as they should. . . . If there are two people, one being a person of color and one being a white, and the person making the choice is white, they are more likely to lean toward whomever looks like themselves. It's just human nature, so I think right now some affirmative action goals we're monitoring, is a positive move.

Here we see a discerning recognition of the existence of "glass ceilings" in employment, coupled with a highlighting of networking and the greater comfort that many unreflective whites have in relationships with those like themselves in regard to such characteristics as color and language. This respondent also indicates his knowledge that some affirmative action programs monitor and thus ensure access to employment for people of certain racial backgrounds, a point not found in numerous other interviews.

Another corporate manager notes that he has had "different opinions at different times" about affirmative action programs, then adds this point about diversification of the workforce: "I think the fact that you're getting blacks, Hispanics, and other minority populations, minority groups, including women, into roles where their diversity can contribute and where they can kind of be the rising tide that lifts all boats, I think its a good thing." Yet he, too, sees some serious problems with these corrective and remedial programs, as he then makes clear.

> I think the part of it that's really bad is the way that the minority leadership has sort of . . . adopted an approach to dealing with society in

general as, "you owe us as such," and I think that example is a pathetic one to be, to be, perpetrating onto people that they represent.... I think it leads to this thing going on and on, longer and longer.

The theme of programs which were once needed dragging on too long and being abused appears again. An additional theme here involves the concern that certain Americans of color, especially leaders, have an ill-advised attitude. The leaders are viewed as communicating this idea to the rank and file. One finds this critique of minority leaders as whining or unfairly demanding in a number of the interviews with these elite respondents, as well as in many media commentaries by other white men. There is more than a hint here of certain blame-the-victim stereotypes that we have encountered in previous chapters.

Some of these elite respondents, who agree that there is indeed a problem with reverse discrimination, also recognize that discriminatory barriers have been faced by Americans of color. For example, when asked if he thinks there is reverse discrimination in the United States, one professor explains that this is "definitely true within academia, and within an awful lot of the professions. Medicine, law, business school, and so forth. And I think it tends to be true in higher-level management within corporations." However, he continues with a broader view and explores a new type of discrimination that has developed against Americans of color.

> Sometimes the minorities are taking up positions which have great visibility, so the company will look like they have a, you know, strong affirmative action program, but then the person doesn't get that much responsibility.... It does mean some sense of whites being displaced from [the fact] that blacks are given preferential treatment— and, in another sense, they are even being discriminated against, because they're put in a position where they're not likely to take further steps up, because they're not getting the sort of training and challenges that they would get in another position ... which they might have been able to get without preferential treatment.

Just putting black employees into highly visible positions, in effect just for show, is seen as yet another form of discrimination, since these employees often do not get the opportunity to move up a job ladder. In effect, the other side of this type of preferential treatment is dead-end discrimination. This type of channeling discrimination is often reported by black employees in various employment settings, such as in Sharon Collins' study of black executives in Chicago.[13] She found that black corporate executives were frequently put into specialized jobs oriented to communities of color, but which did not offer significant opportunities to move up the corporate ladder.

One executive at a major corporation speaks of his "dilemma" in response to a question on whether there is reverse discrimination today.

> To a point, yes. . . . I have a dilemma, where I believe the country probably still needs affirmative action, yet, on the other hand, what bothers me, or what I have a hard time with, is the fact that I think some people that are receiving this affirmative action tend to take it for granted. . . . And . . . think that it's their born right to, to have a certain job without having to, you know, work for it. On the other hand, I think there are very capable whites that are not getting those jobs because people feel that they have to abide by quota. I will tell you, as a manager, when, for example—you can look at it this way, too—when you're doing a downsizing . . . and you're looking at the people you have to let go, in a lot of cases, you don't let go of a black person, or you don't let go of a female. It's easier to fire or lay off a white male because the country has been so conscious of having, you know, quotas and stuff like that.

Then, in response to a question about whether white men are currently the targets of specific racial hostility and discrimination, he comments:

> Well, you know, it's very hard to really think about that for a person like myself. I haven't been put in a situation, through the grace of God, I haven't been put in that situation where I have lost out on anything because—that I felt that a black person got it because that's what they needed and they didn't want a white male. . . . I think you can sit back and try to be a liberal, free-thinking person and say those, those fellows are just using that as a crutch, they're angry or they're bitter, just as I might say the black man is angry and bitter and uses it as [a] crutch . . . because he feels he's being picked on and he can't get ahead because of his race.

While this reflective executive does appreciate that there is probably some need for corrective action for discrimination, he is concerned that some people "take it for granted," a theme we have seen previously. This recurring critique is linked to the similarly familiar idea that the beneficiaries feel they have a "born right" to a certain position and thus do not "work for it." Implied in some of the language here may be the stereotype of black Americans as lazy. Still, while this executive notes that some capable whites are excluded by affirmative action, he himself has not faced such a situation.

Such a personal report is not unusual. Asked if white men are the targets of hostility and discrimination, one broker reacts this way: "I have never personally felt that. I would say that the jealousy—people who are disadvantaged, who don't have things, tend to be jealous. And this jealousy is felt towards people who have it, and I happen to have it." In his interview, he reports that he did experience heated dialogue with some students of color in his college days, but he has not experienced racial hostility per se, just perhaps some jealousy over his achievements and wealth.

Indeed, a few respondents thought the idea of there being any significant racial hostility and discrimination directed against white men was more or less ludicrous. One entrepreneur laughs when asked if he thinks white men are now the targets of hostility and discrimination.

> White men targets of hostility? I ... don't agree with that.... If the market is open, there're going to be minorities that are going to advance if everything is on equal footing. In other words, if it's totally color-blind. You've got to have situations where blacks that are more qualified, that are hotter, that are better.... I won't say the majority of whites, [but] there are certain whites [who,] due to their own inadequacies, are saying, "Well, the only reason he's got the promotion was because he's black." ... It is such a small minority—that here, again, we are paying because of the headline. We're led to believe that it is a problem, and why the entire society on a whole embrace it because of the attention, flamboyant attention has been given to [it in] the media.

This insightful entrepreneur offers an analysis of how some whites use the argument of reverse discrimination to take the blame off themselves for their own inadequacies. This is an ironic reversal of an argument that many more whites use against black Americans. He also clearly discerns that the scattered cases of white employees losing out to black employees in serious ways because of affirmative action have been greatly overstated in the mass media. This is an important insight, and one that shows the interpretive diversity in this sample.

THE POSITIVE IMPACT OF AFFIRMATIVE ACTION

The last respondent's willingness to demur from the standard white argument about a reversal of traditional discrimination shows that some of these influential men, though part of the well-off elite, are aware of exaggerations in conventional white views of affirmative action. Their views of these redress programs are generally more accurate than those of other whites. One also observes here, as elsewhere in the interviews, that there is a liberal wing within this power elite.

Though in the minority, some respondents are consistently or strongly positive about affirmative action programs and about their actual or potential impact within key sectors of U.S. society. In their view, the benefits of affirmative action accrue not only to individual people of color and their groups, but to particular companies and other organizations and generally to the society as a whole. For instance, one research analyst is strong in his praise for affirmative action policies.

> I think that affirmative action is a very positive thing. I personally would support that, because there is no question that given the opportunity—and first you have to have that opportunity—an individual can really catapult himself into a situation. But without it at all, they will never know. Not everyone really has the ability to be able to figure out how to move up the ladder, so to speak, and if you give them a second or third rung in that ladder, you can very well at least get that timing or boost that is necessary to at least get into the next gear of things. So, yes, I believe that affirmative action is very important, and as I said, I would support [it] in any ways that I can.

This understanding of affirmative action envisions it as opening up new opportunities for individuals to move up economically in the society. This analyst makes innovative use of the language of "opportunity," which other respondents employ against the idea of affirmative action. Note, too, another interesting use of metaphor: Affirmative action creates the chance for talented people of color to "catapult" themselves upward, and thus to move up the rungs of the socioeconomic "ladder."

A few respondents include in their probing observations some assessment of the benefits of affirmative action for particular business or government organizations. One government executive offers a positive view of the presence of black employees in U.S. workplaces.

> I interact now with a lot of black people on really all levels in county government and . . . I'd like to see more people of color in positions of authority, because I think . . . we'd deal with issues of race better if we had more people like that in department heads or high-ranking positions. . . . I get to interact with legislators, counselors that are black, department heads that are black, and I think things are better as a result of it.

Seen from this vantage point, particular organizations can deal with racial issues and conflicts better if they have access to the substantial knowledge and experience of employees of color, especially at the higher management levels. Racial diversity in decision-making has major advantages for the successful operation of organizations that must function in an increasingly multiethnic and multiracial society.

In addition, from this perspective, affirmative action programs are essential because of the reality of both past and present discrimination, a point just a few of the other respondents seem willing to make. The respondent adds this comment:

> I don't know how we could, well, how we can ever get over, let's say, the remnants of discrimination if we don't have something like affirmative action. I mean, it's sad when I think about—I mean, how can you tell people that, well, you know, slavery was two hundred years ago, now you're going to have to fend for yourself? And yet, I mean, there's still racism going on and discrimination going on every day, everywhere, and so I don't know how you can not give a little bit of an advantage to people. . . .

This respondent clearly recognizes the hard reality of present and continuing discrimination. He later adds that there are some rather new problems of differential expectations that employees of color often face in historically white organizations.

I'm not excusing it, but its like sometimes when you look at a person of color you expect them to meet some higher standard than—I mean, there are incompetent professors, or incompetent people in the stuff I do, that get promoted, that get hired. And I'm not suggesting people be hired ... that are not competent, but I'm saying it's—like, again, why does a person of color have to meet a higher standard? So I think that there has to be ... some form of affirmative action or what will we say to [later] generations: Well, you're going to have to wait another couple hundred years before you can—I mean, it'll never be equality.

In regard to empathy across the color line, this respondent is among the more sensitive and understanding in this sample of elite white men. After citing the severity of past and present discrimination as an important reason for programs of redress, he raises the issue of many whites' expecting higher performance from employees of color. His rare point about white incompetence is very important for current discussions of remedial programs, for most white analysts who examine affirmative action and its results for employees of color generally ignore the many incompetent or mediocre white employees who hold positions up and down the employment ladders in various organizations.

One prominent member of the elite, a leading corporate executive, stresses the broad range of benefits accruing to the larger society from programs that are aimed at remedying discrimination.

The reason I think they're essential is that I think the only [way] we change people's attitudes about diversity or about integration, segregation—you name [it], whatever you want to call it.... The generations have to grow up, and affirmative action is a way to, because ... the older generations are always the ones in power.

He suggests, as we find in several other respondents' commentaries, that affirmative action and other such programs may over time change the negative racial attitudes of older whites—which would be good for society. Thinking in terms of changes across the generations, he provides some interesting examples from recent U.S. political history.

You know, you got Bill Clinton at—what is he, fifty?—and you got ... whatever that other guy's name, Dole, at seventy-two. I mean ...

they're the people in power. Bill Clinton probably grew up with blacks and women a little bit. He was the first generation. Bob Dole didn't, and the only way . . . an older person like my parents would really change is if the government set those kinds of goals. The younger generation is much more accepting of it and you don't need those kinds of things. So I think goals like affirmative action are essential because [of] social change between the generations.

From this nuanced perspective, younger generations of white Americans have had, on the average, greater experience with a diversity of friends and other social contacts, which is thought to have made them more open and tolerant. Still, later in the interview, this executive adds a point that does qualify his support for affirmative action.

I guess it goes back to my zoology, in sort of the survival of the fittest. And I believe that it is important for the country that we take our smartest minds and allow them the best education possible, and so it's at conflict with affirmative action policy. So, I'm in favor of it, but that's the one place that I have to be very careful. And I think we can work at it differently. We have to [go] back and work at the school systems and bring those people along, but you know there's, it's a pretty complicated situation. It's not just the school system, it's the parents. It's the environment and a lot of things and you can't just change it by changing who goes to what schools. You got to . . . go all the way back.

While he favors affirmative action, he draws here on the idea of the "survival of the fittest" to explain his view that it is important to secure the best talent for society, even if that contradicts affirmative action. In the end of his comment, he accents a point that we have seen in some of the other interviews—that you have to begin at the earliest years of child development.

AFFIRMATIVE ACTION IN THEIR WORKPLACES

In some of the interviews with these members of the white elite, we received reports on how affirmative action programs have worked in their companies, stores, agencies, and other organizations in which they have significant decision-making power or influence. Whether or not they question or reject affirmative action in general, they sometimes describe the important benefits that have come from hiring employees of color in their own particular employment settings.

An apparent contradiction between general opposition and beneficial results can be seen in comments from an executive who had elsewhere expressed negative feelings about affirmative action in general.

> As a matter of fact we've gone out of our way to try and interview and hire, where possible, minority candidates. We interviewed an outstanding candidate not long ago, offered him the job, he turned it down. He didn't think that this young organization has [as] much security as what he was looking for, and I respect that, that's not a problem. But I still don't believe in affirmative action. It's just that we have—we practice it here—and it may be in [a] little bit different manner, in the sense that we're not going to take someone and promote them just because of the color of their skin. But if we can reach out and find candidates of very high character and credentials, then we will hire them or promote them within our organization, which we have done.

This respondent says he does not agree with affirmative action as he understands it, yet his company does practice the outreach model of affirmative action in its actual hiring practices. His position seems illustrative of some misinformation surrounding the topic of affirmative action among many whites. Although he may reject one model (Model I) of affirmative action, he does support yet another version (Model IV). Still, the often skewed media and political framing of such corrective programs seem to have made him into more of an opponent than an ally of proponents of affirmative action. It is significant that there is a clear recognition on his part of the importance of diversity, although he does not see a role for specific racial goals for his company.

Other respondents are also positive in their characterizations of the actual impact of certain types of affirmative action efforts in their organizations. Thus, one executive, who is supportive of affirmative action in general as well, discusses its application in his company's construction projects.

> We have to comply with federal and state laws so we, we do that, and then we've got to, [in] regards to construction, on some construction projects that we've done ... we set goals rather than actual set-asides

> ... and try to have people meet them. We've done that on all the proj-
> ects that I've been involved with, the convention center ... and so
> forth. ... I think it's good, I mean I think ... the community needs to
> have it, especially if we want to have, if we want people of color or
> women to, let's say, be self-sufficient.

Affirmative action is viewed as being good for the health of local communities, in that such programs can increase the number of successful
businesses owned by people of color and women in a community. Evident here is the practical application in an affirmative action program of
preference and outreach efforts ("goals rather than actual set-asides"),
rather than the Model I approach by way of set-aside quotas.

Similarly, another corporate executive, who elsewhere in his interview states that affirmative action is needed to break down white networking, feels that affirmative action in his company has been essential.

> Yes, I think that program has been ... good for the workplace, because
> more diverse people have been moved in the business. And I think
> they wouldn't have been unless we had a program like that. So I wish
> it wasn't necessary, but I think it's been basically good. I think it's
> been more good than bad. ... We have an objective where we try and
> mirror the community in which we operate in the percentage of
> different types of people that we're working [with].

Once again we see a somewhat ambivalent commitment to the idea of
affirmative action, but a firm conclusion that it is necessary in practice.
He, too, recognizes the importance of his company looking more like the
community in which it operates, which is one goal in the self-examination and outreach models of affirmative action.

A powerful manager for another firm, who, as we saw earlier in this
chapter, feels that affirmative action should only seek to bring in the
most qualified and cannot cure "sins of the past," discusses successful
affirmative action in his firm.

> It was affirmative action to the extent that we definitely tried to have
> nonwhites and non-males in jobs that historically they had not
> had. ... And I can think of at least two instances where the same thing
> was done with a nonwhite male over a white male. The nonwhite was
> given the job over the white. It was done to, in part, bring balance
> to the corporation, giving other people opportunities to progress

within the corporate structure.... Well, I would like to say we felt the balance was needed, but at least initially it was a result of federal policies to try to bring more nonwhites and non-males into the managerial ranks.... There was some resentment, but that died fairly quickly. And as long as the people—and both the instances ... which I referred to a while ago, the people were qualified—any resentment died, because the people found out that the people put into these positions were very capable and that was the end of the story.

Federal affirmative action policies are given credit for moving this company in the direction of a more diversified management structure. Interestingly, once the managers of color were put in place and found to be very capable, the overt resentment reportedly died down. This success in hiring is a common report in workplaces across the country, yet such in-place data about the capability of most employees of color do not seem to dampen much the general white negativism in regard to affirmative action programs in the society. Also interesting here is his language, for the previously excluded employees are described in terms of what they are not—that is, as non-males and nonwhites—rather than in terms of what they are.

Another influential respondent indicates that he is opposed to affirmative action programs in higher education. Yet he also recognizes the positive impact of his firm's having numerous black employees in his workplace: "From people in office services and messengers, we've got black attorneys, and by and large, you know, every single one of them is terrific." Asked about affirmative action programs at his firm, he explains:

> We don't have an affirmative action program in the sense of any kind of quotas or any kind of numerical goals. But what we do try and do as a very conscientious effort is to make sure, you know, [in] our job offers, that we try and treat people, number one, without regard to whether they are black or white, for example. But at the same time we are always looking for minority candidates, and if there is a good minority candidate, we will usually go out of our way to try to get him.... Because especially as the country becomes increasingly non-white, in my business, if you have a law firm that is composed of only white males, eventually you are going to have clients who have lots of blacks, lots of women, lots of Hispanics, and lots of Asians in manage-

ment positions, and they are going to say, "Why should we go to an all-white law firm?" They are going to be looking for law firms that have treated people like them equally.... So it is just good, it is just good business for us to be thinking about that, too.

Once again, his general image of typical affirmative action programs seems to be that of the Model I approach, with fixed quotas. Yet, in practice, he supports the more common outreach form of affirmative action. Given the reality of the United States becoming an increasingly multiracial country, this respondent is aware of the practical reasons why his firm should seek to have an integrated workforce. Support for this type of affirmative action among white men at the top of the society, as with other whites, may depend to some degree on the particular societal circumstances. Because of the changing demographics of the country, racial and gender integration plainly makes good business sense.

One senior executive argues insightfully that companies and other organizations cannot in fact be color-blind, however much they may desire to be.

I think for organizations to recognize the difficulty—to recognize cultural differences—to recognize the difficulty of, say, one black person being the first black person in an organization, and maybe hiring two, is an affirmative action step.

Conventional tokenism, which seeks out just one employee of color for an isolated position, is not adequate. He articulates the need for a critical mass of employees of color in an organization, one of the few respondents to make this argument. He then describes his hiring of numerous health care professionals for his company.

And, you know, when we did have an opening for [an] ... intern, we hired a young black woman. I mean we ... reached out, and we were glad to do that.... I think we polarize in this country around so many issues, and I think this whole thing with, with affirmative action, that if everybody does a little bit, then it would work and [we] wouldn't need quotas.... No, it wasn't color-blind, if we ... want to bring in minority-group people into our workforce. So in this case ... [the] paradigm that ... if you know two people, being equal, if two people really are equal, then to the extent possible I would give the edge to the minority person, just now, because we don't have many of them.

In practice, he suggests, affirmative action programs should involve reaching out in a color-conscious way to give people of color a chance when they are at least equal in basic qualifications. This is the essence of the outreach and preference models of affirmative action. Here is an overt rejection of the color-blind ideology that we find explicit or implicit in many of the other respondents' commentaries. In his reflective assessment, if all employers did this color-conscious outreach on a gradual basis, society-wide change would come with less conflict and debate.

Some of these influential respondents report only a modest impact from the affirmative action programs that have been implemented within their companies or organizations. For instance, when asked if affirmative action had helped his company or those where he had previously worked, one executive replies in these terms:

> I don't think it's had much of an impact. There have been some instances, I think, at [names company], where some really top minority employees have surfaced because of it, but I would say it's also created some ill will between the races, and I don't think that was healthy. I really don't.... In the hiring process, a district manager, for example, who's looking for a sales representative is told to hire a minority, period. Not the best person for the job, hire a minority, or hire two. And I don't think that's healthy. I think it creates ... a dual standard.

Even this highly placed respondent, a critic of affirmative action, notes that certain affirmative outreach efforts in his company have brought in a few excellent employees of color. Yet, in his evaluation of what some companies may do (apparently not his own), he emphasizes the negative aspects of a type of affirmative action (Model I) that involves actual quotas. In his view, such programs create ill will on the part of white employees. Thus, he feels that other business criteria must take precedence over such affirmative action.

CONCLUSION

The majority of these elite white male respondents have at least some misgivings about the use of affirmative action programs as public policy. While many comprehend something of the rationale for putting such programs in place in prior decades, and while some still remain support-ers, many others take the position that they are inappropriate or no longer needed. Once again, we see a type of group ideology, a common perspective on racial matters, for these men often adopt similar interpre-tations or language to make their key points.

One might speculate that in the absence of the adversarial framing of affirmative action in the mass media and by conservative politicians as mostly a Model I phenomenon (with "rigid quotas" seen as seriously disadvantaging white men), the majority of these men might publicly support much affirmative action as such, since the most commonly practiced models of affirmative action accent self-study, outreach, and modest preference for qualified candidates of color. Indeed, they do of-ten indicate some support for these latter types of programs, if without labeling them as "affirmative action."

For a time after their initial implementation in the late 1960s and 1970s, many affirmative action programs were effective in bringing at least token-to-modest numbers of people of color and white women into historically white, male workplaces or other institutions, places where most white male decision-makers would otherwise have made little or no effort to desegregate. The data indicate that government contractors made more progress in desegregating their workforces than those firms that did not do business with the government.[14] However, data gathered since the conservative resurgence in the 1980 Reagan election indicate that this progress has slowed significantly. Over the last two decades, affirmative action programs have been cut back significantly, and those still in effect have had much weaker effects in many economic sectors than one might expect from the often intense public rhetoric about them. For example, since that time, only a few major penalties have been imposed by government agencies or courts on noncomplying compa-nies doing business with the federal government. Meanwhile, one U.S. Department of Labor compliance review examined 4,179 companies as of the mid-1990s and found some three-quarters of them to be violating federal regulations by not recruiting widely, by discriminating in hiring, or by not even having any affirmative action plan.[15]

Affirmative action in employment rarely seems to cause white male employees significant problems. For example, Alfred Blumrosen did re-search on some 3,000 federal court decisions dealing with discrimination for a multi-year period in the 1990s. Fewer than 100 were "reverse discrimination" cases involving white men; less than thirty of these resulted in a victory for the plaintiffs, about 1 percent of the total cases. Other recent reports also indicate that less than 2 percent of the Equal Employment Opportunity Commission's inventory of complaints of discrimination come from white men.[16]

Discrimination targeting white men, especially at the hands of white women or people of color, remains relatively infrequent across the United States. Most importantly, it is not institutionalized and pales in comparison with the impact of the traditional institutionalized discrimination against Americans of color and women. Perhaps the clearest indicator of this is the demographic bottom line. Thus, after decades of affirmative action, some 90-100 percent of the top positions in most major economic, political, and educational organizations are still held by white men. For example, one study found that only 5 percent of 7,314 powerful positions in U.S. society were held by white women or people of color. Only twenty were black, far less than 1 percent of the total. According to the 1990s Glass Ceiling Commission report, some 95 percent of the holders of corporate positions at the level of vice president or higher were white men.[17] Another study found that white men were dominant in the political sphere, holding 77 percent of House and Senate seats and 92 percent of state governorships. White men were also found to be dominant in the mass media, holding about 90 percent of newspaper editor positions.[18] Such data suggest that a very serious policy problem for the country is the general failure of public and private attempts since the 1960s to substantially desegregate most of the country's major institutions, particularly at their upper levels.

8

THE MULTIRACIAL FUTURE

When one looks for who holds the lion's share of powerful positions and socioeconomic resources in this society, the answer is still clear. White men remain very much at the helm of society's ship. Upper-middle-class and upper-class white men, though a modest proportion of the population, are generally dominant in most major institutions. This is a striking indication of just how deep and systemic the patterns of racial and gender discrimination have been over the long course of U.S. history and down to the present day.

Yet, as the song says, "the times they are a-changing." Over the next several decades, this white male dominance of U.S. society will increasingly be challenged. Whites of European descent now comprise a decreasing portion of the U.S. and world populations. They are a statistical minority of the population in half of the largest U.S. cities, as well as in larger geographical areas such as the states of California, Texas, New Mexico, and Hawaii. By no later than the 2050s, if the rate of population growth for Americans of color does not decrease significantly, Americans of European descent will be a statistical minority in the country. This will mark a very dramatic change; not since the 1700s have whites been a minority of the North American population.

In order to assess adequately whether these increasing numbers of people of color over the next half-century will bring about significant changes in the landscape of white male domination, it is useful and important to understand the views and experiences of powerful white men in regard to a range of racial and ethnic issues. Are they becoming increasingly insightful on racial and ethnic issues? Are they ready and willing to share significant power and resources with those who are racially unlike themselves? Under what conditions will they actually do so? Our interviews with some of these elite white men bring us one step closer to answering such questions.

Very few in our sample express the more blatantly racist views that many whites openly expressed in the past, and that some still do in the present. Instead, most of these well-educated and influential men hold in their minds, and presumably express in their actions, a complex blend of racial ideas and understandings. One recurring pattern is the respondents' use of apparently nonracial or color-blind language to contextualize or sanitize what are in effect racial understandings. This emerges on issues ranging from black family values, to their own identities as whites, to public policies such as affirmative action. Because white men in the elite play a critical role in shaping the country's racial discourse, most of these men generally understand the necessity of speaking in seemingly in-offensive or qualified ways on numerous racial matters.

Yet, in part because of their isolation from sustained equal-status contacts with people of color, many cling to certain misunderstandings and stereotyped notions about what it means to be an American of color today, particularly an African American. Their general isolation from ongoing and meaningful interpersonal communications with people of color—life in a "white bubble," as it were—has often resulted in a lack of full understanding of the persistence of racial prejudice and discrimination as everyday realities for Americans of color. This, in turn, means a general reluctance or inability to comprehend the pain and other individual and family costs, as well as the countering strategies, that are forced daily on Americans of color in a society that is still pervaded by racial bias and discrimination. For most whites, including a majority of these respondents, there seems to be a recurring lack of expressed empathy for the painful experiences of those across the color line.

Another pattern is that of apparent contradictions in numerous respondents' key racial beliefs, understandings, or proclivities. For example, black school acquaintances, servants, coworkers, or employees are frequently seen as likable, hardworking, family-oriented, and admirable, while black Americans as a group are still often viewed as more or less lacking in work ethic and family values. Opposition is voiced by many to "affirmative action," yet certain remedial actions that diversify their workforces—and are, in effect, affirmative action—are willingly carried out or even applauded by the same respondents.

These and other contradictions on racial matters seem to reflect a tension between their concrete experiences as individuals, and the collective reality or consciousness of privileged whiteness, with its pressures for conformity to the views of important reference groups, including views constantly expressed in the media. We see in these examples, as well as in many other contexts, how the problem of "race" is not merely the sum of the racial attitudes of white individuals, but rather is a racialized system reinforced by the pressures within, and the cohesion of, the dominant racial group. In this book we emphasize the group character of white understandings about racial matters, understandings that are centered around a sense of group position in a racialized hierarchy. When most whites remain in substantial isolation from sustained equal-status contacts with people of color, and are imbedded in groups more or less entirely composed of other whites, the racialized system is maintained not just through overt expressions of racial bias, but also through a seemingly benign conformity to (or unwillingness to confront) the racial understandings, propensities, and sensitivities of these other whites.

A more hopeful theme spanning these chapters is the presence of antiracist convictions and propensities among some of these elite men. Although their voices are in the minority, they are strong and often insistent in their desire to eliminate racial prejudice and discrimination for present and succeeding generations of Americans. Even some of those who often accept some of their groups' racial stereotyping and imagery do, on occasion, put forth an anti-bias or antidiscrimination argument. Despite a recurring adherence to the racial status quo on the part of many of these respondents, some periodically exhibit an ability to move away from the racial understandings of their groups and toward a more overtly antiracist position. This potential for new understandings is a promising finding, offering some hope for change toward a more democratic society in the increasingly multiracial future.

NONRACIAL LANGUAGE, COLOR-BLINDNESS, AND CULTURAL DEFICIENCY

The men in our sample are generally highly educated, and many hold graduate degrees. As such, many seem to view it as inappropriate to be too racially explicit when discussing matters of public policy and social relationships. Very few express old-fashioned stereotypes and views linked to racist thinking accenting biological and genetic differences. Yet they often convey a somewhat updated or more moderate version of conventional white positions on key issues. For example, they often express opposition to affirmative action and interracial marriage, or reveal the assumptions that blacks as a group are indolent, morally challenged, or criminal—albeit often without resorting to the old-fashioned racist language, and even, at times, while expressing some concern for the families and communities of black Americans.

Archie Bunker of television fame might say that black Americans do not deserve affirmative action programs because they are racially and intellectually inferior. However, many of these elite white male respondents oppose affirmative action programs for different reasons, as hurtful to whites or to national ideals, and frequently use color-blind language such as "everyone should have a fair chance regardless of race." Similarly, while the Archie Bunkers of the world might say that whites and blacks should not date or intermarry because that "degrades the white race," those elite respondents who express opposition to interracial relationships generally take a much different tack, tending to couple their opposition with some concern about potential cultural and social challenges such interracial relationships might bring to the parties involved.

Still, the end result of this modernized version of opposition to affirmative action or interracial relationships is more or less the same. The use of a color-blind discourse does not change the negative effects of generally preserving the racial status quo or of resisting major change in the inegalitarian or discriminatory conditions faced by black Americans and other Americans of color. This discourse primarily changes the way in which whites can view themselves and the society itself. Whites are able to adhere to sincere beliefs about themselves, and their country, as nonracist, while Americans of color continue to be impacted heavily by continuing problems with racial animosity, discrimination, and inequality.

Consider this comment by one professional who was asked whether he believes the stereotype that black Americans as a group do not work as hard as others: "I think that's not a race issue, it's an upbringing issue. They're shiftless and lazy, yes [joking tone], but it's because of their upbringing." Like numerous other respondents, this professional asserts the view that black indolence has nothing to do with racial characteristics per se; rather, it has to do with family "upbringing." One repeatedly sees this framing of racial understandings in terms of reworked cultural-deficiency concepts. Recall from chapter 4, for example, that numerous respondents use concepts like "culture," "family values," or "family background" to insist that negative generalizations about black Americans and other Americans of color are not race-related, but rather are accurate evaluations of their sociocultural conditions. The language of contemporary racial understandings among whites relies heavily on much apparently nonracial language, and many code words, in order to communicate understandings that are still substantially negative or racially stereotyped.

Constructing one's understandings of contemporary racial matters in terms of a nonracial language or color-blind rhetoric not only allows whites to see themselves and their society as nonracist, but also generally prevents them from seeing the great impact of racial animus and discrimination in the everyday lives of Americans of color. For example, in chapter 6 we reviewed different responses by these elite men to a hypothetical incident in a store where waiting black customers are bypassed for a white customer. Recall that many respondents chose to interpret this event as a nonracial slight. Several excuses are proposed for the white sales clerk's behavior: He did not see the black customers, or he saw a preferred customer. Even when more clearly negative stereotypes shape the respondents' listed excuses, they often strive to offer their interpretations using code words that do not mention racial characteristics directly, such as by noting the clerk's worries about being robbed or not being able to make a high-dollar sale. Again, these are often characterized as socioeconomic judgments, even though the stereotypes of blacks being poor or robbers are in the background. Even those who do not make excuses for the sales clerk's unfair behavior frequently think the slight should not be viewed in racial terms. They prefer to see racial characteristics as irrelevant or insignificant, with statements to the effect that, regardless of color, the black customers were there first and should have been served first. Whether they feel the white clerk's behavior was right or wrong, many respondents prefer to seek out more or less nonracial interpretations of the event, rather than describe it as a possible or probable case of racial discrimination.

Framing events from a white point of view, and often using a distinctive color-blind language, large numbers of white Americans seem to view incidents of differential treatment of Americans of color as either justified on nonracial grounds or as unfortunate brushes with bad luck, rather than as linked to the continuing reality of systemic racism. The belief that most serious racial discrimination ended in the decade or two after the 1960s civil rights legislation, and that most whites now live by principles of fairness or equality, is a sincere but fallacious view to which the majority of whites now appear to subscribe.

That many white men of high class standing hold to similar beliefs has definite implications for the future of public policies on racial discrimination and its impact. These powerful and influential men are likely to see future public or private initiatives that attempt to address contemporary discrimination aggressively as unnecessary and inappropriate. Recall that a couple of the respondents viewed their workplaces as racially peaceful, until a person of color was employed there and dared broach the problem of discrimination. If they see themselves and their white counterparts in the workplace as generally color-blind and fairminded, then white managers and other supervisors are less likely to see discriminating white employees as the culprits in regard to such disturbances, and more likely to view employees of color who bring up the matter of discrimination as the source of the problem. As such, a color-blind perspective can therefore lead to antidiscrimination efforts being misinterpreted, and, thus, often rejected as viable workplace options.

Ultimately, this type of color-blindness does render whites blind, but blind to their own racialized understandings and biases, which are masked by nonracial code words and other obfuscating language. It also makes them blind to the need for much greater antidiscrimination efforts by private and public organizations in a still-racist society.

SOCIAL ISOLATION AND THE LACK OF EXPRESSED EMPATHY

A blindness to the harsh realities still faced by African Americans and other Americans of color is easy to maintain when no alternative perspectives are readily available. That most whites, including most elite men, have few truly sustained and close equal-status contacts with black Americans or other people of color indicates their substantial racial isolation, individually and as a group. Living in the "white bubble," many of them admit that they receive their information about important matters from generally white-controlled media sources like television and newspapers. Thus, research studies show that such media sources are often laden with anti-black stereotypes and other negative racial imagery, and do not give nearly the same level of positive coverage to African Americans and their communities as to white Americans and their communities.[1]

Indeed, much mass media coverage of racial matters focuses on conflict and divisive issues, with little attention to instances of cooperation and coalition, especially cooperation and coalition in the service of major social change. Recall that our respondents generally relied upon media representations of the O.J. Simpson trial that often cast it as a racial matter and portrayed black opinions on the not-guilty verdict as being diametrically opposed to white opinions. When a black civil rights leader and minister such as Jesse Jackson only gets media attention while highlighting racial discrimination in voting, policing, or some other area, we again see the white-controlled media emphasizing adversarial stories of blacks versus whites.

There is little room in this storytelling format for whites to see African Americans as *fellow* Americans with similar personal, family, and community values and concerns. There is also little in the mainstream media approach that encourages whites to be as outraged about continuing racial injustice as they often are about such matters as corrupt corporate executives cheating the public. If the majority of whites in their racial isolation rely on racially skewed and white-controlled local news accounts, radio talk shows, and movies as primary sources of information about Americans of color, there is typically little impetus for them to develop strong empathy with those Americans who live across the color line.

Empathy is a strong positive emotional response to the experiences of other people. Empathy connects us to those beyond us, such that we can feel some of their joy or pain ourselves. It is important to note that the aforementioned spatial and social isolation of many elite white men from people of color seems to result in significant emotional isolation. Emotions are not just individual biochemical processes, they are also socially constructed. When watching a news story about some company's tires causing fatal auto accidents, for example, most whites can automatically picture themselves as the family who could have been riding in the vehicle when the accident occurred. It is relatively easy for them, then, to have an empathetic response to the injured family, coupled with a sense of anger at something unfair happening. However, the same response may not occur while watching a story about a black teenager who is unjustly shot and killed by white police officers. Our interviews as well as national opinion surveys indicate that many whites agree with the view that black Americans complain too much about discrimination or other manifestations of racism, and this is often the framework from which whites are likely to interpret such a police incident. As the grieving black parents on the television screen demand justice for their teenager, whites' social and emotional isolation can often prevent them from feeling strong empathy for a fellow parent who just lost a child, perhaps seeing instead a mere "complainer."

Recall that one manager quoted in a previous chapter describes a situation where a black employee of his resigned, apparently because of racial insensitivity on the part of a white supervisor. In his interview comments, this manager did not seem to connect emotionally with the black employee's feelings about a difficult workplace climate, but instead expressed concern for the white supervisor. This difficulty in substantially understanding the impact of the color line seems to be common among whites, as can be seen in their uncomprehending reactions to discriminatory situations at work or in other institutional settings. Indeed, it may account for the difficulty that many black Americans face in trying to get redress from uncomprehending white executives and other supervisors for discrimination in their workplaces, or from white judges and juries in the U.S. justice system. Human emotions flow into, and out of, actual social interaction, and thus often follow the contours of the color line.

Interestingly, researchers have found that strong antiracist attitudes and antidiscrimination commitments on the part of some white Americans often spring from significant empathy with people of color that is deve-loped through close equal-status relationships, such as those with a close friend, a spouse, or other family member. That is, when whites significantly emerge from the spatial and social isolation that characterizes the majority of white lives, they are often able to connect emotionally with those who experience discrimination and develop some sense of injustice about that discrimination. Interestingly, research shows that some white women, in particular, develop empathy with people of color through "overlapping approximations"—that is, they are able to relate to racial injustice by drawing on their experience of gender discrimination in their own lives.[2] Because of their social status, however, elite white heterosexual men as a group may be the most removed from this type of approximating, and potentially empathetic, experience. The number of our respondents who reported close or intimate contacts with people of color, especially in their adult lives, is small. Unless more whites, including those in the elite, break out of the social isolation that generally characterizes their entire lives, we can expect this serious lack of empathy across the color line to continue, and the blindness to much racial discrimination to persist.

CONTRADICTIONS: THE WHITE "DYSFUNCTIONAL FAMILY"

Clearly, the men who speak throughout this book are complex and often insightful in their assessments of racial and ethnic issues. Though shaped by their early and continuing socialization, and thus their social environments, they are by no means cut out of the same cloth. Whether intermittently or consistently, numerous respondents show some awareness of the realities of the racial prejudice and discrimination remaining in this society, and they are on occasion sensitive, albeit to varying degrees, to the troubling racial experiences of people of color as fellow human beings. Indeed, even as numerous respondents express opposition to such matters as interracial dating or marriage, they still have some sense of the importance of societal contexts, for they often blame society for making these interracial liaisons difficult. They often indicate genuine admiration for certain people of color as national figures or respected employees and coworkers. While they may subscribe to certain media-fostered stereotypes of black Americans as criminals or indolent individuals, they may also describe a few African Americans that they have actually met or worked with as hardworking and morally upstanding. Many echo the media commentators' disdain for affirmative action as comprised of rigid "quotas," yet they may also, as employers, value other diversifying actions or express a desire for diversity in their workplaces. Consistent in these contradictions is a tension between a certain open-mindedness about some racial matters and experiences on the one hand, and the power of the white collective's stereotyped imagery and racial ideology over individual convictions and experiences on the other.

These frequent contradictions play out in a variety of interesting ways. Recall the respondent in an earlier chapter who resolves some dissonance in his mind by creating two categories of black Americans. There is the negative category of the "urban blacks," who, from a few interpersonal contacts (and perhaps the media), he sees in terms of negative images of rudeness and deviance. Then there is the positive category he calls "white blacks," illustrated by a few black Americans with whom he had pleasant contacts in his community of origin. Many whites seem to make this type of distinction among black Americans, with the urban blacks category often based on fleeting or no contacts. This category is developed or greatly reinforced by media imagery of urban black Americans as deviant and threatening. In contrast, the category of "white blacks" seems to express some sense of shared humanity that whites feel for a few black Americans with whom they have some experiences at school or work. Indeed, because their experiences with the latter blacks are contrary to much that is defined as "black" in public discourse, even the term "black" may not seem to fit—so some, like this respondent, choose alternative terms like "white blacks." Like many other whites, numerous men in the sample periodically appear to be caught between their own more positive, or semi-progressive, images or impulses and the powerful racial ideology that greatly exaggerates the social and moral differences between white and black Americans—in favor of the former racial group.

Nowhere is this influence of or allegiance to the white collective, despite individual misgivings, more evident than when respondents discuss times when they have been passive observers or bystanders to racialized incidents. This preference for preserving harmony with other whites can be strong or weak, but it is common. Even when whites like our respondents are more outspoken about the racist animosity or actions that they witness, they may prefer to express their dissent to the people of color who are targeted or offended, rather than confront another white person, who may be a clerk, employee, coworker, relative, or friend.

If we posit that the larger white collective is often like an insular "family," then we might regard the racial stereotyping and discriminatory propensities within it as unspoken "family secrets" (perhaps like alcoholism) that everyone notices, but which few are willing to confront, out of fear of disrupting the sense of family unity and harmony. However, this sense of uniformity and harmony in the white family is a sincere fiction, as the dissenting voices among whites, including some of our respondents, sometimes illustrate. Nonetheless, it remains an ideal that many whites seek to preserve, often at a high cost to traditional ideals of fairness and justice. This family secret of continuing white stereotyping, racial bias, and discrimination is obvious to those people of color outside the white family who must experience its impact. Still, the white collective generally clings to the notion that most whites are fair-minded and egalitarian, despite regularly observing individuals and incidents obviously to the contrary.

The rewards of conformity are evident in the higher class strata wherein these white male respondents reside. It appears that many white men's favorable views of people of color may be more or less played down or suppressed as they move through their corporate and professional careers and spheres, where they may fear to challenge openly racist whites who often play a critical role in shaping their personal careers and successes. Even as their individual observations may teach them that African Americans and other Americans of color are hardworking, moral human beings who yet must face discriminatory barriers, their conformity to or silence about the racially stereotyped and biased views of those whites for whom they work or with whom they regularly interact must seem almost obligatory.

We do not mean to suggest that those whites—like many of the respondents—who accept, perpetuate, or allow racial stereotyping and bias are just the victims of other whites who shape their careers or patronize their businesses. Rather, the complexity of the views of large numbers of whites, including many of these respondents, encompasses their inability to disentangle their own frequently antibias or anti-discriminatory inclinations from the understandings pressed on them by the influential racial ideology constantly reiterated and reinforced in key white reference groups. This is evident when we consider those respondents who indicate individual disapproval of racial bias or discrimination, yet cannot seem to act forcefully against it, even when their social and economic positions would allow or require them to do so. In this regard, we see that the racist system in the United States is greater than the sum of its individual parts.

We conceptualize contemporary racism as a system of bias, discrimination, and resource inequalities in which elite white men as a group play a very important part. They did not create this system, for they were born into it. Yet, now that they are adults, they generally have great power and influence, and they are first among those who maintain, reinforce, and, periodically, act to change this system. They are the Americans with the greatest ability to bring changes in a racially oppressive system that contradicts the articulated, if often rhetorical, American ideals of fairness and justice for all.

While systemic racism is certainly perpetuated by anti-black attitudes and overt practices, the status quo of continuing racial inequality is also maintained through the social inheritance over generations, by whites like the ones we have interviewed, of power, privileged networks, and material resources. Simply by remaining largely unresisting members of these often powerful social networks, many elite white men play a critical role in the continuance of systemic racism, despite the convictions they may personally hold about fairness and justice.

The white collective, and particularly the white power structure, currently rewards those who generally conform to its views and standards. There is no motivation or reward within the white collective for those who dare to speak out against discrimination or who seek to develop active antiracist agendas. Instead, the pressure of the collective is toward keeping quiet about racial animus and discrimination in all but extreme cases, that is, to not "rock the boat," or question or reveal the "family secrets." Most elite white men have reaped the rewards of silence and inaction in regard to racial animosity or discrimination. Indeed, however they may feel personally about these matters, they enjoy great economic prosperity and social status substantially because of the long history of racial inequality benefiting them and their white ancestors. Until the economic, educational, and political institutions of the United States actually reward effective antiracist organization and actions, the egalitarian rhetoric will continue to have little effect, because there is little significant motivation for most whites to act against the overt racial animosity or discrimination of other whites, as their individual consciences may often suggest.

The leading constitutional scholar, Derrick Bell, has suggested that the racial problem for black Americans is not just about a matter of anti-black animus and discrimination, but even more about racial nepotism on the part of whites—that is, whites' seemingly benign preference for constantly supporting one another.

> Racism is more than a group of bad white folks whose discriminatory predilections can be controlled by well-formed laws, vigorously enforced. Traditional civil rights laws tend to be ineffective because they are built on a law enforcement model. They assume that most citizens will obey the law.... But the law enforcement model for civil rights breaks down when a great number of whites are willing—because of convenience, habit, distaste, fear or simple preference—to violate the law. It then becomes almost impossible to enforce, because so many whites, though not discriminating themselves, identify more easily with those who do than with their victims.[3]

Writing provocatively from a perspective that he calls "racial realism," former Harvard law professor Bell proposes a "Racial Preference Licensing Act." This law would allow whites to openly practice the racial nepotism that they often engage in covertly. Under this law, employers, business owners, and managers of housing facilities could then pay the federal government for a license to legally exclude people on the basis of their racial characteristics. They would then have to pay a tax on income derived from their whites-only operations, and this money would go into an "equality fund" to support the start-up of black-owned businesses, interest-free home loans, and college scholarships for African Americans. While this system might be seen as encouraging the white collective to continue its discrimination, Bell argues that it may in fact have the opposite effect.

By requiring the discriminator both to publicize and to pay all blacks a price for that "right," the law may dilute both the financial and the psychological benefits of racism. Today even the worst racist denies being a racist. Most whites pay a tremendous price for their reflexive and often unconscious racism, but few are ready to post their racial preferences on a public license and even less ready to make direct payment for the privilege of practicing discrimination. Paradoxically, gaining the right to practice openly what people now enthusiastically practice covertly, will take a lot of the joy out of discrimination and replace that joy with some costly pain.[4]

As he often does in his analyses, Bell develops what seem like outrageous proposals and scenarios for the purpose of getting the often hidden realities of racism into the open for fuller public discussion. Putting the dynamic of racial nepotism into the spotlight goes against its ability to continue through inertia, unexamined preferences, and comfort levels.

Clearly, whether it is done through positive or negative reinforcement, a major change in the dynamic of whites' allegiance to one another must take place before the United States can address systemic racism in a fundamental way. It is clear that attitudinal changes among whites have so far been insufficient to accomplish this task, when the material privileges of whiteness, and the collective dynamics that maintain both those privileges and persisting inequality, are deeply entrenched.

THE ANTIRACIST POTENTIAL IN WHITE AMERICA

In the United States today, only a modest number of white men, including elite white men, seem to view the moral rewards of acting aggressively and consistently in accord with their antiracist impulses and consciences as more important than the socioeconomic rewards gained by maintaining or ignoring the persisting system of racial inequality. Still, those elite white men who do consistently and openly act against their groups' pressures have managed to achieve economic success and high status without having to abandon antiracist goals and ideals. Although they are less numerous than those men who prefer the cultural-deficiency or color-blind perspectives, those of our respondents who adopt a more or less consistent antiracist perspective are important to focus upon, since they provide alternative visions of whiteness among the powerful. They also demonstrate that the "iron cage" of the white collective is not inescapable.

The popular nonracial discourse by which many white Americans now convey their racialized beliefs frequently paints those who bring up issues of racial prejudice and discrimination and other racial matters as villains or culprits. Those who articulate an antiracist perspective, who are most often people of color, are thus viewed as paranoid, as complaining too much, or as introducing racial tensions where there otherwise would be none. Not surprisingly, then, when asked whether black Americans complain too much about racism, many whites still agree with this characterization. They thus conform to the white collective's desire to maintain the status quo by denying or ignoring the problem of widespread discrimination.

However, a few of the respondents do understand the importance or necessity of speaking out against continuing discrimination. Commenting on this question, one professional sees the consequences of not speaking out as greater than those of being silent.

> If you feel like somebody's racist, you can't complain too much.... [Blacks] are as guilty of stereotyping white people as we are of stereotyping them, but the consequence for the black community is so much greater than the consequences [for] the white community of [not complaining,] because the white community continues to control most of the engines of the social order.

While he does articulate the common view held among whites that blacks stereotype as much as whites, this professional understands that inaction in the face of racism has great consequences for black Americans. Given their relative lack of power in society, it is important for black Americans to complain about the racism they face.

Commenting on this point more sharply, one corporate executive views this speaking out as a useful springboard for solution-focused action.

> I think that they have a right to complain about racism because I think that it still exists. We haven't stamped out racism by any stretch of the imagination, and it exists in daily life. I think that not just racism, but all kinds of prejudice, continues to exist in this country. So I don't think that they are complaining too much. I don't think

that anybody who speaks out against things that are unjust and not right should be labeled as complaining too much. I think that we need to listen to what people have to say, because usually when people are, as you say, "complaining," there is a reason. And we ought to see what that reason is and see [what] we can do to fix the problem and not just sugarcoat the complaint.

Breaking from the white collective's norm of not talking candidly about the problem of racism, this man advocates speaking out—and not labeling that as complaining—as a form of positive protest against in-justice that needs to be heard by society. Rejecting more conventional framing and nonracial language, he feels that racism should not be sugar-coated but remedied.

As we have seen in previous chapters, a common white perspective focuses on the cultural deficiencies of blacks, a point of view that tends to minimize the existence of racial discrimination. Those whites who openly and strongly acknowledge contemporary racial discrimination as a major problem worth addressing have broken the hold of this dominant ideology on their own thinking, and are thus taking an important step in the direction of societal change.

Antidiscrimination Actions in the Workplace

Although acknowledging racial prejudice and discrimination as serious societal problems is an important step, the next steps are considering how to take significant action, and then taking action, directed at remedying these problems. Some of these elite respondents have actually taken one or both of these additional steps against discrimination. More than just embracing the idea of diversity, these men illustrate the ways that whites can take concrete actions against racial prejudice or discrimination in particular institutional settings.

We have discussed how infrequent sustained and close equal-status contacts with black Americans are for most elite white men. Taking antiracist action in one's own organizational setting might thus begin with remedying this isolation problem by substantially diversifying the labor force at all organizational levels, thereby challenging the glass ceiling that often exists for those in entry- and mid-level positions. Recall from a previous chapter the executive who advocates for this view: "I'd like to

see more people of color in positions of authority, because I think ...
we'd deal with issues of race better if we had more people like that in department heads or high-ranking positions." Elsewhere in his interview,
when reflecting upon the hypothetical white clerk who ignores black
customers, he suggests the need for more cross-racial friendships: "If
that salesperson actually had a close black friend, it would make a difference ... he might see things a little differently." Breaking out of the white
bubble of isolation can begin with implementing significant workplace
diversification, which might then have the ripple effect of influencing
some whites who interact in an ongoing equal-status way with new black
employees to think differently, at least some of the time, about racial
matters in other spheres of their lives.

Those elite white men who understand this value of diversity in the
workplace are often situated to implement that vision through their own
hiring practices. For instance, one professor thinks it important to give
people of color a hiring preference when all else is equal, in order to correct for the glass-ceiling effect at his institution.

> If it became to the point where there were two individuals, one was
> white and one was black, I'd pick the black person without question.
> But I try to take the person who is best qualified for the job regardless
> of skin color, giving underrepresented minorities the benefit of the
> doubt as much as I can. [Q: Why do you think that's important?]
> Well, I think for the very reason we talked about this institution. Most
> of the service personnel are black. So the only way to upgrade them
> in a serious manner is to get them jobs with greater responsibility.
> And we should make every effort to do that.

In effect, this respondent is supporting an affirmative action approach
that is often rejected by other whites. Moreover, many whites, including
some other respondents, overestimate the extent to which whites are becoming outnumbered in better-paying positions in the U.S. workplace.
Yet, the job categories where black Americans are numerous seldom involve significant organizational power. In contrast, this respondent recognizes the need for black Americans in more influential positions.

Another respondent recounts his use of his hiring power to help one
black woman achieve self-sufficiency when she had much going against
her.

> This woman came . . . and so I hired her as an intern. The reason that I hired her was not because she had any skills that would help in the workplace, but . . . she was a single mother going back to school, and . . . was receiving fifty dollars a week from the government for public assistance. . . . And so we employed her on a part-time basis. . . . She's now mainstreamed . . . she's self-supporting, she's doing very well, got a nice job. [In the] transition through several jobs, [she] had some problems with those jobs. [They] would always call, [and] I'd always protect her.

Elsewhere in his interview, this committed professional discusses choosing a career path in "civil justice," where he could help victims of discrimination seek redress through the courts. He reflects eloquently on the reasons for this commitment: "Early on, I realized that the whites were not the good guys. But I always felt I was a good guy, and I always felt [and] I still feel that I can change things. Okay, not . . . all by myself, but we all have to make that commitment. We can't stand around." This respondent paints an ideal picture, in which elite white men use their positions to effect social change. Still, only a few of these elite men report in their interviews that they have been this strongly committed and proactive in regard to current racial discrimination, in their workplaces, communities, or the larger society.

Antiracist Action Begins at Home

Since relative inaction and passiveness in regard to much contemporary discrimination pervade the accounts of many men in this sample—as would likely be the case in interviews with the majority of elite white men in the society—and since the overt antidiscrimination actions described above are not widespread, it seems important to investigate the experiences that influence some white men to think or act differently from the majority in the white collective. As one executive quoted above suggests, having a close black friend can mean emerging from the white bubble at a personal level. This can be the significant influence that breaks some of an individual's bonds to the dominant white collective and ends some of the white isolation that helps to sustain systemic racism. When whites come to know black Americans or other Americans of color at a close, sustained, more or less equal-status level, they often seem to develop deeper antidiscrimination and antiracist convictions than they otherwise might have.

Several respondents talked about these personal interracial connections and the implications of such relationships for interracial understanding or empathy. Recall this professional's comments in a previous chapter, in which he sees racial intermixing in personal relationships as one key to improving the country's situation.

> [T]he solution to this [racism], if we give it enough time, is for more interracial marriage. Because ... the thing is, that if it's "those people," they're different. But if, well, that's your daughter-in-law, or your son-in-law, or your aunt or your uncle. I remember, you know, when I was growing up, the real biases were against people who were Polish, or Italian or, you know, things like that, and that the real breakdown of it came when my parents' brothers and sisters started marrying people like that.... And [you] find out that they're also like everybody else.

This respondent speaks from personal experience, since not only has he witnessed interethnic marriages in his family, but his own child has also dated a black person, with his acceptance of that situation. Still, there is a major step between tolerating or approving interracial relationships in one's own family and advocating that as *the solution* for societal racism. This position distinguishes him from many others in the sample, who expressed significant reservations about interracial dating or marriage outside or within their family networks.

Another relatively rare position is taken by this white manager, who not only approves of intermarriage but admires those who marry interracially. In contrast to most men in the sample, who are generally isolated from close relationships with people of color, especially in their personal networks, this man has had a rather multiracial social life. When asked how he would feel if a close relative married a black person, he responds:

> No big deal. We have black friends, we're godparents to a black child. We had the family over here after the christening. And the mother and father are black; he's from Africa ... she's black, local. She has two brothers, one of whom is engaged to a white woman, the other one is engaged to another black [person]. They have ... a mixed family, we're in mixed company, we go to their mixed church. I'm probably

as color-blind as you'll find in your study here. We have lots of black friends, we go to their houses, and they come to ours. I wouldn't mind.... I don't have a reaction as some people would. My reaction would be, "Wow, that's cool ... let me meet the person," because ... I recognize that it takes certain moral fiber to get into an interracial relationship in this country today and for anybody to take that risk— there are risks involved with that—to take that risk, it's got to be a special person. I would be interested in meeting somebody that special and seeing why my friend or relative thought that person was that quality.

Bringing such relationships a step closer to home, another respondent indicates that he is in an interracial marriage. We have discussed some of his sage comments in an earlier chapter, where he notes remarking to his African-American wife about an all-white party, "We were the only black people there." He and his wife have a son, and his son's case demonstrates how interracial personal relationships can be an important springboard to taking action against racial prejudice or discrimination. In his interview he explains how he took action when his son was subjected to a pattern of racial harassment. One white boy called his son "a porch monkey and [also] said, 'Your mother is black and your father is white, that's not right.' " One white student at school called him "brown like a turd," and another white boy asked about the location of the family's mailbox. He continues with this account of vandalism: "And then the next day, when my wife came home, there was a dead bird in our mail tube and dog feces in our mailbox. So then that all culminated in our filing a complaint with the school and the police." He notes that one boy confessed, and that he has taken further action "to see if we can do something that's more proactive with the school. And so the school has kind of designed a tolerance teaching that's much larger than ... just this incident." While other parents might want only immediate justice for their son, this man follows through on his antiracist commitments to use this incident as a way to get more active educational efforts on issues of racial prejudice at the local school. These last few accounts indicate that interracial personal relationships can facilitate and foster a level of awareness about the pathology of racism common in the general white population.

It is significant that a few men in this elite sample have built, have sought out, or have been consistently supportive of close and ongoing interracial relationships. Even given their high class positions, these men have not followed the herd. Indeed, they seem to feel both vindicated and comfortable in going against the grain and creating alternative visions of being white and male in U.S. society. Historically, many white analysts and ordinary white Americans have made excuses for the racial orientations or excesses of prominent whites who have been the leaders and pillars of U.S. society. Discussing the country's founding and early years, for example, many people have offered the excuse that "it was a different time" to justify the fact that so many of the "founding fathers" were slaveholders or supporters of slavery. Yet this excuse ignores another critical reality: In the same early period there were also some white men (and women) of high intellectual, social, or political status who were outspoken abolitionists and opponents of slavery. There were also many ordinary white Americans who were open opponents of slavery. The same can be said for the era of racial segregation. While most whites in the North and the South supported or at least tolerated legal segregation in the Southern and border states, numerous white men and women in all social classes worked against it and risked their lives—together with many African Americans—to end that type of institutionalized racism. One need not use the standard of today to judge the actions of white men in the past; one can judge them by the best of their times.

Today, in one way or another, many observers still seem to excuse elite white men, as well as other whites, for their lack of convictions about or commitments to eliminating racial animosity and discrimination in society. In addition to playing down the current significance of racism, some apologists suggest or argue, explicitly or implicitly, that members of the white elite have more important priorities than racism, or that their hands are tied, given the increasingly conservative attitude of the general white population in regard to racial change. Given this head-in-the-sand viewpoint, it is important to underscore the strongly antiracist convictions and antidiscrimination actions of some members of today's white male elite, because these convictions and actions indicate that it is in fact possible to hold such an influential position in society while still challenging institutionalized racism.

VISIONS OF THE MULTIRACIAL FUTURE

Recall the point we made earlier in this chapter concerning the declining proportion of whites in the U.S. population. Given this new demographic reality, it seems likely that major social and political changes are coming to the United States. How fast these changes will come is hard to predict, yet over the next few decades demographic developments may mean an eventual end to white dominance of numerous political, juridical, and public school systems. Democratic institutions such as the vote and the peer-jury system can no longer be relied on by whites to maintain political domination. The new majority of Americans of color will be unlikely to acquiesce politically in continuing white discrimination and oppression. In many areas of the United States we may well see more competition and social conflict, including, perhaps, protests, demonstrations, and even uprisings against continuing patterns of racial animosity and discrimination.

Because of these ongoing demographic changes, the white collective —and thus the white elite—will be under ever increasing pressure to meaningfully integrate the country's major institutions and to redistribute important socioeconomic and political resources. What does the future hold for this country? Certainly, an optimistic scenario for the future envisions a coalition of Americans of color working with supportive whites to bring major changes in the patterns of systemic racism in order to establish truly fair, egalitarian, and democratic social institutions.

However, there are more pessimistic scenarios as well. As we have seen, many members of the white elite do not now seem inclined to take action to meaningfully integrate institutions or to significantly redistribute resources. Even as the numbers of people of color increase in the United States, if the perception of certain key white members of the society is that people of color already have too much—and that whites are somehow losing too much ground economically or politically—they may consider strategies whereby a white minority can maintain ultimate political control, such as that under the old apartheid system of the Union of South Africa. In such a scenario, the increasing diversity of U.S. society would hardly usher in the positive changes to racial relations that our more optimistic and antiracist respondents envision.

We can now return to an examination of the views of these men on the future of this multiracial nation, views discussed earlier in chapter 3. In reflecting on impending demographic changes, they reveal possible avenues for, and probable barriers to, building a truly democratic and egalitarian sociopolitical system. Some are positive about the prospects, while others are neutral, skeptical, or strongly negative.

One influential respondent replies in strong terms when asked about the likely demographic changes over the next half-century.

> I would not welcome that . . . for lots of reasons. The populations that are white in the world—I don't like to use the term "white" in the first place; I use the term Caucasian and Negro; I don't use color—I think the Caucasian countries are advanced, and if you look at the Third World countries and particularly Africa, they are not. When the Dutch were there and the English were there and the Portuguese in Angola, Africa was very progressive. [Since] the Caucasians left, the jungle has taken over. . . . And if you look at cities in our country and areas that are predominantly Negro, you will see that they are crime-infested and backward.

The coming of an America that is not primarily white is very troubling for this respondent, who sees it as leading to a decline in U.S. civilization. Using the outdated term "Negro," this respondent echoes a view of black cultural inferiority and criminality in cities that is held by many other whites today.

He also alludes to the supposed lack of a work ethic on the part of people of African descent. This, too, is a commonly held view among whites, which we see brought out by the following corporate official when he considers the country's increasingly multiracial future.

> Because the strength of the country and the economy is driven by the Anglo-Saxon work ethic heritage, which will be gradually destroyed because these other groups don't have that heritage. . . . Because if you look at the historical integration of the black people into the country, and the Hispanic, they have always, very few of them have been able to operate on a sophisticated income-producing level. [Q: But don't you think that that's the problem of the white people who subjugate them?] I think that is true up until about 1960, 1965, but I don't think this is true in the last twenty, twenty-five years.

Recall that an important implication of the cultural-deficiency view is that it minimizes the significance of present-day racial discrimination. This respondent clearly thinks that institutionalized discrimination did occur up until the mid-1960s or so, but has not been a serious problem in recent decades. This recurring blame-the-victim view doubtless fuels negative reactions to a future multiracial society among many white Americans. Also notice that the last two respondents share a view of the United States as a white (Caucasian) or Anglo-Saxon society, so that a multiracial future seems an unwelcome departure from that supposedly white-centered reality. Here again, we see how specific racial attitudes are imbedded in a more general sense of social-group position in a society.

In recent years, a number of prominent white intellectuals and presidential advisers have expressed more or less similar views about immigration, multiculturalism, and the "browning of America," often in leading publications and journals. For example, Harvard professor Samuel Huntington has argued in the influential journal *Foreign Affairs* that, if multiculturalism ever becomes central in the United States, the country could join the former Soviet Union "on the ash heap of history."[5] In the past, according to Huntington, nativist worries about white European immigrants assimilating were unwarranted, but today the situation is one where major immigrant

> groups feel discriminated against if they are not allowed to remain apart from the mainstream. The ideologies of multiculturalism and diversity reinforce and legitimate these trends. They deny the existence of a common culture in the United States, denounce assimilation, and promote the primacy of racial, ethnic, and other subnational cultural identities and groupings. They also question a central element in the American Creed by substituting for the rights of individuals the rights of groups defined largely in terms of race, ethnicity, gender, and sexual preference.[6]

Huntington makes clear in his analysis that he is explicitly concerned that today most immigrants are people of color "overwhelmingly from Latin America and Asia." Significantly, he does not deal in his analysis with the substantial discrimination and segregation that these Latin American and Asian immigrants receive at the hands of white Americans.

Some of the elite men in the sample are ambivalent or neutral in regard to possible changes in the country's racial and ethnic mosaic. For instance, one corporate manager begins with an acceptance of this multiracial future, but ends his commentary with some concern about immigrants.

> If you look at the statistics and demographics, the nonwhite population is growing in percentage of the total, and that is not necessarily a bad thing. I think one of the things that had made this country what [it] is today is the fact that we do have many ethnic groups, and many cultural groups in the United States, and it had served us well in the past. And I see no reason [why] it will not serve us well in the future. I guess my only concern becomes one of, if we look at any group, white or nonwhite group . . . gaining in terms of sheer numbers, of the ability to control the destiny of the U.S., my only concern would be, are these groups going to be sufficiently educated to represent the whole of America? So if we can take the assumption that they will be educated, then . . . certainly I have no problems with that, and clearly that probably is what is going to happen.

Although his concern about education seems to call up the cultural-deficiency position we have seen in some other comments, for the most part this respondent remains neutral to modestly positive on the topic of the growth of the nonwhite population. Clearly, too, he recognizes the important role of a multiplicity of ethnic groups in the vitality of the United States.

Similarly, reviewing the broad sweep of American history, an attorney finds it neither positive nor negative that whites might be a numerical minority in the future.

> Well, its not a question of whether it's favorable or unfavorable. It's a natural—it's consistent with the history of the country, although I suppose most would say that we are really an Anglo country. You know, we are a colony of the United Kingdom, called England. . . . And the culture was an implantation of the English culture, but that was supplemented over the years with the influx of mostly Europeans. And then we began to see the influence of the Africans once slavery was eliminated, although there was probably influence before this. We've most seen it speed up through the mid-twentieth century. Then we saw influence from other, from Asian cultures, and then

from the South American cultures which are themselves European cultures but not an English culture. It came from Spain primarily, I guess, Spain and Portugal. So, do I think it's good or bad? In a sense of the country, it's not a question of good or bad.... As a whole, the country will adapt to changes like that. Whether its personally threatening, I think we all do feel that any change is [a] threat to our, to each person individually, because we all identify whether we know it or not with the status quo, the background in which we live.

While some elite white men do sense that their group's position is being threatened by demographic changes, men like this respondent remain more or less neutral and do not express much trepidation over the prospect of a multiracial future. They seem to take the pragmatic view—that the country will again adjust, as it always has in the past. Some of these respondents do not exhibit much concern at all in regard to the topic, suggesting they do not think it will affect them personally. One banking executive sums it up succinctly: "I'm not concerned about it at all. I think it's probably going to happen, but I don't think about it, and I don't worry about it. [Q: You don't think it will affect you in any way?] No, I don't. [Q: Not socially, or in the business world?] Nope."

It may be that one consequence of the white elite's isolation from close relationships with people of color is that they often do not really see themselves yet as an integral part of the multiracial mosaic that makes up the United States. While it seems likely that what affects the country will affect all Americans at some point, statements like this last one suggest that some in the elite view themselves as so insulated from populations of color that they will be relatively untouched by the coming demographic changes.

Other respondents are cognizant of the fact that demographic changes could bring shifts in the country's definitions of "race," and draw upon historical examples. For example, this professional says that he feels threatened by the changes, but

> I would probably take a historical perspective. To be perfectly honest, to a degree I find it somewhat threatening. Because you'd think this is my culture ... this is my country. This is the way we do things here. And so to a degree it is threatening, and you would think, gee, I'd hate to see this country become something that it isn't already. But if you take a historical perspective that the people who have always been in

this country have always felt very threatened by new groups of immigrants. But for the most part the new groups of immigrants have become assimilated and have become white themselves or have become a version of white. I mean, there was a time when . . . Sicilians in Louisiana were, like, considered the lowest scum, lowest form of scum of the earth, and now they run the place and are pillars of society.

He accents the broad historical sweep of immigration to the United States. His sense of group position is evident in the way he uses pronouns like "my" and "we" to describe his culture and country, thereby suggesting that the new Americans of color may take away that sense of dominant position and culture. Again, thinking about racial and ethnic groups is linked to the sense of group position, and we glimpse the reality of an individual participating in group understandings about these matters of racial and ethnic change. However, this respondent implies that if the new immigrants do assimilate to white culture like those of the past, and thus identify to a significant degree with the white group, the demographic shifts might not significantly alter the society.

Another respondent also elaborates on the country's history of incorporating certain immigrant groups, such as Jews, into the "white" category. Commenting on the demographic trend, he says, "It's not true. The only reason you can make that assertion is by counting almost all of the Latino immigrants as being nonwhite, but actually a very large percentage of the Latinos are of white ancestry or are considered white. The other thing, whiteness is very relative." Like the previous respondent, this man suggests that "race" is a social construction that shifts over time, thereby sometimes incorporating previously stigmatized groups into the privileged category of whiteness.

Elaborating on this issue, one professional offers this sentiment:

When you say "trend," you have to take into consideration that there are many variables. This is a very complex society that we live in, and there's a diversity of race that basically has been with us at least for the last hundred years, and I think that while that is a possibility, I don't think that it is an inevitable [thing] . . . I don't think that it's a fait accompli. I don't think that, because of the increasing influx of minorities in our country, that this is going to be basically a nonwhite country. I think that minorities as such, and you know, once you—when you say minorities, sometimes you over-generalize. Minorities are defined in relation to whatever you might be talking about. So that, for example, within the African-American community, there are American African Americans—when I say Americans, they have been here for two, three generations; and yet there is a growing influx [from] Third World countries who to the outside world are African Americans, but really aren't. For example, Nigerians. There's a steady increase of Nigerians who come into the country [and] they are a minority within a minority. . . . In other words, I think we over-generalize when we talk about minorities. . . . I think . . . it's going to be a very fluid society and with education available and job opportunity available for all. I think that you're going to have inter—minority/majority—for want of better words—marriages. I think that you're going to have an increase in interracial marriages, and we're going to be a very varied society. And hopefully somewhere down the line we'll drop the nomenclature of minorities and majorities, et cetera.

This professional initially questions whether the immigration trend will lead to a predominantly non-European country. As he reflects on these developments, he seems to welcome them, and envisions that demographic shifts may bring about a society where no one group dominates, intermarriage increases, and education and job opportunities are accordingly more evenly distributed. While this may be an overly optimistic view, he differs from some of his peers who would only feel comfortable with non-European immigration if the core of the U.S. population and the culture remain white. He prefers to view the future of the United States as one where there is so much blending and diversity, and such a balance of power, that "minorities" are no longer an issue.

It is evident from the interviews that these elite white men vary noticeably in terms of how they view the future of non-European immigration and multiracialism in the United States. Numerous respondents continue to ascribe to some version of the cultural-superiority (cultural-deficiency) viewpoint that is common among white Americans, and suggest or aver that a continuing white majority and culture ensure a successful and healthy society. For them, the increasingly multiracial reality is often seen as undermining the work ethic and other traditional aspects of the dominant European-American culture, so as to create yet other societal problems.

With many people in the white elite and the general white population adopting or moving toward this perspective, one might predict some fairly repressive governmental measures in the near future. In fact, we have recently seen a large increase in prison construction and imprisonment of people of color, often for relatively minor infractions, coinciding with people of color becoming the numerical majority in numerous cities. Government spending for imprisonment strategies greatly exceeds spending for employment strategies, which would likely be more effective than imprisonment in reducing economically generated crimes and related problems. Measures that restrict or limit immigration are also likely on the political horizon, and are already being proposed by some conservative commentators and politicians in the elite. Although government steps like severe immigration restrictions are now seen as part of a distant racist past, it is clear that many in the general white population hold attitudes that might eventually lead to support for some variation on these measures again, especially in the wake of the major demographic shifts that are well underway.

One possibly problematic position taken by some elite white men is the view that the influx of immigrants of color and related demographic trends will not impact their lives in a significant way. While their more or less neutral position on these demographic trends may at first glance seem benign, if they see themselves as far removed from these fellow Americans, they may not see repressive government measures directed at immigrants of color or other populations of color as affecting them in any way, either.

Perhaps more hopeful are the views of some elite respondents who see the looming demographic changes and their impact on the racial makeup of the United States as mainly a positive trend. While some in the elite see negative outcomes such as crime and a weakened work ethic when they picture an increasingly multiracial nation, others actually picture positive by-products of the changes, such as an increased national vitality, increased interracial respect and understanding, increased interracial contacts, and a more equal division of societal resources.

New and innovative governmental policies that work to maximize such positive changes, rather than to repress or manage the growing populations of color, could become an important project for the more progressive, diversity-positive sector of the white elite. Clearly, U.S. society needs more activist members of the elite, as well as more activist members of the general population from all racial and ethnic backgrounds, working on innovative ideas and progressive policies to counter the current negative and repressive strategies being implemented in many cities and states, and by the federal government, partly in response to the continuing demographic shift. We review some ideas about what such innovative policies and actions might look like in the concluding section.

PROSPECTS FOR CHANGE

The outlooks of many elite white men on racial matters often resemble those of the larger white population. These men usually hold to the common individualistic perspective that asserts that it is color-blind, and that anyone can make it up the socioeconomic ladder in U.S. society. As a rule, these apparently nonracial understandings are mixed with uninformed views about the sharp decline or absence of racial discrimination in the United States and with notions of the cultural inferiority of darker-skinned Americans in terms of such things as work ethic, family values, or desire for more education.

That most whites, men and women, do not know or think seriously about the pervasiveness of racial discrimination today, or about the similar values, personalities, and aspirations held by African Americans and other people of color, is one direct result of their often great spatial and emotional segregation. Elite white men generally have more power and influence than ordinary white Americans, yet they, too, are often trapped within and by the institutions they play a role in running. That they share certain racial viewpoints with many other whites arises from the fact that they are affected by the dominant culture and institutions that they have helped to manage or sustain. That is, they, too, are influenced by the public discourse on racial matters that constantly appears in media, conventional politics, and various other mainstream settings. If many frequently sound like the majority of white Americans, it is because they or their brethren have often set the tone for how the rest of society should think about a range of racial issues. Regardless of their class standing, it is troubling when whites hold stereotyped attitudes and racial propensities that are detrimental to the ideal of a just and democratic country, but it is especially troubling and problematic when these well-educated white elites think this way, because of their power to bring or hinder change in a progressive direction.

However, as in the larger white population, there are significant elements of antiracist hope to be found within the white elite. There are white leaders with an antiracist bent, such as attorneys who dedicate their careers to fighting for civil justice and some executives and other employers who consistently make it a point to hire employees of color in order to diversify their firms at all levels. There are those in the elite who seek out multiracial situations and relationships. These men have intentionally taken paths different from those of many of their peers. They are learning to listen to, work with, and value the views of people of different racial and ethnic backgrounds from their own.

Often, the white men who hold strongly antiracist views and have taken significant actions against discrimination in the workplace or other public spheres have broken out of the "white bubble" of social isolation in their own personal lives. They are no longer just a passive part of the white reference groups into which they were born. They generally have had close, and more or less equal-status, relationships with black Americans or other Americans of color, such as a college roommate, a godchild, a relative by marriage, a spouse, or a child. These are typically relationships with significantly more sustained interpersonal and emotional connections than those involving an employee or coworker. While many elite men may have more or less equal-status contacts with a few employees of color at work, they can still remain in social or emotional isolation from them because they do not see them on a sustained basis, as they would in home or neighborhood settings. They are thus unlikely to hear the often deeply painful stories of incidents of discrimination they face, nor are they likely to observe up close their spirituality, work values, family values, and friendship connections outside of the workplace. These more superficial contacts do not necessarily help to generate antidiscrimination and antiracist commitments among whites in the ways that the more intimate interracial contacts often seem to do.

While those men in our sample with strongly antiracist sentiments and activist inclinations are themselves making some changes in the racist patterns of U.S. society, their small numbers are plainly not enough to alter patterns of discrimination and oppression on a larger scale. A potential "critical mass" lies in the much larger group of elite whites who embrace substantial racial equality in theory, but appear to have difficulty putting it into practice more aggressively in their lives because of the continuing and heavy influence of their powerful reference groups. Given the power of this white social context, the feelings and dilemmas of other whites seem to attract their sympathies and empathies first. As a result, their actions on racial matters tend to protect their own kind, if only through remaining passive bystanders rather than pressing actively for the equality that they may believe in at a more abstract level.

Perhaps one key to unlocking more changes in the system of racism in the United States is for this larger group, those in the "white middle" as it were, to feel much more connected to those outside the white collective and thus empowered to act as their consciences dictate, instead of acting to protect the white "dysfunctional family." Clearly, such a shift from abstraction to action requires support and rewards from the larger society for actively antiracist thought and antiracist actions.

Interestingly, Jeffrey Kelly, a researcher who has studied the group dynamics that sometimes lead to people changing deeply ingrained habits, has noted that it is not so much the knowledge of facts that alters behavior, but rather changes in people's perceptions of what is socially acceptable and legitimate. "By reshaping the norm, you can shift the behavior of the whole group."[7] Cigarette smoking was once very legitimate and widely practiced among Americans, yet that began to decline when most people came to feel that many others were giving up the deadly habit. Knowing that it was the way of their peers not to smoke influenced people to give up smoking or to not start in the first place.

Such findings suggest one innovative approach to the continuing and serious problem of racial prejudice and discrimination. In media organizations, institutions of higher education, and corporations, for example, key leaders and opinion makers—or youth who will soon be leaders and opinion makers—can be trained to recognize and understand the highly costly and damaging realities of contemporary racial discrimination both for those targeted and for the larger society. They can also be taught how to incorporate a range of antiracist actions into their everyday lives. As respected and influential leaders and opinion makers, they can then pass on those new understandings about the many costs of systemic racism and the benefits of dismantling that racism to their families, friends, acquaintances, employees, and coworkers. This can perhaps be done most effectively in small group settings where each leader will be responsible for educating a few associates, who in turn can become opinion leaders, and so on down the line. In this way, what is now considered acceptable and legitimate behavior in white-dominated peer groups, workplaces, schools, neighborhoods, and larger communities will give way to a more antiracist standard, and we can begin to envision a much less racist society.

Of course, we realize that changing racial attitudes and proclivities to discriminate will be much harder than changing attitudes on such behavior as smoking, in large part because most whites benefit substantially from the privileges of the racist system. Still, finding ways to influence and shift the white collective's norms and inclinations in regard to racial prejudice and discrimination can be a step toward creating a more just and equitable future for the United States. The white collective's norms and inclinations have shifted in the past in a progressive direction, and they can shift yet again.

Other steps are clearly required to break down the white-generated and white-maintained system of racism. As with the last suggestion, they will involve not only the white leadership, but also the white population generally. Indeed, it is from this general white population that much opposition to, and new leadership against, racial oppression have arisen in the past. One major step today involves the creation or expansion of important incentives to act against persisting racist thought and practice. Building rewards for antiracist behavior into major U.S. institutions can help to generate and reinforce antiracist actions in the ongoing operations not only of these institutions, but also of the larger society. Already, a few private agencies, corporations, and branches of the military have made it a criterion for promotion to the next rank or level that many employees show how they have worked against discrimination or furthered racial and gender diversity as part of their job-related tasks. When these programs work effectively—and, unfortunately, that is often not the case—a person cannot expect to move to positions of greater responsibility until they have made a significant effort to increase racial and gender diversity or to end organizational discrimination.

Even if these limited organizational experiments are far from perfect, they do show that whites, and especially white men, can in fact change and act to bring down some of the structures of racial prejudice and discrimination in their organizations. These programs also allow us to realistically envision a future in which people have to document their antidiscrimination and pro-diversity efforts in order to get promotions, maintain their jobs, keep their business licenses, and maintain professional licenses such as in medicine or law. If more institutions made such efforts a requirement, a critical mass of whites and others willing to work against systemic racism, against the grain of the larger society, might well develop.

Yet it is important to note that changes at the workplace, while important, will not be enough to break through the social isolation that results from most whites' lack of close personal relationships across the color line. True desegregation and integration of residential neighborhoods and local educational institutions—places where close interracial relationships can be formed—will be necessary to minimize the significant isolation that currently separates most white Americans from black Americans and many other Americans of color. Such meaningful desegregation will require much more effective and vigorous enforcement of U.S. civil rights laws, especially fair housing laws, than now exists. If white political and business leaders, as well as other influential whites, actually make the enforcement of civil rights laws a priority, then residential neighborhoods and local schools will eventually be places where people of all racial groups form sustained equal-status relationships with those in numerous other groups, leading to the much more blended society that some respondents would welcome. Subsequently, many white Americans will likely develop much more empathy for the difficult lives and discriminatory experiences of Americans of color, and they will likely come to realize how much they share with them in the way of values and family concerns. They will also be more likely to come to one another's aid, whenever their common humanity is assaulted because of discrimination linked to the color of one's skin.

We recognize that we are calling for major societal changes. Yet they are the kind of changes that eroding the age-old system of racism requires, since it is so deeply ingrained into every white-controlled institution and into most white hearts and minds. Just as the group that our respondents represent controls much of society's socioeconomic resources, so that group also has substantial control over the future of racial oppression in its hands. Whether or not they use this power to break down racial prejudice and discrimination, the numbers of Americans of color will continue to increase, thereby all but guaranteeing an increasing scrutiny of currently racialized decisions and discriminatory policies at all levels of U.S. institutions. It remains to be seen whether more major conflicts and recurring confrontations between white Americans and their leaders, on the one hand, and Americans of color and their leaders, on the other, lie on the American horizon. They likely do, unfortunately for all concerned.

Still, there is a possibility that the number of progressive white Americans will grow, and that they will learn to work with those in racially oppressed groups to reduce and eventually end racial discrimination. This is not an unrealistic hope, for the U.S. has a long history of multiracial organizations and coalitions against racial oppression. Multiracial organizations have helped to bring significant changes in racist patterns, as in the case of the abolitionist movement of the 1850s and the civil rights movement of the 1960s. For three centuries, many whites, blacks, and other Americans of color have organized to break down institutionalized racism and expand social justice. For example, from its beginning in 1911, the National Association for the Advancement of Colored People (NAACP) has had black and white leaders, and many nonblack members. The black-led civil rights movement of the 1960s had participants from numerous racial and ethnic groups, including many whites. In recent decades, antiracist whites have often participated with other Americans in numerous local organizations working against racism. The Institutes for the Healing of Racism, to take one major example, are more than 150 multiracial groups now working across the country to educate local citizens about how to dismantle discrimination in their communities. The People's Institute for Survival and Beyond (PI), founded by two black men, is a community-oriented group that sets up multiracial workshops that have trained more than twenty thousand local officials and community activists, half of them white, to understand how they can reduce racial discrimination in their organizations and communities. While their objectives have varied, numerous other multiracial organizations have recently pressed for changes in institutionalized racism across the United States.[8]

One next step in building a broad antiracist strategy for the United States is to expand the number of these multiracial organizations and to connect them into a national association working against systemic racism. As we see it, the democratic future of the country likely lies in the ability of progressive and antiracist Americans of all backgrounds to build much greater understanding across the color lines—and to use that understanding to create large-scale coalitions of Americans from many different racial, ethnic, gender, class, and other backgrounds, coalitions seeking to break down the several major oppressions that have long cost this country much of its human energy and potential creativity. It is certainly our hope that this occurs, so that the vaunted national creed of justice, fairness, and equality will eventually become a reality after all.

NOTES

INTRODUCTION

1. David M. Halbfinger, "Lott Acknowledges 'Misbehavior,'" *New York Times*, December 17, 2002; retrieved at www.nytimes.com/2002/12/17/politics/17SHOW.html.

2. "Clinton: GOP Criticism of Lott Hypocritical," *USA Today*, December 18, 2002; retrieved at www.usatoday.com/news/washington/2002-12-18-clinton-lott-gop_x.htm.

3. Robert Novak and Joe Conason, as quoted in "Media Advisory: Media Play Catch-up on Lott's Latest Endorsement of Racism," December 11, 2002; retrieved at www.fair.org/press-releases/lott-advisory.html.

1. "RACE" IN AMERICA

1. Gunnar Myrdal, *An American Dilemma*, Volume 1 (New York: McGraw-Hill, 1964 [1944]), pp. lxxv–lxxvi.

2. Toni Morrison, *Playing in the Dark: Whiteness and the Literary Imagination* (New York: Vintage Books, 1992), pp. 11–12.

3. Louis Wirth, "Preface," in Karl Mannheim, *Ideology and Utopia* (London: Routledge and Kegan Paul, 1960 [1936]), pp. xxiv, xxx; Georges Gurvitch, *The Social Frameworks of Knowledge*, trans. by Margaret Thompson (New York: Harper & Row, 1971), p. xxxv.

4. See Debra Van Ausdale and Joe R. Feagin, *The First R: How Children Learn Race and Racism* (Lanham, Md.: Rowman & Littlefield, 2001).

5. Edward Ball, *Slaves in the Family* (New York: Ballantine Books, 1999), p. 14.

6. Pierre Bourdieu, *The Logic of Practice* (Stanford: Stanford University Press, 1980), pp. 113–126. Here we draw on joint theoretical work by Hernán Vera and Joe Feagin. See Joe R. Feagin and Hernán Vera, "Rethinking Institutionalized Racism: The U.S. Educational System," unpublished research paper, University of Florida, 1994.

7. Kenneth O'Reilly, *Nixon's Piano: Presidents and Racial Politics from Washington to Clinton* (New York: Free Press, 1995), p. 11.

8. Herbert Blumer, "Race Prejudice as a Sense of Group Position," *Pacific Sociological Review* 1 (spring 1958): 5.

9. Richard Herrnstein and Charles Murray, *The Bell Curve: Intelligence and Class Structure in American Life* (New York: Free Press, 1994).

10. Donald R. Kinder and David O. Sears, "Prejudice and Politics: Symbolic Racism Versus Racial Threats to the Good Life," *Journal of Personality and Social Psychology*, 40 (1981): 414–431; Leslie Carr, *'Color-Blind' Racism* (Thousand Oaks: Sage, 1997); and Eduardo Bonilla-Silva, *White Supremacy and Racism in the Post-Civil Rights Era* (Boulder, Colo.: Lynne Rienner, 2001).

11. See the surveys cited in Joe R. Feagin, Hernán Vera, and Pinar Batur, *White Racism: The Basics* (2nd ed.; New York: Routledge, 2001), pp. 187–189.

12. See Jennifer Hochschild, *Facing Up to the American Dream* (Princeton, N.J.: Princeton University Press, 1995), chapter 8.

13. Ralph Ellison, *Invisible Man* (New York: Vintage Books, [1947] 1989), p. 3.

14. See the summary in Jennifer Hochschild, *Facing Up to the American Dream* (Princeton, N.J.: Princeton University Press, 1995), pp. 56–57, 59–60.

15. Ibid., p. 60.

16. Jessica Benjamin, *The Bonds of Love: Psychoanalysis, feminism, and the Problem of Domination* (New York: Pantheon, 1988), pp. 12, 15. We draw here on collaborative work with Hernán Vera. See Joe R. Feagin, Hernán Vera, and Nikitah Imani, *The Agony of Education: Black Students at White Colleges and Universities* (New York: Routledge, 1996), pp. 14–15.

17. Hochschild, *Facing Up to the American Dream*, p. 68.

18. David O. Sears, "Symbolic Racism," in *Eliminating Racism*, eds. Phyllis A. Katz and Dalmas A. Taylor (New York: Plenum, 1988), pp. 55–58; John B. McConahay, "Modern Racism," in *Prejudice, Discrimination and Racism*, eds. John F. Dovidio and Samuel L. Gaertner (Orlando, Fla.: Academic Press, 1986).

19. Richard Morin, "Misperceptions Cloud Whites' View of Blacks," *Washington Post*, July 11, 2001, p. A01; "Washington Post/Kaiser/Harvard Racial Attitudes Survey," *Washington Post*, July 11, 2001, p. A1.

20. Cited in Robert J. Blendon, John M. Benson, Mollyann Brodie,

Drew E. Altman, and Mario Brossard, "The Public and the President's Commission on Race," *The Public Perspective* (February, 1998): 66.

21. Myrdal, *An American Dilemma*, p. 4.

22. Teun van Dijk, *Elite Discourse and Racism* (Newbury Park, Calif.: Sage, 1993), pp. 6, 20.

23. Hochschild, *Facing Up to the American Dream*, p. 55 and passim.

24. Lani Guinier and Gerald Torres, *The Miner's Canary: Enlisting Race, Resisting Power, Transforming Democracy* (Cambridge: Harvard University Press, 2002), p. 42.

25. Derrick Z. Jackson, "Unspoken During Race Talk," *Boston Globe* (December 5, 1997): A27.

26. See Feagin, Vera, and Batur, *White Racism*, pp. 4–5.

27. Anti-Defamation League, *Highlights from an Anti-Defamation League Survey on Racial Attitudes in America* (New York: ADL, 1993), pp. 8–25; see also Paul M. Sniderman and Thomas Piazza, *The Scar of Race* (Cambridge: Harvard University Press, 1993, pp. 41–45.

28. Lawrence Bobo, "Inequalities that Endure?: Racial Ideology, American Politics, and the Peculiar Role of the Social Sciences," paper presented at conference on "The Changing Terrain of Race and Ethnicity," University of Illinois, Chicago, October 26, 2001.

29. See Patricia G. Devine and A. Elliot, "Are Racial Stereotypes Really Fading? The Princeton Trilogy Revisited," *Personality and Social Psychology Bulletin* 21 (1995): 1139–1150.

30. See Lawrence Bobo, "Group Conflict, Prejudice, and the Paradox of Contemporary Racial Attitudes," in *Eliminating Racism*, eds. Katz and Taylor, pp. 99–101.

31. Eduardo Bonilla-Silva and Tyrone A. Forman, "I Am Not A Racist But . . .: Mapping White College Students' Racial Ideology in the U.S.A.," *Discourse and Society* 11(2000): 51–86.

32. Maria Krysan, *Public Opinion Quarterly* 62 (Winter 1998): 506–544; and Kristen A. Myers and Passion Williamson, "Race Talk: The Perpetuation of Racism through Private Discourse," *Race and Society* 4 (2001): 3–26.

33. Patricia G. Devine and E. Ashby Plant, "The Regulations of Explicit and Implicit Racial Bias: The Role of Motivations to Respond without Prejudice," *Journal of Personality and Social Psychology* 82 (2002): 835–848; Jody David Armour, *Negrophobia and Reasonable Racism: The*

Hidden Costs of Being Black in America (New York: New York University Press, 1997), p. 41.

34. See Patricia G. Devine, "Stereotypes and Prejudice: Their Automatic and Controlled Components," *Journal of Personality and Social Psychology* 56 (1989): 5–18; Elliot Aronson, Thomas D. Wilson, and Robin M. Akert, *Social Psychology,* 4th ed. (Upper Saddle River, N.J.: Prentice-Hall, 2002), pp. 473–474; and Yolanda Flores Niemann and Paul F. Secord, "Social Ecology of Stereotyping," *Journal for the Theory of Social Behaviour* 25 (March 1995): 2–7.

35. Armour, *Negrophobia and Reasonable Racism*, pp. 132–135.

36. Adrian Piper, "Passing for White, Passing for Black," *Transition* 58 (1992): 28.

37. See Kurt Eichenwald, "Texaco Executives, On Tape, Discussed Impeding a Bias Suit," *New York Times* (November 4, 1996): A1.Bari-Ellen Roberts, *Roberts v. Texaco: A True Story of Race and Corporate America* (New York: Avon Books, 1998), pp. 1, 283; Kurt Eichenwald, "The Two Faces Of Texaco," *New York Times* (November 10, 1996): Section 3, p. 1.

38. Floyd Allport, *Social Psychology* (Boston: Houghton Mifflin, 1924), p. 6.

39. Mannheim, *Ideology and Utopia*, p. 3.

40. Blumer, "Race Prejudice as a Sense of Group Position," pp. 3–7.

41. Lawrence, "The Id, the Ego, and Equal Protection," pp. 323–324.

42. Maurice Halbwachs, *On Collective Memory*, edited and translated by Lewis Coser (Chicago: University of Chicago Press, 1992), pp. 38, 52.

43. Quoted in Herbert Aptheker, *The Unfolding Drama: Studies in U.S. History*, edited by Barbara Aptheker (New York: International Publishers, 1978), p. 136.

44. Douglas S. Massey and Nancy A. Denton *American Apartheid: Segregation and the Making of the Underclass* (Cambridge: Harvard University Press, 1993), pp. 221–223; John R. Logan, Brian J. Stults, and Reynolds Farley, "Segregation of Minorities in the Metropolis: Two Decades of Change," unpublished research report, Center for Social and Demographic Analysis, University at Albany, 2002.

45. Tom W. Smith, "Measuring Inter-Racial Friendships: Experimental Comparisons," GSS Methodological Report, National Opinion Research Center, University of Chicago, no. 91 (1999).

46. See Gordon Allport, *The Nature of Prejudice* (Abridged ed.; Gar-

den City, N.Y.: Anchor Books, 1958), pp. 251–253; Aronson, Wilson, and Akert, *Social Psychology*, pp. 494–497.

47. Robert M. Entman and Andrew Rojecki, *The Black Image in the White Mind: Media and Race in America* (Chicago: University of Chicago Press, 2000), p. 49.

48. Ibid., pp. 8–9.

49. *Merriam Webster's Collegiate Dictionary* (Springfield, Mass.: Merriam Webster, 1993), Tenth edition, p. 375.

50. In the chapters we have disguised names and places of the respondents to protect their anonymity. We trained the college student interviewers with practice interviews, then told them to choose two white men in "elite positions" in the social networks available to them.

51. All respondents have annual incomes of at least $100,000, and usually much more. The interviews were approximately one to two hours each and were transcribed by the student interviewers. A research assistant scanned the important sections of the interviews for computer analysis. Although we have kept them anonymous here, we are greatly indebted to these students for their assistance in this project. We should note that in quoting from the interviews we have disguised names and places, using pseudonyms where necessary. We have also edited the quoted comments to reduce false starts and stutter words like "ah" and "you know," and sometimes added clarifying words in brackets.

2. THE WHITE BUBBLE: LEARNING ABOUT WHITENESS AND THE RACIAL OTHERS

1. See, for example, Joe R. Feagin, Hernán Vera, and Pinar Batur, *White Racism: The Basics*, 2nd ed. (New York: Routledge, 2001), especially chapters 7 and 8.

2. For an earlier assessment of some of these views, see Rhonda F. Levine, "The Souls of Elite White Men: White Racial Identity and the Logic of Thinking on Race," paper presented at the Hawaii Sociological Association Meetings, February 14, 1998, Honolulu, Hawaii.

3. Judith Rollins, *Between Women* (Philadelphia: Temple University Press, 1985).

4. See Debra Van Ausdale and Joe R. Feagin, *The First R: How Children Learn Race and Racism* (Lanham, Md.: Rowman & Littlefield, 2001).

5. Douglas S. Massey and Nancy A. Denton, "Trends in Segregation of Blacks, Hispanics and Asians, 1970–1980," *American Sociological Review* 52 (1987): 802–825; Douglas S. Massey and Nancy A. Denton, *American Apartheid: Segregation and the Making of the Underclass* (Cambridge: Harvard University Press, 1993), pp. 221–223.

6. Feagin et al., *White Racism,* chapters 7 and 8, and endnote citations.

7. Joe R. Feagin, Hernán Vera, and Nikitah Imani, *The Agony of Education: Black Students at White Colleges and Universities* (New York: Routledge, 1996).

8. Gordon Allport, *The Nature of Prejudice,* abridged ed. (Garden City, N.Y.: Anchor Books, 1958); Elliot Aronson, Thomas D. Wilson, and Robin M. Akert, *Social Psychology,* 4th ed. (Upper Saddle River, N.J.: Prentice-Hall, 2002), pp. 473–474.

9. Joe R. Feagin, *Racist America: Roots, Current Realities, and Future Reparations* (New York: Routledge, 2000), p. 254.

10. Sharon Rush, *Loving Across the Color Line* (Lanhom, Md.: Rowman & Littlefield, 2000).

3. PERSPECTIVES ON WHITENESS

1. Ruth Frankenberg, *White Women, Race Matters* (Minneapolis: University of Minnesota Press, 1993), p. 149.

2. See Peggy McIntosh, "White Privilege and Male Privilege," in *Race, Class and Gender,* ed. Margaret L. Andersen and Patricia Hill Collins (New York: Wadsworth, 2001), pp. 97–98.

3. See John Yinger, *Closed Doors, Opportunities Lost,* (Thousand Oaks, Calif.: Russell Sage Foundation, 1995).

4. See Jennifer Hochschild, *Facing Up to the American Dream* (Princeton: Princeton University Press, 1995), chapter 8.

5. McIntosh, "White Privilege and Male Privilege," p. 95.

6. Quoted in David D. Porter, "What Must Blacks Go Through? An Experiment Will Let You See," *Orlando Sentinel,* September 13, 1989, p. G1.

7. See the citations in John Sibley Butler, *Entrepreneurship and Self-Help among Black Americans* (Albany: State University of New York Press, 1991).

8. Maurice Halbwachs, *On Collective Memory*, edited and translated by Lewis Coser (Chicago: University of Chicago Press, 1992), p. 52.

9. Glass Ceiling Commission, *Good for Business: Making Full Use of the Nation's Human Capital* (Washington, D.C.: U.S. Government Printing Office, 1995), pp. 12, 60–61; and Joe R. Feagin, *Racist America: Roots, Current Realities, and Future Reparations* (New York: Routledge, 2000), chapters 4–6.

10. See Richard E. Lapchick with Kevin J. Matthews, "The 1997 Racial Report Card," in *Rethinking the Color Line*, ed. Charles A. Gallagher (Mountain View, Calif.: Mayfield, 1999), pp. 395–397, 399–400.

11. See Lawrence Bobo, "Group Conflict, Prejudice, and the Paradox of Contemporary Racial Attitudes," in *Eliminating Racism*, eds. Phyllis A. Katz and Dalmas A. Taylor (New York: Plenum, 1988), pp. 99–101; Richard Morin, "Misperceptions Cloud Whites' View of Blacks," *Washington Post*, July 11, 2001, p. A01; and "Washington Post/Kaiser/Harvard Racial Attitudes Survey," *Washington Post*, July 11, 2001, p. A01.

12. See Barbara Ehrenreich, "The Silenced Majority," *Zeta Magazine* 2 (1989): 22.

4. PERSPECTIVES ON AFRICAN AMERICANS AND OTHER AMERICANS OF COLOR

1. Herbert Blumer, "Race Prejudice as a Sense of Group Position," *Pacific Sociological Review* 1 (spring 1958): 4.

2. See, for example, Howard Schuman, Charlotte Steeh, and Lawrence Bobo, *Racial Attitudes in America* (Cambridge: Harvard University Press, 1988).

3. See Donald R. Kinder and David O. Sears, "Prejudice and Politics: Symbolic Racism Versus Racial Threats to the Good Life," *Journal of Personality and Social Psychology* 40 (1981): 414–431; Leslie Carr, "*Color-Blind*" *Racism* (Thousand Oaks, Calif.: Russell Sage Foundation, 1997); and Eduardo Bonilla-Silva, *White Supremacy and Racism in the Post–Civil Rights Era* (Boulder, Colo.: Lynne Rienner, 2001).

4. Jessica Benjamin, *The Bonds of Love: Psychoanalysis, Feminism, and the Problem of Domination* (New York: Pantheon, 1988), pp. 12, 15.

5. Marilee Taylor and Thomas Pettigrew, "Prejudice," in *Encyclope-*

dia of Sociology, eds. Edgar F. Borate and Marie L. Borate (New York: Macmillan, 1992), p. 1,538.

6. Kinder and Sears, "Prejudice and Politics: Symbolic Racism Versus Racial Threats to the Good Life."

7. See Joe R. Feagin and Clairece B. Feagin, *Racial and Ethnic Relations,* 7th ed. (Upper Saddle River, N.J.: Prentice-Hall, 2003), pp. 185–188.

8. Nijole V. Benokraitis, *Marriages and Families: Changes, Choices, and Constraints,* 3d ed. (Englewood Cliffs, N.J.: Prentice Hall, 1999), p. 332.

9. See, for example, Mary Ann Schwartz and Barbara Marlene Scott, *Marriages and Families: Diversity and Change,* 3d ed. (Englewood Cliffs, N.J.: Prentice Hall, 1999), p. 373.

10. See William J. Chambliss, *Power, Politics and Crime* (Boulder, Colo.: Westview Press, 2001), p. 82.

11. James M. Henslin, *Sociology,* 4th ed. (Boston: Allyn and Bacon, 1999), p. 512; see also Harriet Pipes McAdoo, "African-American Families," in *Ethnic Families in America,* ed. Charles H. Mendel, Robert W. Shorenstein, and Roosevelt Wright, Jr. (Englewood Cliffs, N.J.: Prentice Hall, 1998), pp. 375–6.

12. Elizabeth Martinez, "Seeing More than Black and White," *Z Magazine* (1999): 56–60.

13. This is also the view among Western Europeans. See Marimba Ani, *Yurugu: An African-Centered Critique of European Cultural Thought and Behavior* (Trenton, N.J.: Africa World Press, 1994).

14. Jonathan Alter, "White and Blue," *Newsweek,* October 16, 1995, pp. 66–7.

15. Martin Kasindorf, "A Great Divide," *Newsday,* October 1, 1994, p. A3.

16. Muriel Perez-Stable and Mien Urinate, "Cubans and the Changing Economy of Miami," in *Latinos in a Changing U.S. Economy,* ed. Rebecca Morales and Frank Bonilla (Thousand Oaks, Calif.: Russell Sage Foundation, 1993), pp. 133–159; and Feagin and Feagin, *Racial and Ethnic Relations,* chapter 9.

17. See B. Suzuki, "Education and the Socialization of Asian-Americans," in *Asian-Americans: Social and Psychological Perspectives,* eds. R. Endo, S. Sue, and N. Wagner (Palo Alto, Calif.: Science & Behavior Books, 1980), 2:155–178; William Petersen, "Success Story, Japanese-

American Style," *The New York Times,* January 9, 1966, p. 21; "Success Story of One Minority Group in the U.S.," *U.S. News & World Report,* December 26, 1966, pp. 73–76.

18. We are indebted to Sharon Rush for pointing out this distinction.

19. See Joe R. Feagin, *Racist America: Roots, Current Realities, and Future Reparations* (New York: Routledge, 2000), chapter 8.

20. Patricia G. Devine, "Stereotypes and Prejudice: Their Automatic and Controlled Components," *Journal of Personality and Social Psychology* 56 (1989): 5–18; Elliot Aronson, Thomas D. Wilson, and Robin M. Akert, *Social Psychology,* 4th ed. (Upper Saddle River, N.J.: Prentice-Hall, 2002), pp. 473–474; and Yolanda Flores Niemann and Paul F. Secord, "Social Ecology of Stereotyping," *Journal for the Theory of Social Behaviour* 25 (March 1995): 2–7.

21. Jody David Armour, *Negrophobia and Reasonable Racism: The Hidden Costs of Being Black in America* (New York: New York University Press, 1997), pp. 132–135.

5. ISSUES OF INTERRACIAL DATING AND MARRIAGE

1. National Opinion Research Center, *General Social Survey* (Chicago: National Opinion Research Center, 1990).

2. John Briggs and F. David Peat, *Turbulent Mirror: An Illustrated Guide to Chaos Theory and the Science of Wholeness* (New York: Harper and Row, 1990), p. 154.

3. Ninety percent of the subgroup answered "approve" to the short-survey question. Eduardo Bonilla-Silva and Tyrone A. Forman, " 'I Am Not A Racist But...': Mapping White College Students' Racial Ideology in the U.S.A.," *Discourse and Society* 11 (2000): 51–86; Kristen A. Myers and Passion Williamson, "Race Talk: The Perpetuation of Racism through Private Discourse," *Race and Society* 4 (2001): 3–26.

4. See Jennifer Hochschild, *Facing Up to the American Dream* (Princeton, N.J.: Princeton University Press, 1995), pp. 56–57, 59–60.

5. Joe R. Feagin, Hernán Vera, and Pinar Batur, *White Racism: The Basics,* 2nd ed. (New York: Routledge, 2001), p. 203.

6. See Joe R. Feagin and Clairece B. Feagin, *Racial and Ethnic Relations,* 7th ed. (Upper Saddle River, N.J.: Prentice-Hall, 2003), especially chapters 5–11.

7. Ibid., p. 7.

8. Quoted in Theodore Cross, *Black Power Imperative: Racial Inequality and the Politics of Nonviolence* (New York: Faulkner, 1984), pp. 157–158.

9. These points were made by communications scholar Robert Entman, in Greg Braxton, "TV Finds Drama in Interracial Dating," *Los Angeles Times*, March 22, 2000; retrieved at judgingamy.tripod.com/amy/news/a000322la.htm.

10. Ralph Ellison, *Invisible Man* (New York: Vintage Books, [1947] 1989), p. 3.

6. SITUATIONS OF POSSIBLE DISCRIMINATION: ACTION AND INACTION

1. Joe R. Feagin and Hernán Vera, *White Racism* (New York: Routledge, 1995), pp. 9ff.

2. Joe R. Feagin, *Racist America: Roots, Current Realities, and Future Reparations* (New York: Routledge, 2000), chapter 5.

3. Eduardo Bonilla-Silva, *White Supremacy and Racism in the Post-Civil Rights Era* (Boulder, Colo.: Lynne Rienner Publishers, 2001), p. 196.

4. Ibid., pp. 149–150.

5. Lawrence Bobo, James R. Kluegel, and Ryan A. Smith, "Laissez-Faire Racism: The Crystallization of a Kinder, Gentler, Antiblack Ideology," in *Racial Attitudes in the 1990s: Continuity and Change*, ed. Steven A. Tuch and Jack K. Martin (Westport, Conn.: Praeger, 1997), pp. 15–40.

6. See Joe R. Feagin and Melvin P. Sikes, *Living with Racism* (Boston, Mass.: Beacon, 1994), chapter 2.

7. Quoted in Daniel Kurtzman, "The Lone Ranger," *Jewish Monthly* (November/December 1997): 36.

8. Jody David Armour, *Negrophobia and Reasonable Racism: The Hidden Costs of Being Black in America* (New York: New York University Press, 1997), pp. 39–40.

9. Feagin and Sikes, *Living with Racism*, chapter 2.

10. P. R. Klite, R. A. Bardwell, and J. Salzman, "Local TV News: Getting Away with Murder," *Press/Politics* 2 (1997): 102–112; Franklin D. Gilliam, Jr. and Shanto Iyengar, "Prime Suspects: the Effects of Local

News on the Viewing Public," unpublished research paper, University of California (Los Angeles), n.d.

11. See Daniel Romer, Kathleen H. Jamieson, and Nicole J. de Coteau, "The Treatment of Persons of Color in Local Television News," *Communication Research* 25 (June 1998): 286–290.

12. Robert M. Entman, "Violence on Television: News and Reality Programming in Chicago," report for the Chicago Council on Urban Affairs, May 9, 1994.

13. We are indebted to Hernán Vera for suggesting the inclusion of such a hypothetical question in our project.

14. See Dinesh D'Souza, *The End of Racism* (New York: The Free Press, 1995), pp. 278–287.

15. Armour, *Negrophobia and Reasonable Racism*, pp. 39–40. See also Farai Chideya, *Don't Believe The Hype* (New York: Plume, 1995).

16. Melvin L. Oliver and Thomas M. Shapiro, *Black Wealth/White Wealth* (New York: Routledge, 1995), p. 107.

17. Jeffrey Goldberg, "The Color of Suspicion," *New York Times Magazine*, June 20, 1999, p. 51.

18. Joe Barndt, *Dismantling Racism* (Minneapolis: Augsberg Fortress, 1991), p. 65.

19. Kristen A. Myers and Passion Williamson, "Race Talk: The Perpetuation of Racism through Private Discourse," *Race and Society* 4 (2001): 3–26. The other project referenced here is being conducted by Leslie Houts and Joe Feagin, with the current working title of "Racist Thought and Action: Backstage versus Frontstage" (University of Florida, 2003).

7. VIEWS ON PUBLIC POLICY: AFFIRMATIVE ACTION AND "REVERSE DISCRIMINATION"

1. Sidney Verba and Gary R. Orren, *Equality in America: The View from the Top* (Cambridge: Harvard University Press, 1985), p. 63.

2. Patrick Buchanan, *The Death of the West: How Dying Populations and Immigrant Invasions Imperil Our Country and Civilization* (New York: St. Martin's Press, 2002), pp. 218–220.

3. Elisabeth Lasch-Quinn, *Race Experts: How Racial Etiquette, Sensi-*

tivity Training, and New Age Therapy Hijacked the Civil Rights Revolution (New York: Norton, 2001), p. 186; for citations and reviews of studies on the pervasiveness of discrimination, see Joe R. Feagin, *Racist America* (New York; Routledge, 2002).

4. See Leslie Carr, *"Color-Blind" Racism* (Thousand Oaks, Calif.: Russell Sage Foundation, 1997), pp. 109–143.

5. David Oppenheimer, "Distinguishing Five Models of Affirmative Action," *Berkeley Women's Law Journal* 4 (1989): 42–61.

6. See Marc Bendick, Jr., "Social Policy: Affirmative Action," http: www.spaef.co/IJED_PUB/v2n2/v2n2_social.html (ret. March 7, 2003).

7. For a discussion of these many connections, see Feagin, *Racist America*, chapters 1, 2, 7, and 8.

8. Surveys are cited in Arlie Hochschild, *Facing Up to the American Dream: Race, Class and the Soul of the Nation* (Princeton: Princeton University Press, 1995), pp. 101–102.

9. See, for example, Joe R. Feagin and Melvin P. Sikes, *Living with Racism* (Boston: Beacon, 1994), chapters 4, 5, and 7; and *Double Burden: Black Women and Everyday Racism* (New York: M.E. Sharpe, 1998).

10. For more evidence on this, see Feagin, *Racist America*.

11. See, for example, Melvin L. Oliver and Thomas M. Shapiro, *Black Wealth/White Wealth* (New York: Routledge, 1995).

12. See Jill Quadagno, *The Color of Welfare: How Racism Undermined the War on Poverty* (New York: Oxford University Press, 1996).

13. Sharon M. Collins, *Black Corporate Executives: The Making and Breaking of the Black Middle Class* (Philadelphia: Temple University Press, 1997); see also Feagin and Sikes, *Living with Racism*, chapter 4.

14. According to the U.S. Labor Department, an estimated 5 million workers of color are probably in higher occupational classifications today because of affirmative action programs. See Kevin Merida, "Reverse Discrimination Rejected: Study Finds Many Claims by White Men 'Without Merit,'" *Houston Chronicle*, April 1, 1995, p. A5. See also Collins, *Black Corporate Executives*, pp. 20–23.

15. Summarized in Pamela Mendels, "Up for Evaluation: Is Affirmative Action Still Working After 30 Years on the Job?" *Newsday*, June 13, 1995, p. 6.

16. Alfred Blumrosen on CNN News, April 4, 1995, Transcript No. 909–10. See also Associated Press, "Reverse Discrimination Complaints

Rare, Labor Study Reports," *New York Times*, March 31, 1995, Section A, p. 23; and Nancy Montwieler, "EEOC: Casellas Says New Litigation Procedure Will Free Commission for More Policy Work," *Daily Labor Report* (Bureau of National Affairs), April 21, 1995, p. D5.

17. Thomas Dye, *Who's Running America?*, 4th ed. (Englewood Cliffs, N.J.: Prentice Hall, 1986), pp. 190–205; and see the summary of the Glass Ceiling Commission's findings in "Federal Panel Reveals That Most Top Jobs Are Still Held By White Men," *Jet* (April 3, 1995): 2–4.

18. David Gates, "White Male Paranoia," *Newsweek* (March 29, 1993): 48.

8. THE MULTIRACIAL FUTURE

1. Robert M. Entman, "Violence on Television: News and Reality Programming in Chicago," report for the Chicago Council on Urban Affairs, May 9, 1994; see also Robert M. Entman and Andrew Rojecki, *The Black Image in the White Mind: Media and Race in America* (Chicago: University of Chicago Press, 2000).

2. See Eileen O'Brien, *Whites Confront Racism* (Boulder, Colo.: Rowman and Littlefield, 2001); and Joe R. Feagin and Hernán Vera, *White Racism* (New York: Routledge, 1995).

3. Derrick Bell, *Faces at the Bottom of the Well* (New York: Basic Books, 1992), pp. 55–56.

4. Ibid., pp. 61–62.

5. Samuel P. Huntington, "The Erosion of American National Interests," *Foreign Affairs* (September/October 1997), pp. 28ff.

6. Ibid.

7. Cited in D. Gelman, "The Young and the Reckless," *Newsweek*, January 11, 1992, p. 61.

8. See Nathan Rutstein, *Racism: Unraveling the Fear* (Washington, D.C.: The Global Classroom, 1993), pp. 225–228; O'Brien, *Whites Confront Racism*; and Michael Omi, "(E)racism: Emergent Practices of Anti-Racist Organizations," paper presented at American Sociological Association Meetings, San Francisco, Calif., August 1998.

ACKNOWLEDGMENTS

We would especially like to thank the many college students who conducted the interviews or otherwise assisted us in this longterm research project. We are grateful for their interest and efforts. We would also like to thank the many respondents who took time out from busy lives to provide their views on a variety of issues important to the present and future of this country. We are also indebted to a number of scholars across the country who have helped us by reading various draft chapters and by providing other types of research assistance, including helping us with copyediting problems and bibliographic references. In particular, we would like to thank Hernán Vera, Bernice McNair Barnett, Leslie Houts, Sharon Rush, and Vicki Vinther for this research assistance and suggestions at various stages of our project. We are also grateful to Danielle Dirks, Kristi Lowery, William Smith, John Foster, and Donny Barnett for their important suggestions on particular chapters of this manuscript. We are heavily indebted to Rhonda Levine for her substantial help in the original data gathering, for her insightful comments on several drafts of the manuscript, and for her constant input and support in shaping and completing this research project.

Joe Feagin is especially grateful for the ongoing support of his family in these writing projects on racial matters in the United States. He would like to thank especially his colleagues Hernán Vera and Bernice McNair Barnett, who have patiently examined his data or listened to his views on these matters, and always responded with insight and encouragement. They are among the wisest scholars on these matters in our generation.

Eileen O'Brien is grateful for the support of her loving family, her partner Kendall James, and her department chair Joan Spade. Most importantly, she is thankful for her new daughter, Kaya O'Brien-James, who kicked in her belly as she wrote chapters and nursed as she did final editing. Kerry O'Brien was a helpful aunt, holding a newborn Kaya while the conclusion was written. Kaya, who is both African American and white, is a constant inspiration, reminding us of the possibility of a more harmonious racial future for the United States.